Practice the *Presence*

Practice *the* Presence

Chris Michaels

Edward Viljoen

Awakening World Enterprises

Kansas City, Missouri

Awakening World Enterprises
1621 West Fiftieth Street
Kansas City, Missouri 64112

Printed in China
Published August 2009

ISBN 0-9742256-3-0
Library of Congress Control Number 2003111103

Design by Randall Friesen

An Interactive Journal

Practice is the repeated performance or systematic exercise of something for the purpose of acquiring skill or proficiency. The phrase "Practice makes perfect" suggests that by repeatedly engaging in an activity, you get better at it. In the phrase "Practice the Presence," we refer to activities that help us become more conscious of the tangible Presence of Divinity.

This interactive journal offers you daily opportunities to reflect on that Presence in whatever manner you experience it. By taking a moment each day this week, and the next week, and the week after that, you will achieve one full year of spiritually focused living. By the end of the year, you will have authentically practiced being aware of the Presence that animates you and sustains your life.

As you practice in this way, you will become aware of your thoughts and actions in different areas of your life. By taking the time each day to reflect upon your life, you will begin to notice the activity of Divinity in everything from the very ordinary activities of your day to the extraordinary moments you may not have noticed before.

Edward Viljoen, Santa Rosa, California

Spiritual Practice

Because we are, first and foremost, spiritual beings, our relationship with God requires more than just a Sunday-morning commitment. In order for it to be truly beneficial, this relationship must be nurtured on a regular basis. Like all human relationships, our relationship with God requires time and frequent communication in order to remain healthy and vital. We have to take the opportunity each day to pray and meditate in order to hear that one, pure voice of Spirit alive within us. In other words, if we expect to live well and prosper, we have to make more room for God in our lives.

This is where a daily spiritual practice becomes imperative. Taking time out of each day to tend to your spiritual self not only brings you closer to God, it also gives you a greater sense of belonging and purpose. The long-term benefits are healthier choices and a happier life.

Maybe you can't stop five times a day to pray. But you can take a few moments of each day to remember that you are a spiritual being and not merely a human body. The truth is, attending to your spiritual needs each day will probably take you less time than it does to shower, brush your teeth, and get dressed. If you have the time to tend to your body, you can certainly take time to create a daily ritual that addresses your spirit as well.

In addition to daily prayer and meditation, journaling is a way to record and ritualize your spiritual growth. Writing in a journal each day calls on you to be more conscious of the insights that occur daily on your spiritual path. It gives you an opportunity to examine your beliefs and be mindful of your choices. It allows time to reflect on your day and think about the choices you have made. Journaling can be a cathartic experience that releases judgment and self-condemnation. It can also offer a place to confess your true feelings about someone or something in your life.

My friend, Jane, has had self-esteem issues her whole life. Even though she attends church regularly and has taken a plethora of workshops and classes on the subject, she was never able to reach the root cause of her low self-esteem. Because of this, she carried more weight on her body than she was comfortable with and had begun to have health challenges. Every diet she tried failed, and she used each failure as another excuse to mentally beat herself up, thereby reinforcing her low self-opinion. The merry-go-round of guilt and shame frustrated her incredibly.

After trying everything to resolve the issue, she picked up a journal one day and started to write. Having a safe place to confess her feelings and explore her thoughts more honestly, she was finally able to understand the limited beliefs that continued to block her good. Inevitably, the pounds began to fall away and, to this day, have not returned. If you ask her how she lost the weight, she'll tell you, "I just got to a place where I didn't need it anymore."

Jesus said, "The truth will set you free." In Jane's case, that's exactly what happened. Her journal became her best friend. It was the place she went to tell the truth without fear of judgment or condemnation. Knowing she would never share what she wrote with another human being freed her to be brutally honest with herself. And in that honesty, she found her healing.

Somehow, writing things down in a journal makes them more real to us. When we take time to write down our goals and explore our dreams, we see that what we've written is actually a self-fulfilling prophecy. That's the power of journaling. It's one more way to express your experience as a human being.

Many famous people have used journaling as a way to express themselves more fully. Leonardo da Vinci was a voracious journal writer. His genius flowed onto the pages, complemented by drawings of his latest inventions. Today, just one of the pages from his journal is worth millions of dollars.

There will never come a time in life when you can say, "I am done now." Each of us is a work in progress. We are all on different paths, making unique choices and learning powerful truths. Knowing this can set you free from comparison to others and will bring greater peace and acceptance to your heart. Realizing it will allow you to more greatly appreciate the unique person God has created you to be.

Because we are spiritual beings, made in the image and likeness of God, our souls have infinite depth. And that means each day brings a new discovery. Every day is a new opportunity to grow and change. Every new experience in life calls to the surface some previously unknown or hidden talent. And every new person we meet is another opportunity to express God's love.

The Bible says, "Behold, I make all things new." For us, that means we are made new all of the time. Like aging, though, it's difficult to notice all that's changed about you in a single day. However, if you take time to write your thoughts down in a journal, looking back on it later, you'll be amazed at your progress.

In a universe governed by a Perfect Intelligence, there can be no errors, mistakes, or coincidences. Everything in your life has been perfectly synchronized to unfold the highest good, whether you are aware of it or not. Each experience that you claim to be either good or bad contributes to your growth as a spiritual being. The key is to live consciously and pay attention to the patterns that show up in your life.

Journaling is an excellent way to stay awake. It provides a record of your thoughts and feelings that can be looked back on to measure your progress. Create a new spiritual practice, and journal your way to a more conscious life. Make more room in your life for God and see what happens. In no time, you'll have new insights that will change your life forever.

Chris Michaels, Kansas City, Missouri

JANUARY

Practice *the* Presence *through* Sacredness

January 1

Believing is the brush that converts your dreams into a masterpiece of reality.
Picasso

BELIEVING

Believing is having confidence in the truth, the existence, or the certainty of something, without definite proof that one is right in doing so. Sometimes we believe things that are not true. Other times, we cannot explain why we believe a certain thing.

At the beginning of this journey, it may be helpful for you to investigate what you believe. Make a list of the top beliefs you have about life, and try to explore how it is you came to believe these things.

January 2

Do you think that you shall enter the Garden of Bliss
without such trials as came to those who passed before you?
Scott Reed

BLISS

Bliss is supreme happiness, utter joy, or contentment. In spiritual terms, bliss is thought to accompany a complete realization of unity with Divinity. Daily spiritual practice, such as contemplation, meditation, prayer, and journaling, is thought to lead us to an experience of the Presence.

This journal offers one of many possible devotional activities that you might use to practice feeling the Presence. Take time each day to read these journal entries and record your own reflections.

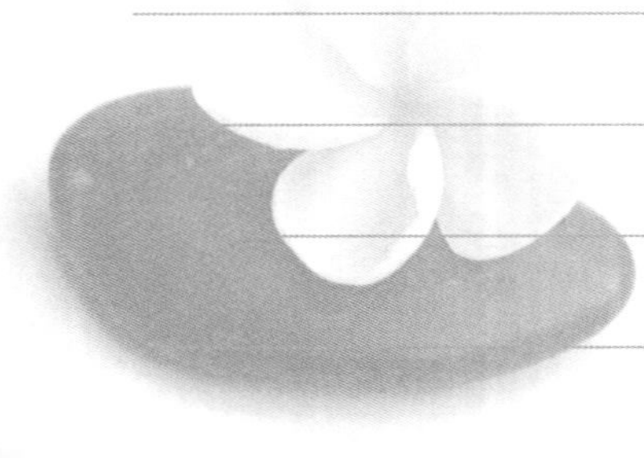

JANUARY 3

The problems of the world cannot possibly be solved by skeptics or cynics whose horizons are limited by the obvious realities. We need men who can dream of things that never were.
John Fitzgerald Kennedy

BROADENING HORIZONS

To practice awareness of the Presence of Divinity calls us to look beyond what is obvious, normal, and routine. To begin, imagine what it might be like to be born into a different culture or in a different age. How would your beliefs differ from those you have today? What would your life be like if you were a different gender, and what do you think would be the advantages and disadvantages? Try to imagine how your current beliefs about the world may be limited. Is there some way you can broaden your horizons today?

JANUARY 4

The important thing is not to stop questioning. Curiosity has its own reason for existing. One cannot help but be in awe when he contemplates the mysteries of eternity, of life, of the marvelous structure of reality. It is enough if one tries merely to comprehend a little of this mystery every day. Never lose a holy curiosity.

Albert Einstein

AWE

Awe is an attitude of mind that allows us to see things differently. An attitude of awe includes appreciation for detail, beauty, and significance. It is the feeling of reverence or admiration that comes from witnessing something grand like a canyon, sublime like a dance, or powerful like a thunderstorm.

You can practice awe by taking time to truly look at something and list all its qualities. Choose something in your personal environment right now. Really look at it, and attempt to describe it to someone who is not present. How would you convey every detail of the object, as well as the feelings you have when you touch it or see it?

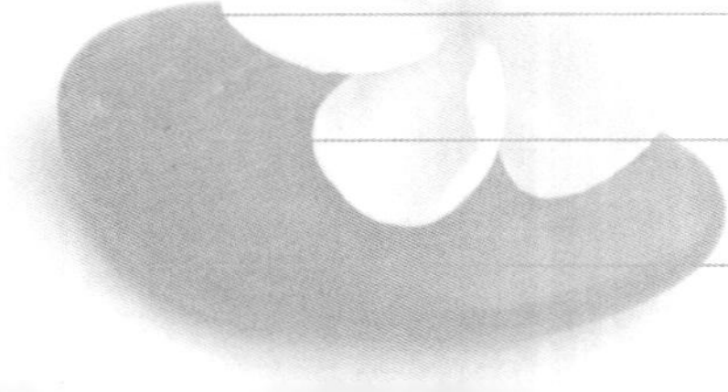

January 5

He who can no longer pause to wonder and stand rapt in awe, is as good as dead; his eyes are closed.
Albert Einstein

WONDER

To wonder means both to be filled with admiration and amazement, and to speculate or be curious about something. Pick someone you admire today to wonder about. Ask yourself what the qualities are that you admire about this person and why these qualities are interesting to you. Then, take a moment to list examples in your own life where you have exhibited these same qualities. Be sure to note how you feel when you both admire and embody these qualities.

January 6

A friend should be one in whose understanding and virtue we can equally confide, and whose opinion we can value at once for its justness and its sincerity.
Robert Hall

CONFESSING

When we take responsibility for our experience of the Presence, it is like a form of confession. In this way, we declare or acknowledge that we are part of something larger and begin to come out of the shadows of secular life to join an ever-growing company of like-minded people who share a love of life.

Our confessions of awe, wonder, belief, and experience contribute to the beauty of the world. Discovering in ourselves the warmth of feeling connection to All That Is—taking time to embrace and share it—is a way of practicing awareness of the Presence. When did you last share with someone something that is really important to you?

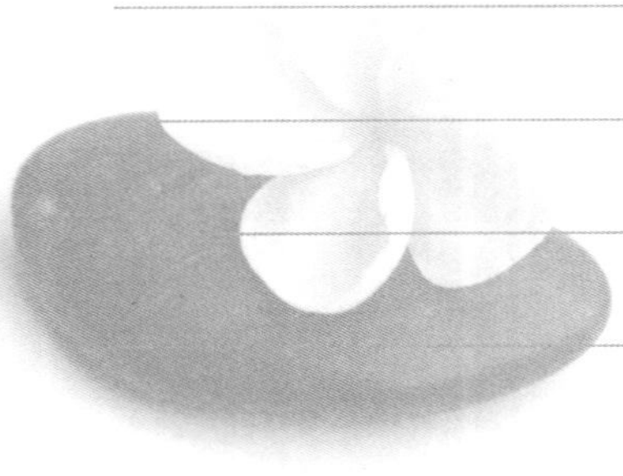

January 7

Dedicate some of your life to others. Your dedication will not be a sacrifice. It will be an exhilarating experience because it is an intense effort applied toward a meaningful end.

Dr. Thomas Dooley

DEDICATION

The human potential movement is based on two beliefs: that an extraordinary potential lies largely untapped in most people, and that social change can be brought about when individuals dedicate themselves to the cultivation of their individual potentials. William Longwood wrote: "Dreams and dedication are a powerful combination." This reminds us to be mindful about what we are dedicated to. Dedication solely to the personal self can result in powerful growth. Dedicating a part of your life to others and assisting them to release their own potentials are powerful contributions to society. Dedicating a part of your life to the Presence is a way of staying in touch with Reality.

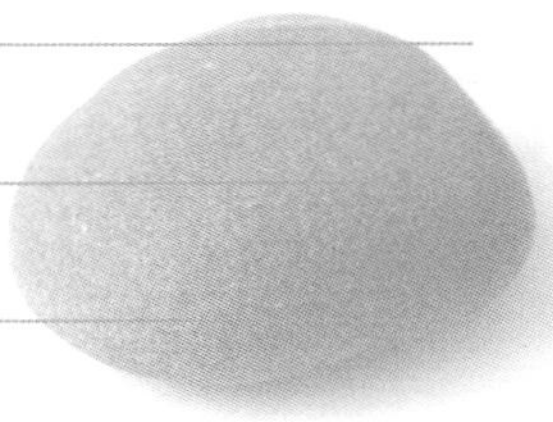

January 8

Yes, Virginia, there is a Santa Claus. He exists as certainly as love and generosity and devotion exists, and you know that they abound and give to your life its highest beauty and joy.
Francis P. Church

DEVOTION

"*Yes, Virginia, there is a Santa Claus"* is the opening phrase of one of the more celebrated editorials written for *The New York Sun*. Responding to an eight-year-old girl's question about the existence of Santa, the editorial served then, as it does today, as a reminder that the real and enduring things in the world are those that we cannot necessarily see, but which we experience.

Devotion is something you cannot see, yet you experience its results. It is a practice of ardently, often selflessly, giving time and attention to a person or a principle. When, in your daily routine, you give attention to a pet or a plant or a person, over time, a natural love for the object of your attention will arise within you. If, in your daily routine, you apply the same practice of giving attention to the Presence in whatever way makes sense to you, a natural love called *devotion* will arise within you.

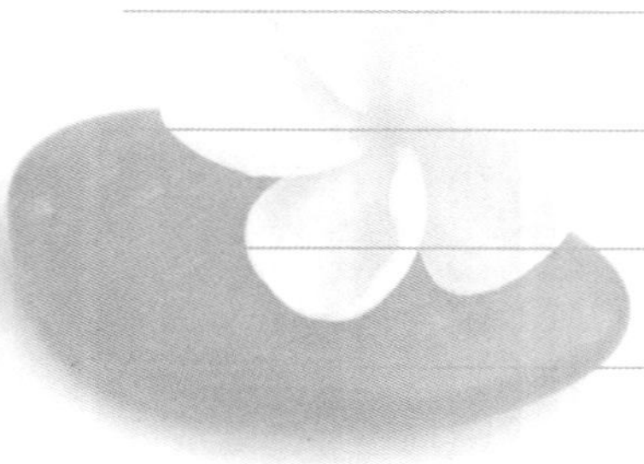

January 9

I feel an indescribable ecstasy and delirium in melting, as it were, into the system of beings, in identifying myself with the whole of nature.
Jean-Jacques Rousseau

ECSTASY

Over time, kindness develops into affection. Over time, affection deepens to love. And over time, when love is given selflessly or unguardedly, a deeper love reveals itself, a love that has no agenda for personal gain or control. When you first become aware that you are loving, you feel as if a rush of joy has flooded in, a rush that reminds you of your natural-born capacity to care about others.

Logan Pearsall Smith wrote that it is "through the cracks in our brains that ecstasy creeps in." To me, that means ecstasy cannot be planned or pursued with rational thoughts, goals, or intentions. It is the natural by-product of innocent loving. The ecstasy that comes from loving people is inspiring. The ecstasy that comes from loving the Presence is something deeply personal that each person must discover and experience for themselves.

January 10

When you come to the edge of all that you know and are about to drop off into the darkness of the unknown, faith is knowing one of two things will happen: There will be something solid to stand on, or you will be taught to fly.

Patrick Overton

FAITH

At some point in life, everyone is brought to their knees. Eventually, we each come to a place where everything we've tried has failed, or everything we've known is no longer applicable. It is in this place that we find God.

When we come to the end of our inflated and insignificant ego-achievements, we find ourselves standing in awe of the sacred life of our Creator. And it is here that humility and faith meld within us to form a confidence that all is well.

What is happening in your life to challenge you? How will it strengthen your faith?

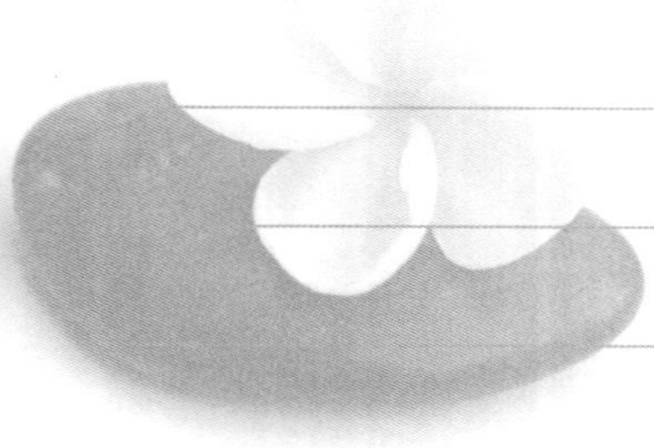

JANUARY 11

Life is too short to be little. Man is never so manly as when he feels deeply, acts boldly, and expresses himself with frankness and with fervor.
Benjamin Disraeli

FERVOR

The universe burst into existence with passion and boldness. The Spirit of God thrust its infinity outward to form the galaxies and create the planets. Its fervor demonstrated the sheer joy of creation. God acts boldly! It does not fear Its own expression.

Since you have been created in God's image, your fullest expression will also come about from bold action. Do not fear your dreams. Do not be afraid to take risks. Great women and men become great by fully expressing what God has placed inside them.

What do you feel deeply about? Where is your passion? What bold action can you take today?

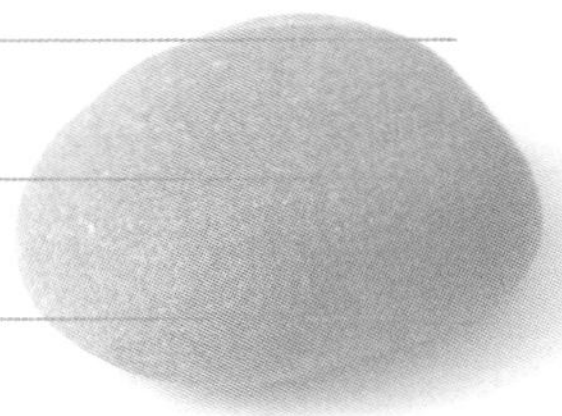

January 12

Heaven is under our feet
as well as over our heads.
Henry David Thoreau

HEAVEN

Many people approach life as if it is a quest for all that's good. They search long and hard for their hearts' desires. They look for love in other people. They try to purchase happiness. They wait for the doctor's report to determine their well-being. What if we have looked too far away for our good? What if God has put it somewhere closer? What if it's true that the kingdom of heaven is within?

I liken the spiritual journey—the quest to find God that so many people seem to be on—to a fish in the ocean, setting out on a long journey to find water. The thing for which we hunt so long and hard is the very thing we're surrounded by and immersed in.

If you want to find heaven, don't look up; look down. The ground you walk on is holy.

January 13

Nature is my manifestation of God. I go to nature every day for inspiration in the day's work.
Frank Lloyd Wright

INSPIRATION

When you are inspired, you are in Spirit. When you lack inspiration, you have taken yourself too far away from Spirit's Presence. Inspiration can be found everywhere. It surrounds you. Look for it in the morning sky or the colors of dusk. Look for it in the eyes of the one you love. Find inspiration in music, nature, or art.

As a spiritual being, your real effort is to stay inspired. By doing so, you will remain in God's Presence. And in God's Presence, all is well.

What really inspires you? What can you do today that will bring you inspiration?

January 14

Participate joyfully in the sorrows of the world. We cannot cure the world of sorrows, but we can choose to live in joy.
Joseph Campbell

JUBILATION

Every day, you ride the roller coaster of human emotions. One day you're happy; the next day you're sad. The circumstances of life vary every hour. Each event provides a choice: Will I let this bring me down? Or, will I choose joy?

At the very center of your heart lies pure joy. Return there each day. Become as a little child again. Don't be afraid to express joy. Who cares if people think you're crazy? You don't have to walk all of the time. You could skip!

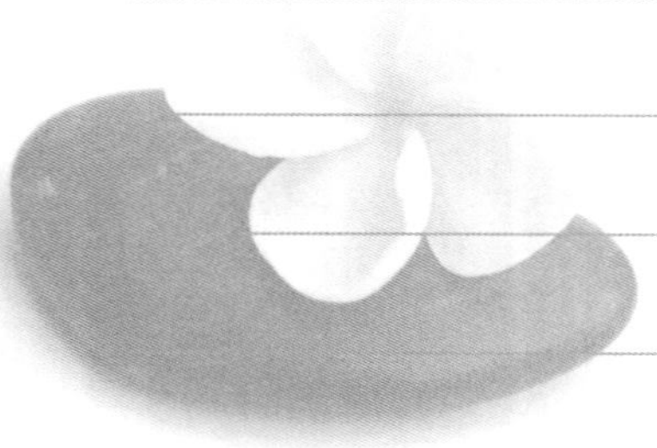

JANUARY 15

Those who danced were thought to be quite insane by those who could not hear the music.
Angela Monet

PASSION

In ancient days, the church sought to subdue the people, believing that they were too weak to control their own desires. Church doctrine warned against the evil of men's passion. Stoicism and piety were not only encouraged, but greatly commended. Sacrifice and submission was the order of the day. However, all of this effort was to no avail. Boys will be boys, and girls will be girls!

There is passion in our souls. It has been placed there by God. It need not be feared nor controlled. It needs healthy expression. It guides us to fuller expression.

How can you express your passion today? What do you fear might happen if you do?

January 16

The more you praise and celebrate your life, the more there is in life to celebrate.
Oprah Winfrey

PRAISING

To praise means to lift up, shine the light on, and give thanks for. When you praise something or someone, it's like saying to God, "Yes, this is what I want to see more of in my life." It creates a willingness to receive your good.

Find things that are praiseworthy in your life. Look for the good in life and you will find it. And when you do, give praise for it. What person or circumstance is worthy of your praise?

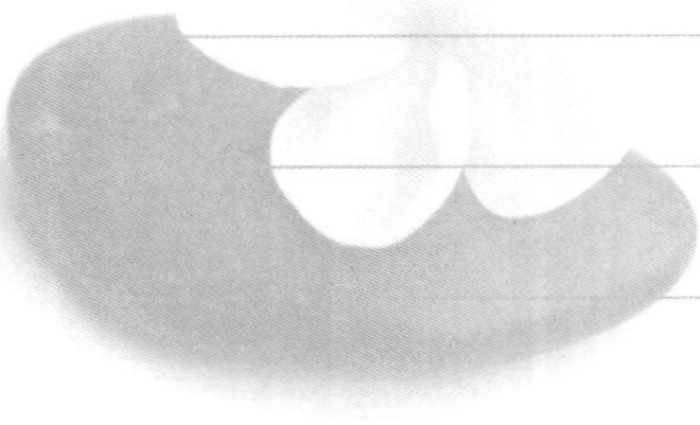

January 17

You pray in your distress and in your need; would that you might also pray in the fullness of your joy and in your days of abundance.
Kahlil Gibran

PRAYING

Too often, prayer is associated with times of difficulty or response to a specific need. There are other times to pray than when we are in need, and there are additional forms of prayer than those that petition for help. Personal devotional prayer, like a poem, is a form of expressing one's love and appreciation for All That Is. This prayer neither asks for anything nor complains and cries out for help. It is a practice of describing all that is holy, good, and beautiful. Performed daily on a regular schedule, prayer is a most satisfying practice and serves as an infusion of energy and appreciation. William Law wrote: "He who has learned to pray has learned the greatest secret of a holy and happy life."

Consider writing a poem about whatever you are praying for today. Or simply express what you love about the state of being alive, and call that your prayer.

January 18

I cannot believe in a God who
wants to be praised all the time.
Friedrich Nietzsche

PRINCIPLE

That which is infinite, eternal, and everywhere present defies definition in a single term. That's why, in this journal, you will encounter different terms to describe Divinity. We have chosen to call it *Presence*, as a shorthand term for what some people call God or Spirit or the Ground of All Being. Although *Presence* defies finite definitions, attempting to describe it is in itself a spiritual practice, giving us the opportunity to investigate what we think and believe about Divinity. Early concepts of *Presence* adorned it with human qualities, such as the need for obedience, praise, and sacrifice. More contemporary concepts frequently describe *Presence* as the principle of anything that appears, or, in other words, the cause that produces it.

In the end, the definition you choose will be the one most important and valuable to you. How do you define *Divinity*, and what does it mean to your life?

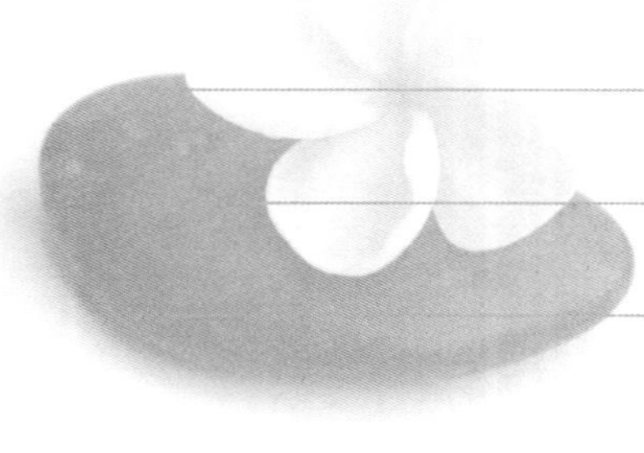

January 19

We can work together for a better world with men and women of goodwill, those who radiate the intrinsic goodness of humankind.
Wangari Maathai

RADIATING

When Wangari Maathai received the Nobel Prize in 2004, the Committee said that "her unique forms of action have contributed to drawing attention to political oppression—nationally and internationally. She has served as inspiration for many in the fight for democratic rights and has especially encouraged women to better their situation." In one of the photographs taken at the award ceremony, Wangari seems to radiate a joy and power that seems incredible for someone who has been knocked unconscious for protesting, thrown in jail for being outspoken, attacked for her beliefs, and vilified by her government and husband. Most photographs of her show a radiant joy that seems to light up everything around her. She is quoted as saying: "All of us have a God in us, and that God is the spirit that unites all life, everything that is on this planet." In 1976, she introduced the idea of planting trees to prevent soil erosion. Since then, thirty million trees have been planted in that project.

What causes you to radiate joy and light?

January 20

We're so engaged in doing things to achieve purposes of outer value that we forget the inner value, the rapture that is associated with being alive, is what it is all about.
Joseph Campbell

RAPTURE

Rapture is the state of being carried away—so deeply absorbed in an activity that we forget the ordinary demands of life. It is a state of expanded awareness, one of deep satisfaction. As lofty as this description seems, the reality is that rapture can be found in the most ordinary of things and experiences, as well as in the most beautiful and sublime.

Take some time today to recall and write about a time when you were in a state of extreme happiness. Describe the experience in detail, including the environment, who was present, and what you were wearing and feeling.

Remembering moments of happiness is an effective method of practicing alertness and makes you receptive to experiencing them again.

JANUARY 21

Being religious means asking passionately the question of the meaning of our existence and being willing to receive answers, even if the answers hurt.
Paul Tillich

RELIGIOUSLY

Doing something religiously conjures up images of strict adherence—perhaps even blind obedience—to a belief system. In common language, when people say, "I do it religiously," they are referring to an activity that occupies an important role in their daily routines, one that they are not likely to avoid for any reason. In spiritual terms, *religiously* refers to the faithful and reverential discharge of a duty, such as regularly attending worship service, burning incense as a form of offering, or serving food at a mission.

The power of any task, when done religiously, lies in the doer's decision to allow nothing to disrupt the activity, as well as the respect they give to the activity. When you perform a task of practicing the Presence religiously, you elevate the importance of the practice in your life, allowing it to occupy a powerful position in your mind and bestowing on your practice a sense of respect and heightened value.

JANUARY 22

Your sacred space is where you can
find yourself again and again.
Joseph Campbell

SACREDNESS

The word *sacred* has its roots in a Middle English word which means to consecrate or to set aside for a spiritual purpose. In your daily practice of journaling, it can refer to how you prepare yourself to be undistracted for deep thought and reflection. You can achieve this by reducing interruptions or by listening to music that inspires peace. Practicing sacredness can have the effect of influencing how you carry out the ordinary activities in your life by introducing a single-minded approach to everything.

How do you create a sense of sacredness within and around you for your daily practice?

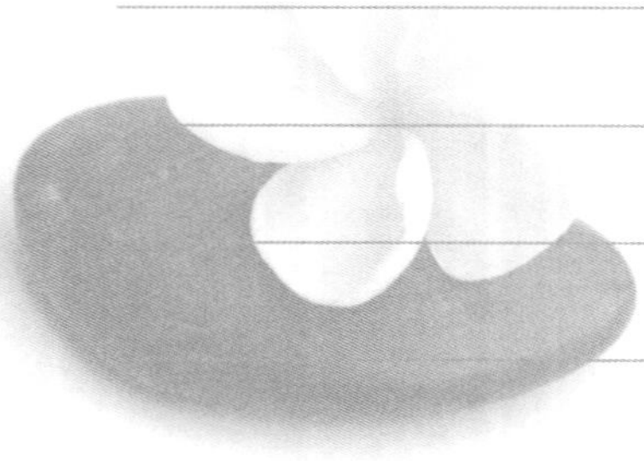

January 23

True religion is real living; living with all one's soul,
with all one's goodness and righteousness.
Albert Einstein

SOULFULNESS

When you practice giving your full attention to whatever you are doing, you receive the reciprocal feeling of being profoundly filled up by the activity. Think of this as *soulfulness*—the deep feeling that comes from being absorbed in the object of your attention. When the object of your attention is a profound awareness of the Presence, the feelings that arise are those that remind us of our natural state of connectedness with all of life and all beings.

In your daily practice, you will achieve a fuller experience when you give yourself the opportunity of being undivided in your work for ten or twenty minutes. Turn off all devices and place yourself in an environment where there is little to distract you from the joy of exploring the Presence.

January 24

Spirituality is a constant, consistent attempt to feel the Presence of God in everything and in everyone.
Dr. Ernest Holmes

SPIRITUALITY

Many people say, "I'm not religious; I'm spiritual." They understand that there is more to life than what meets the eye. Whether claiming religious affiliation or not, they recognize that there is a greater cause and a creator of life.

Spirituality is this recognition put into practice. It is an attempt to see deep into the spiritual nature of life, beyond physical appearances. The goal is to be able to see God in everything and in every person. This takes practice and faith.

It's easy to see God in the people we love or the things we find beautiful. The challenge of spirituality is to be able to see God in those we don't love and things we find ugly. That takes practice.

How do you practice your spirituality? What can you do today to feel the Presence of God in your life more deeply?

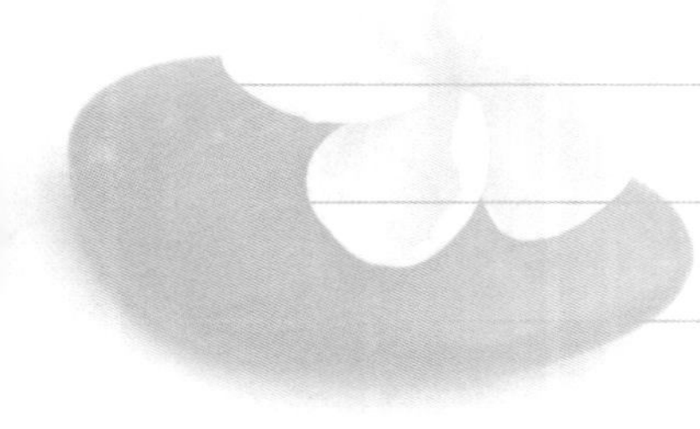

January 25

I was always looking outside myself for strength and confidence, but it comes from within. It is there all of the time.
Anna Freud

STRENGTH

The strength to bear your burdens and overcome your challenges does not flow from the outside. It comes from a deep well inside of you. It rises up from within to greet the challenge and assert its power over it. There is only one true source of strength and power, and that is the Presence of God within you.

Do you think of yourself as a strong person? Where do you gain strength? What person in your life gives you strength? What person relies on your strength?

January 26

And we are now men, and must accept in the highest mind the same transcendent destiny; and not pinched in a corner, not cowards fleeing before a revolution, but redeemers and benefactors…let us advance on chaos and the dark.

Ralph Waldo Emerson

TRANSCENDING

There is more to you than your mortal body. Your true identity lies hidden underneath a temporary shelter of flesh. The greatest part of you can't be seen with the naked eye. It transcends physicality. It is only your spirit that is real and lasting.

Genius is invisible. Power is invisible. All things that really matter are invisible; love, joy, peace, ease, and beauty. Nothing that is real can be seen, and everything that can be seen is not real. Do not be tricked by appearances.

Move toward your goals valiantly. Live boldly. Life is too short to hide in a corner. Charge forward into the new day with heroic power!

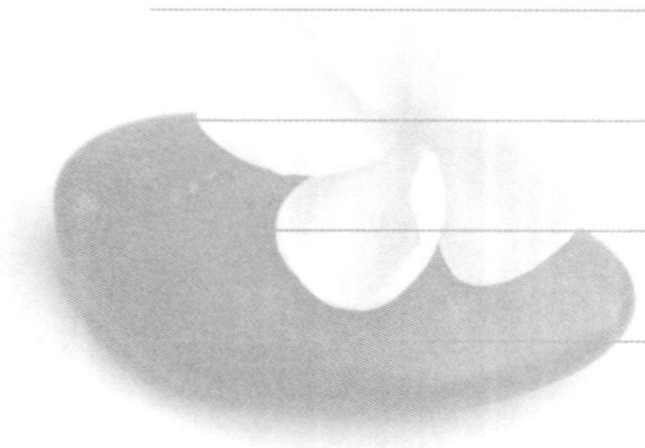

January 27

God is like a warm fire on a cold night. The closer you get to the fire, the warmer and brighter your life becomes. However, the further you get away from it, the colder and darker your life will seem.

Chris Michaels

WARMTH

God never abandons Its creation. It is always present in your life, as close to you as your breath. However, you have a choice as to whether or not you will stay close to God. The closer you are to the Source of your good, the better your life will be. The farther you get away from it, the worse it will become.

Think of God not as a person, but as Love and Joy. The closer you are to what you love and what brings you joy, the nearer you are to God. Every day, you must choose where to invest your time. What will you do with it today?

JANUARY 28

When I admire the wonder of a sunset or the beauty of the moon, my soul expands in worship of the Creator.
Indira Ghandi

WORSHIP

God is not an egomaniacal deity that requires inferior human beings to bow down in worship. It did not create the human race as servants who live eternally in fear and submission.

Worship means honoring or showing respect for something. You do not respect or honor God by living a small, insignificant life. The greatest homage you can pay to your Creator is to live well, be happy, and show compassion. You worship God every time you choose love over hate, faith over fear. You worship God each time you admire beauty or walk in the reverence of nature.

How do you worship? What holds your highest regard? How do you show respect?

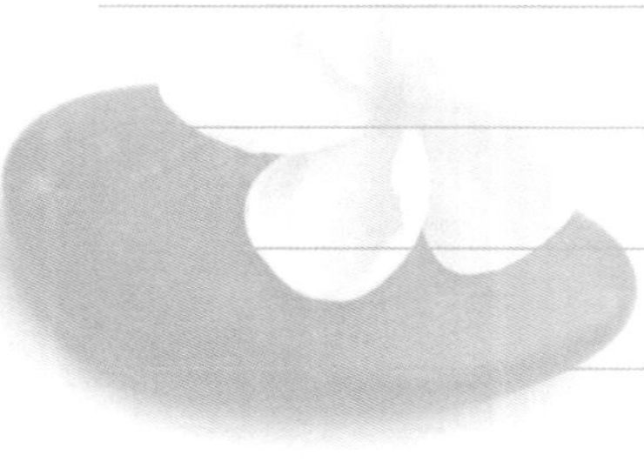

January 29

And it is very much lamented, Brutus,
That you have no such mirrors as will turn
Your hidden worthiness into your eye.
William Shakespeare, Act I, *Julius Caesar*

WORTHINESS

What determines a woman's worth? Who designates the worth of a man? Is it determined on a daily basis or at the end of a lifetime? Must our worth be proven to some distant deity sitting on high who calculates the value of each thought, deed, and action?

The Universe knows your worth. It has already been assessed by God, and your actions can't change it. God's decision is final. You do not have to prove yourself worthy. There's nothing you can do to earn your good. It is a gift, freely given by a Force intent on giving Itself away.

You decide each day whether or not you are worthy. Stop suffering to prove your worth. Stop jumping through hoops trying to earn a good life. Accept that you are worthy right now, and start living the life you have always been entitled to live. It's time for you to live well, be happy, and fall in love.

January 30

Awake my soul! Stretch every nerve, and press with vigor on;
a heavenly race demands thy zeal, and an immortal crown.
Philip Doddridge

ZEAL

It is easy to be lulled to sleep by the monotony of everyday human life. Before you know it, you catch yourself sleepwalking through the day, passing obliviously through it instead of being present in it. For some contests, you do not have to be present to win. But that's certainly not the case in life. Your Presence is required.

Where is your gusto? Where is your fierceness? Have you forgotten who you are?

Stay awake. Move forward in joy. Follow love. Look for the fulfillment of your dreams. Expect miracles. Be present.

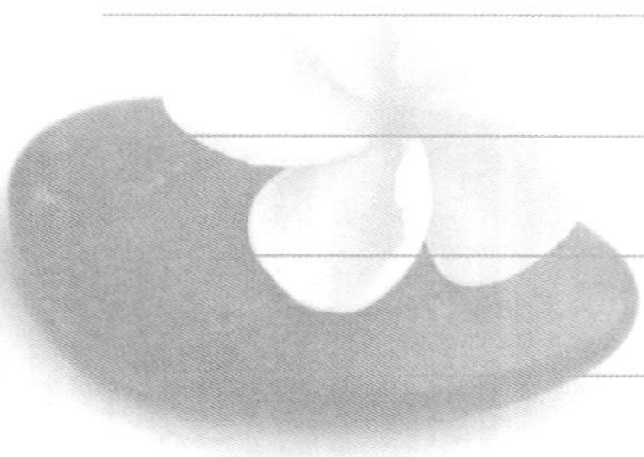

JANUARY 31

Just to be is a blessing;
just to live is holy.
Abraham J. Heschel

HOLINESS

These past thirty days of journaling have been a meditation on sacredness as a way of practicing awareness of the Presence. While exploring holiness, it is worthwhile to consider that it is to be found in everything, not only in practices and places set aside for spiritual purposes. Practice seeing the Presence in the people you meet this week, and also in the tasks of which you are least fond. Attempt to be present for whatever life brings your way, with an attitude of openness and adventure.

FEBRUARY

Practice *the* Presence *through* Love

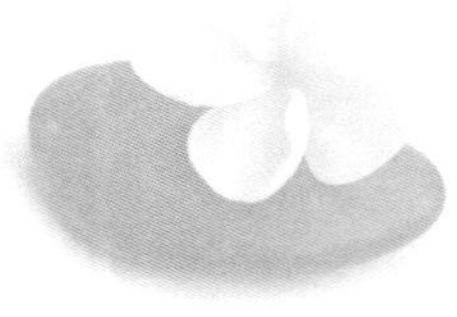

February 1

Real life isn't always going to be perfect or go our way, but the recurring acknowledgement of what is working in our lives can help us not only to survive but surmount our difficulties.
Sarah Ban Breathnach

ACKNOWLEDGING

This month, our attention shifts to the practice of loving. Becoming better at loving others is a powerful way to understand the Presence within us. A particularly effective practice is to regularly acknowledge the good in others as well as in ourselves, regardless of whatever difficulties and challenges are present. We can more powerfully experience the Presence in others when we practice acceptance and compassion, because these attitudes of mind allow us to see beyond our preferences and projections. When we pause daily to consider and acknowledge other people, they become portals through which we see the activity of the Presence.

Who in your life deserves your acknowledgement right now, and how might you express your appreciation of how they have contributed to your well-being?

FEBRUARY 2

To laugh often and much; to win the respect of intelligent people and the affection of children…to leave the world a better place…to know even one life has breathed easier because you have lived. This is to have succeeded.
Ralph Waldo Emerson

AFFECTION

Albert Einstein wrote, "A human being is part of a whole, called by us the Universe, a part limited in time and space. He experiences himself, his thoughts and feelings, as something separated from the rest—a kind of optical delusion of his consciousness. This delusion is a kind of prison for us, restricting us to our personal desires and to affection for a few persons nearest us. Our task must be to free ourselves from this prison by widening our circles of compassion to embrace all living creatures and the whole of nature in its beauty."

In what way can you expand the circle of caring that you express? Is there something you can do today that would increase the amount of affection you contribute to the world around you?

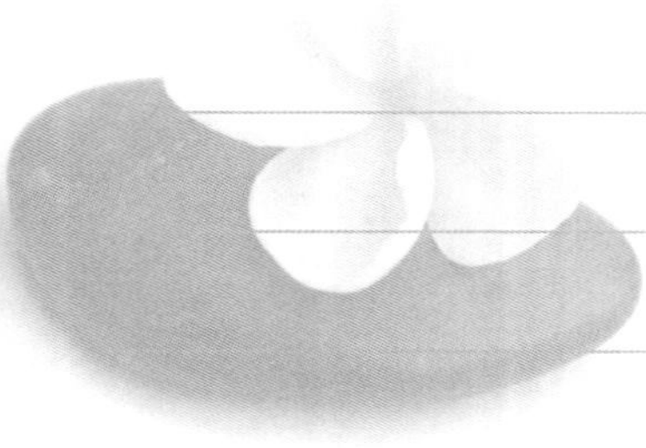

February 3

One who is too insistent on his own views,
finds few to agree with him.
Lao Tzu

AGREEING

One method of practicing love is to agree with others. This is not the same as giving up your individuality or your point of view. It is not the same as becoming a pushover for those who would control you. It is the careful investigation of where you have points of agreement with another being. From these shared points of agreement come a softening of boundaries and an opening to understanding the life, trials, and victories in the people around us. It gives rise to a feeling of safety and belonging in the world.

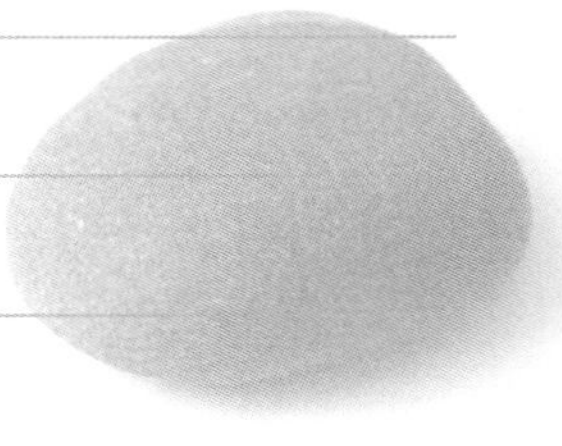

February 4

Mathematics knows no races or geographic boundaries;
for mathematics, the cultural world is one country.
David Hilbert

BOUNDARIES

Being aware of personal boundaries is a healthful way to approach life. It gives us a sense of self and helps us avoid both intruding on another person's space and exhausting our emotional and mental resources by giving too much away. There is a dark side, though, to having inflexible boundaries. If we never allow ourselves to go beyond the comfortable realm of the familiar, we miss part of the luxurious diversity in our world.

Without compromising your safety, where can you go beyond your comfort level in order to express more love in the world?

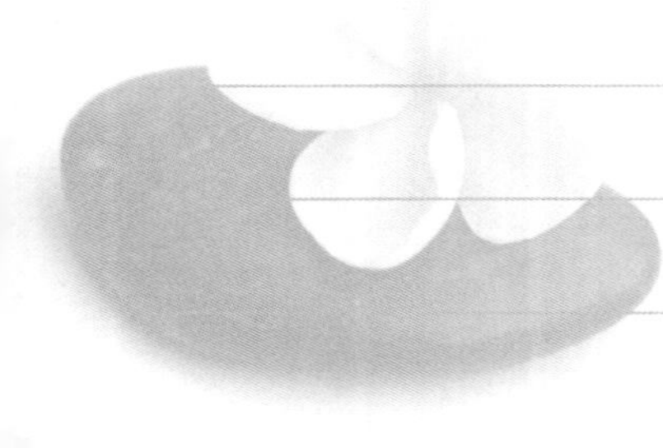

February 5

Do more than belong: participate. Do more than care: help.
Do more than believe: practice. Do more than be fair: be kind.
Do more than forgive: forget. Do more than dream: work.
William Arthur Ward

CARING

To practice caring about other people inevitably leads to the desire to contribute to their well-being. Practicing caring without following the impulse to contribute is only half of the work of becoming aware of the Presence. The Presence is continuously active in all of life all the time. Its desire to express good in the world will continue to nudge you into activities and practices that lead you into participation and acts of kindness.

True caring is the recognition of the innate perfection in others. It is more than the feelings of love and kindness we have for those closest to us. It is the feeling of kinship with all of life, and it is the response to the call we feel inside to love the life that appears in others.

February 6

Life cannot subsist in society but by reciprocal concessions.
Samuel Johnson

CONCEDING

In fostering a life in which love is expressed freely and regularly, you will find that certain skills grow to be ever more important. Skills, such as the ability to forgive and concede, allow us to navigate through the complex world of relationship and the diverse feelings, beliefs, and projections that surround and inhabit us. The act of yielding to another's choice or desire can be a powerful gift of love if it is exercised without resentment or bitterness.

An old adage asks, "Would you rather be happy or right?" A more powerful approach is to concede that different opinions exists among people and that both may be right without negating each other. Maturity allows us to accept that paradox without having to insist that our way be heard or agreed with.

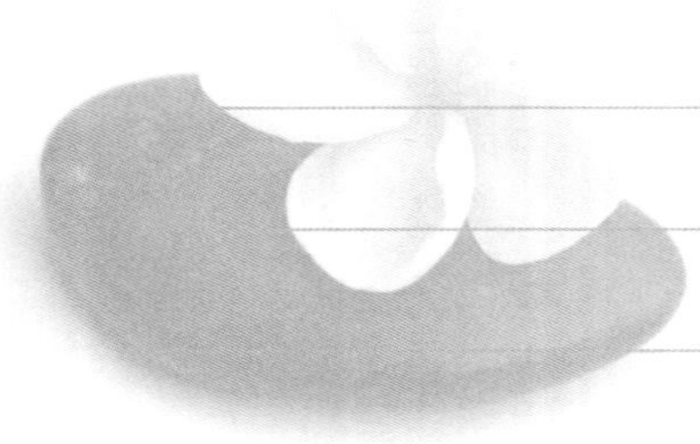

February 7

There's something so accessible about heroes who have faults.
Laura Dern

ACCESSIBILITY

Being accessible and open to life is one of our greatest challenges. It's easy to get stuck in a rut and limit yourself to the same group of people—those who go to the same places and do the same things as you.

Do you want to be accessible to other people? Are you open to love? Are you eager to accept new ideas? Do you welcome change?

Try something new today. Be open to meeting someone new. Do something differently than you have ever done before. Go somewhere new. Open your life to spontaneity. Practice being open and accessible.

FEBRUARY 8

The promises of this world are, for the most part, vain phantoms; and to confide in one's self, and become something of worth and value is the best and safest course.
Michelangelo

CONFIDING

Do you have someone in whom you can confide? Is there a person in your life to whom you can reveal your greatest dreams and worst nightmares? Are you someone else's confidant?

It has been said that confession is good for the soul. Everybody needs someone in whom they can confide, someone to tell the whole story to. Confessing your transgressions is extremely cleansing. It releases the negative energy trapped within you.

What secret have you not told anyone? What are you afraid to admit? Find a safe, nonjudgmental person to confide in, and feel the weight of the world be lifted from your shoulders.

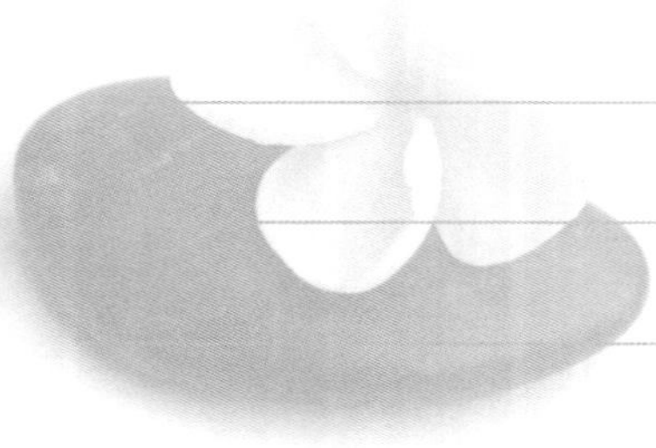

February 9

Secret forces are bringing
compatible spirits together.
I Ching

DATING

Love has its own agenda for your life that resists your strategies. It will not appear on demand. It is not convenient. It will not be coerced or forced.

Relationships are great testing grounds for spiritual growth. They show us our strengths and weaknesses. They create vulnerability and openness. They build character through cooperation and compromise. Dating is one way to prepare you for love. It shows your willingness. It invites people into your life who may have the capacity to love you as you are. It provides you with an opportunity to show compassion, understanding, and forgiveness.

Ask someone out on a date. Enjoy the process of getting to know someone new. Throw caution to the wind, and open your heart to love. Trust in love and its timing for your life.

February 10

Most of us, swimming against the tides of trouble the world knows nothing about, need only a bit of praise and encouragement—and we will make the goal.

Robert Collier

ENCOURAGING

Your friends and family do not need your advice. They don't need your judgment or criticism. They will not thrive on your unsolicited opinions. The only thing that will fuel their growth is love and encouragement.

What we need most from each other is acceptance and compassion. We don't need others to fix our problems or overcome our challenges. We just need them to say, "You are going to make it through this. I believe in you."

How encouraging are you to others? Who needs your encouragement? What will you do to show it?

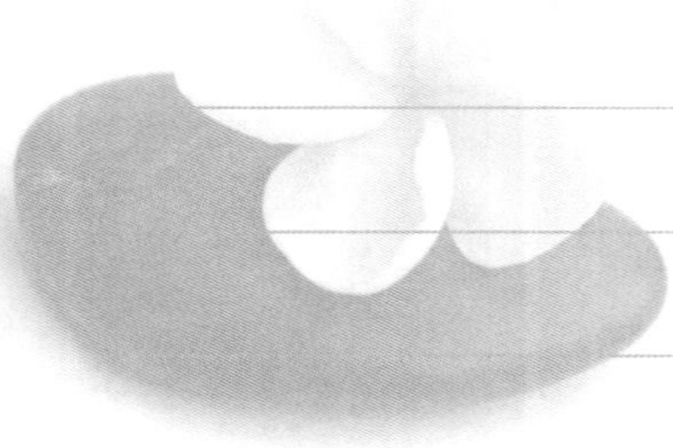

February 11

Feedback is the
breakfast of champions.
Ken Blanchard

FEEDBACK

Good communication is the key to successful relationships. Without it, all that's left is confusion and speculation. If you want to feel close to someone, share your feelings. Tell the truth. Give feedback. Make sure to be constructive, not just critical.

It is equally important to request feedback from those you admire and respect. Ask for their thoughts and feelings about your choices. Request input, with the stipulation that it be compassionate, not cruel.

With the love and support of others, you can accomplish great things. Knowing you are loved and accepted as you are gives you self-confidence and authority. You will walk taller, breathe easier, and worry less.

If you want to make friends and influence people, give feedback only when it is requested or solicited. Otherwise, it is best to keep your opinions to yourself.

February 12

An art which isn't based on feeling
isn't an art at all.
Paul Cezanne

FEELING

Wisdom and order bring structure to our lives. Without them, we would have chaos. But logic and intelligence are only one side of the human equation. Without feeling, our lives are meaningless.

The Eastern symbols of *yin* and *yang*, as well as the Western science of right-brain/left-brain thinking, demonstrate proper balance. One side is the thinker; the other side is the feeler. One without the other results in a lack of balance.

Do you maintain a healthy balance between your thoughts and feelings? Which part is overdeveloped? Which part is underdeveloped? What can you do to create greater symmetry?

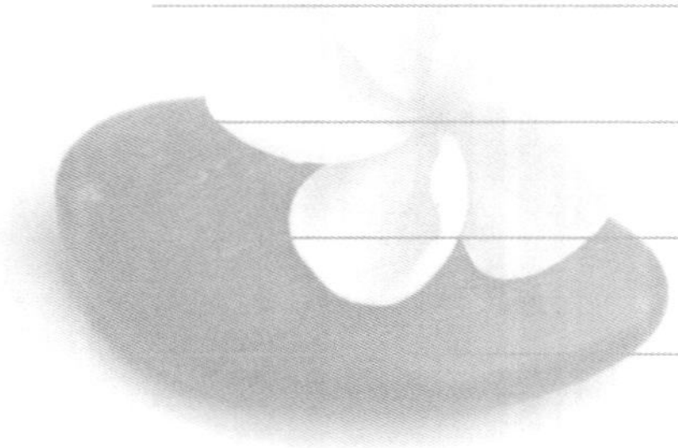

February 13

Many people have a wrong idea of what constitutes true happiness. It is not attained through self-gratification, but through fidelity to a worthy purpose.

Helen Keller

FIDELITY

Many relationships today mirror our disposable culture. People stay devoted to a relationship as long as their own personal needs are being met. But if a challenge comes to the relationship, such as a job loss or a physical problem, they head for the hills.

People are not meant to be discarded. Relationships are too valuable to be thrown away. Like fine wine, they increase in quality as the years progress. Our solid relationships prepare us for an even greater Lover. Through loving each other, we meet the Presence of a third party—God.

If you want to be temporarily entertained, go to Disneyland. But if you want a sense of lasting joy, give your love and devotion to someone worthy of it. Stay in it for the long haul.

February 14

All cruel people describe themselves as paragons of frankness.
Tennessee Williams

FRANKNESS

Tennessee Williams's point of view may be extreme; however, it serves as a reminder that direct communication can be used as an unkind weapon under the guise of honesty. Love-centered frankness is the act of open and sincere communication in a straightforward way. It is the genuine desire to disclose one's thoughts freely and is often accompanied by the willingness to deal with difficulty or unpleasant issues.

When you communicate without sensitivity, you may deliver a message that is antithetical to practicing the Presence. Love-centered frankness leads to intimacy, trust, and appreciation.

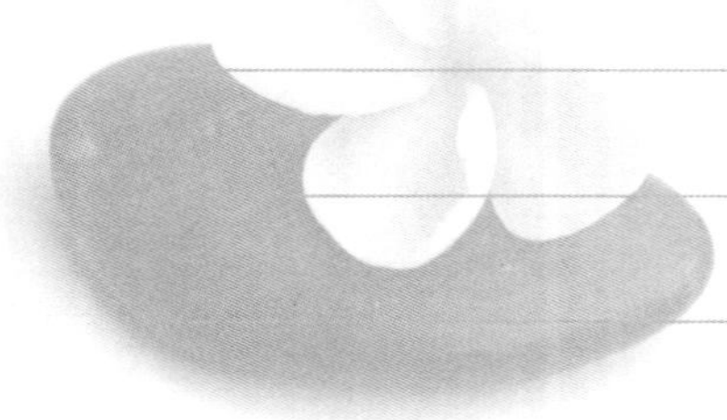

February 15

What is uttered from the heart alone, will win the hearts of others to your own.
Johann Wolfgang von Goethe

HONESTY

William Shakespeare wrote, "The good I stand on is my truth and honesty." Thomas Jefferson called honesty "the first chapter in the book of wisdom." John Lyly warned us that those who lose their honesty have nothing else to lose. By *honesty* we mean more than the direct revelation of facts. We mean what Goethe references in the quote above: that which is consistent with our hearts.

Through this practice of daily journaling, as you investigate what is important to you and how your values drive your participation in the world, you are acquainting yourself with your heart. The more you become aware of the inner world, the easier it becomes to know your heart and express it.

February 16

So when you are listening to somebody, completely, attentively, then you are listening not only to the words, but also to the feeling of what is being conveyed, to the whole of it, not part of it.

Jiddu Krishnamurti

INTEREST

One way to practice being aware of the Presence through love is to give your attention fully to other people. So many people are never truly listened to.

Try the following experiment. Ask your friends to tell you about something that is important to them. Ask them to omit no details. Invite them to start at the very beginning and take as much time as they like to share everything. And then listen to what is being revealed to you beyond the words.

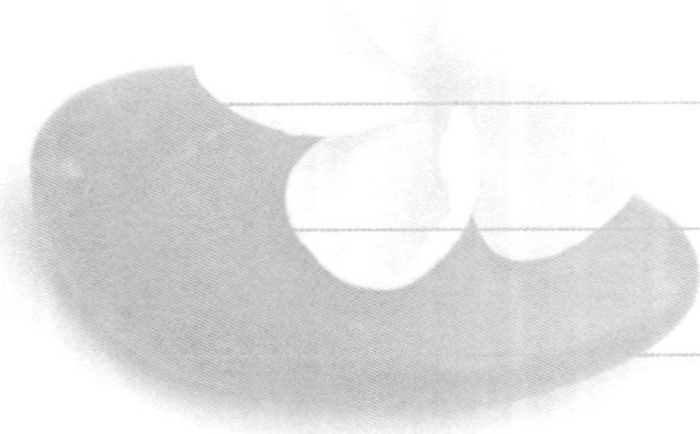

February 17

Any man who can drive safely
while kissing a pretty girl is simply
not giving the kiss the attention it deserves.
Albert Einstein

INTIMACY

In class, a student once made the humorous observation that the word *intimacy* sounds vaguely similar to the phrase "Into me you see." At the time, the comment was extremely appropriate, because we were practicing active listening skills. The phrase has stuck with me ever since, and whenever I am attempting to listen to another being, I try to remember that this person's soul expression is contained in more than the words I'm hearing. I have to listen with more than my physical ears. It is difficult for me to see into another person if I am thinking my own thoughts at the same time as the other person is sharing.

February 18

There is safety in reserve, but no attraction. One cannot love a reserved person.
Jane Austen

LIBERTY

Can you call to mind someone in whose company you feel completely free to be yourself? What do you think the contributing factors are that create the kind of liberty that allows people to reveal their cares, concerns, and joys unreservedly? How do you exhibit those qualities?

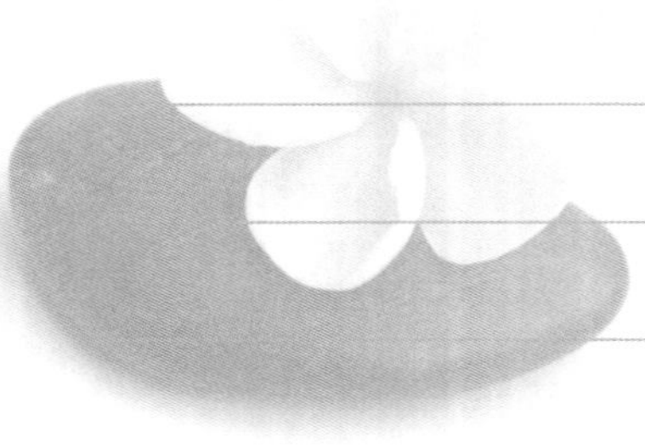

February 19

A true friend is one who knows all about you and likes you anyway.
Christi Mary Warner

LIKING

American psychologist Carol Giligan is quoted as saying, "I've found that if I say what I'm really thinking and feeling, people are more likely to say what they really think and feel. The conversation becomes a real conversation." Real conversations open the pathway to true friendship and the possibility of liking each other despite differences.

Think about the people in your life whom you really like. Possibly they have many qualities you do not like, and yet you like them anyway. What is it that allows you to continue liking them?

February 20

Before you speak, listen.
William Arthur Ward

LISTENING

Abigail Van Buren gave an excellent insight when she said that the less we talk, the more we are listened to. It is my experience, too, that being conservative with my opinions allows people to feel comfortable enough to inquire about my point of view. If only I could more consistently remember to speak less and listen more.

Winnie the Pooh's advice for dealing with people who, like me, sometimes talk too much and listen too little is this: "If the person you are talking to doesn't appear to be listening, be patient. It may simply be that he has a small piece of fluff in his ear." Something about this gentle and lighthearted advice reminds me to lighten up about the whole thing—to struggle less and to accept that the spiritual practice of becoming aware of the Presence can be joyful and simple, too.

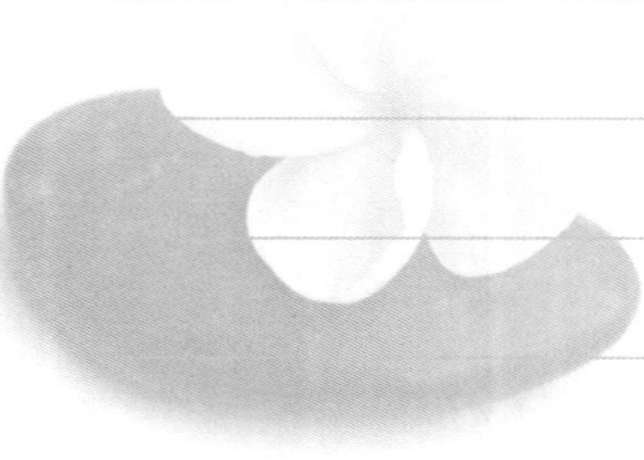

February 21

Loving can cost a lot, but not loving always costs more.
Merle Shain

LOVING

The primary purpose of your life is to love. From a Cosmic perspective, everything else you do or accomplish is nonessential. At the end of the day—as well as at the end of your human life—the question must be asked, "How much did you love?" How do you express love? In what ways are you loving? How do you show your affection?

At times, the price we pay to love seems high, but really, the opposite is true. It costs a great deal not to love. When we choose not to love, we pay for it with a loss of soul and a deep feeling that our lives are meaningless. The best way to practice the Presence is to give love. Start today!

February 22

Lack of loyalty is one of the major causes of failure in every walk of life.
Napoleon Hill

LOYALTY

Of the thousand steps it takes to succeed, most people give up on the nine hundred ninety-ninth. If only they had taken one more step, they could have manifested their dreams. Loyalty is the key to dreams coming true. And it is the one ingredient many people lack.

In order to succeed, you must remain loyal to your best ideas. Pursue them regardless of appearances. Keep moving. Don't stop. Never give up. God would not have given you the dream if there were no way for it to become manifest.

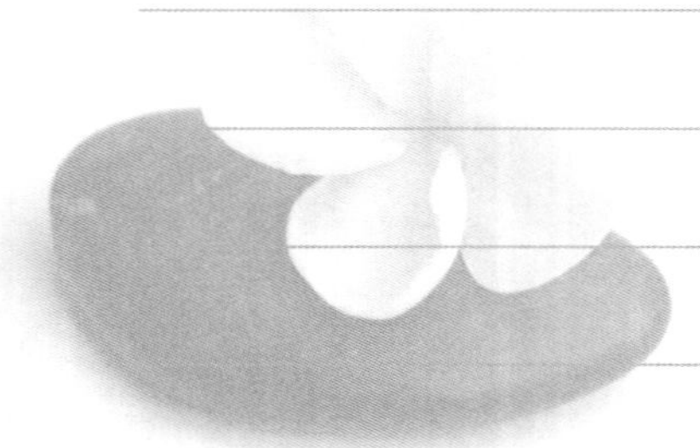

FEBRUARY 23

I must write it all out, at any cost. Writing is thinking.
It is more than living, for it is to be conscious of living.
Anne Morrow Lindbergh

NOTICING

Writing can be quite therapeutic. It allows you space to process and rethink the events of a day. It gives you time to review all that you noticed, and, perhaps, even a few things that went unnoticed.

Staying awake and conscious keeps you from ever being a victim. When you notice what happens around you and your responses to those things, you place yourself in the driver's seat of life. You can choose how you want to respond, rather than react as victims do.

What did you notice today that was kind or loving? What did you notice that you liked and approved of? What experiences do you want to repeat, and which ones do you want to avoid?

February 24

Spirit has fifty times the strength and staying-power of brawn and muscle.
Mark Twain

STAYING

Stay close to Spirit. Don't let your ego take you on the journey of fools. Stay close to your heart's desire and all that you love. Remain steadfast in your thoughts, keeping them centered only on that which you want to see manifest in your life.

Put down your tools and armor, and allow the Presence to do the work for you. All of your pushing and forcing is getting in the way. Allow and invite the Presence to go before you this day, smoothing things out and readying life for your arrival.

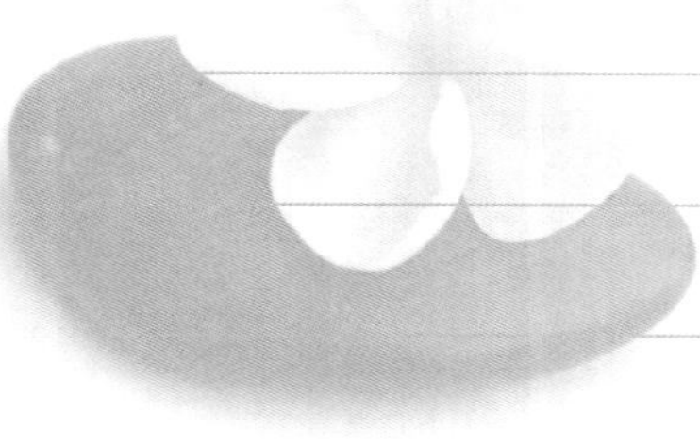

February 25

Don't flatter yourself that friendship authorizes you to say disagreeable things to your intimates. The nearer you come into relation with a person, the more necessary do tact and courtesy become.
Oliver Wendell Holmes

TACT

Not every opinion you have has to be relayed to your family and friends. Sometimes the greatest act of love is in what is not said, rather than what is. If a truth must be told, wrap it in kindness before it is delivered. Speak to others as you would like to be spoken to.

February 26

When a woman is talking to you,
listen to what she says with her eyes.
Victor Hugo

TALKING

Women are powerful. They have strengths that men can only dream of. They intuit things that men can't understand. They feel things that men can't feel. They have a unique authority that is sourced from a deep, inner well of intuition. The Presence of a woman can unite what has been divided and calm what has been chaotic.

If you are a man, listen to women. Don't discount their wisdom before you hear what they have to say. Listen between the words. Watch their eyes. They tell stories of peace and love.

If you are a woman, speak up! Share your wisdom with the world. It is working. The male-dominated culture is falling apart and learning to incorporate your foresight into a healthier, more balanced society.

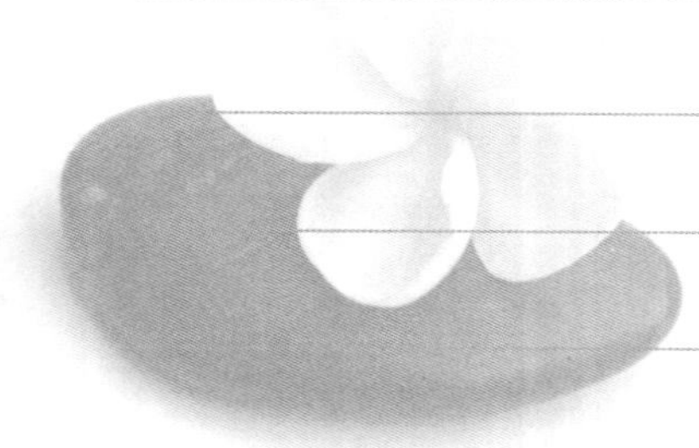

FEBRUARY 27

Life has taught us that love does not consist in gazing at each other, but in looking outward together in the same direction.

Antoine de Saint-Exupery

TOGETHERNESS

Do you know what's happening in the lives of movie stars? Do you watch television talk shows or read *People* magazine? If so, you are like many people in our celebrity-obsessed culture. They know more about the details of the lives of the people they don't know than they do of their own families or friends. They can tell you which movie star got arrested or divorced, but they don't know a thing about their next-door neighbors.

Perhaps we should get to know the people around us better. Maybe we should invest more time in them than we do in television personalities and actors. If we strengthen the ties of the people nearest to us, maybe, together, we can build a better world.

February 28

I think we enjoy the camaraderie as much as anything.
It's just about getting out, getting exercise, and enjoying the friendship.
Chuck Newman

CAMARADERIE

This month's focus on love concludes with a simple invitation to spend more time with the people you enjoy. Without any plan to grow spiritually or to get anything specific accomplished, go out and "be" with people you enjoy.

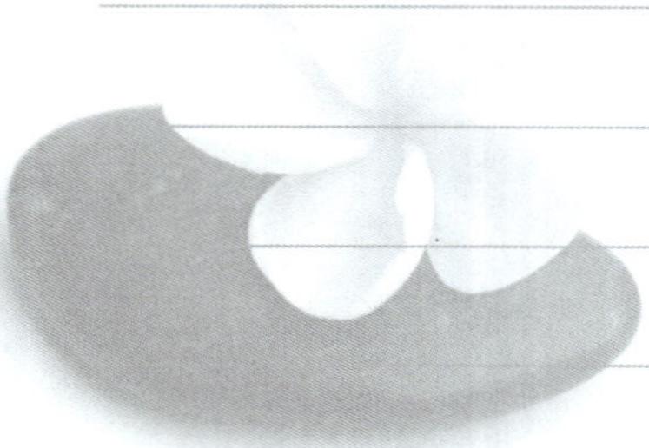

MARCH

Practice *the* Presence *through* Temperance

March 1

Use, do not abuse; neither abstinence nor excess ever renders man happy.
Voltaire

ABSTINENCE

Our focus shifts this month to a particularly powerful practice—that of exercising moderation. On a spiritual level, temperance is the ability to restrain ourselves with the ultimate purpose of having a deeper experience of the Presence. Abstinence is a voluntary restraint from excesses for both practical reasons and spiritual value. In this culture of excess, the conscious decision to practice moderation has health and mental benefits that are well-documented. Spiritually, abstinence has been practiced in many faith traditions in the form of periodic fasting or abstaining from certain activities on a regular schedule. The idea is that the practice elevates our thought, engenders appreciation, and helps us moderate the influence of desire in our lives.

As an experiment, try abstaining from something in your life for a specified period of time. Give up your cell phone for one day. Spend twenty-four hours without speaking. Eat a vegetarian diet for a week. Afterward, reflect on what the practice produced in your thoughts and feelings.

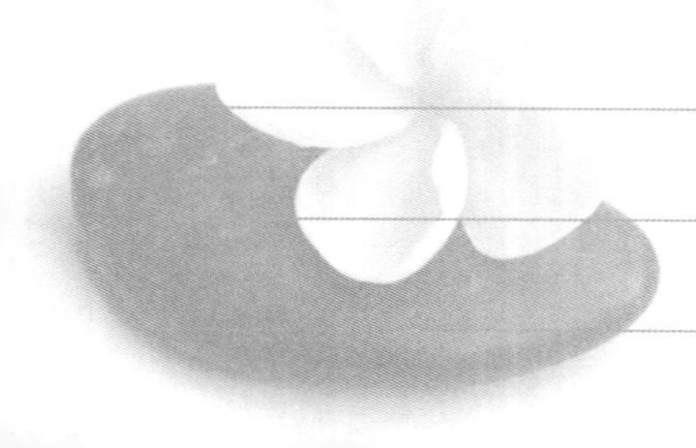

March 2

Necessity dispenseth with decorum.
Thomas Carlyle

DECORUM

American philosopher Ernest Holmes wrote, "We should read, study, think, and meditate upon those statements which tend to calm, to give poise and confidence, and erase all thought of fear and tension." The word *poise* reminds me of a state of readiness in which a person who has thoroughly practiced spiritual contemplation is prepared to take on just about anything life presents. I think of poise as an essential part of decorum.

When I was growing up, decorum was required from me at formal occasions. This is probably why I so intensely rebel at the concept now; some part of me still resists conformity for the sake of appearances. Today, I understand that there is also decorum of the soul that is available to us. This inner "right and correct behavior" is not one dictated by anyone else, but is a rightness that comes from our own spiritual understanding of who we are in the world. Over time, and with practices such as journaling and sitting quietly, we can become acquainted with the behavior and choices that are best for us, and then for our world.

March 3

Eminence without merit earns deference without esteem.
Chamfort

DEFERENCE

As we explore the practice of temperance as a pathway to knowing the Divine, we will encounter qualities of being that seem to be double-edged swords. These qualities can be empowering and sincere on the one hand, yet affected and forced on the other, to the point that, over time, they may assume negative associations in your mind. You may come up with concepts of your own to add to this category, such as discipline, humility, justice, and many of the topics that form the titles in the upcoming month. It is the purpose of these pages to guide you into investigating these concepts with a willingness to learn how, when applied, they can bring you to a closer relationship with your inherent Divinity.

Respect and courtesy are powerful when given without resentment or fear. Yielding to the opinion or will of an elder is a talent that our contemporary culture has long abandoned. Yet, in these activities lies the secret to complying with the spiritual laws of the universe. Having the wisdom to agree with the way things are is a power in itself which is most at home in a heart that understands the value of deference.

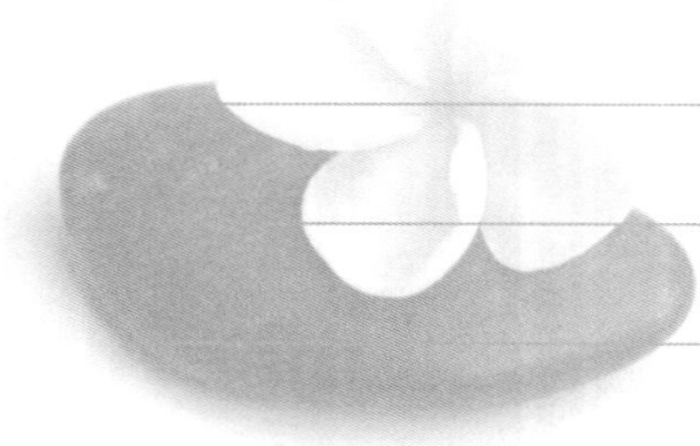

March 4

What we hope ever to do with ease, we must learn first to do with diligence.
Samuel Johnson

DILIGENCE

Diligence, like many of the topics we explore this month, has two sides. Mark Twain calls diligence a good thing, but says "taking things easy is much more restful." Benjamin Franklin said of diligence that it "overcomes difficulties, while sloth makes them." Buddha enjoined us to work out our own liberation with diligence by being our own lamps.

It is worthwhile to temper diligence with play and rest, especially when diligence starts to become an unrelenting effort to accomplish something. In spiritual practices, unrelenting effort is counterproductive. Earnestness and attentiveness is productive. Somewhere between being a fan and being a fanatic is the pathway that leads perfectly to an enduring awareness of the Presence.

March 5

To behave with dignity is nothing less than
to allow others to freely be themselves.
Sol Chaneles

DIGNITY

Dignity is an inner attitude toward life that is present in those who have based their self-respect on who they are, not on who they know, what they possess, or what learning they have achieved. Dignity draws itself from both the awareness that each person possesses the same animating principle of life we call the Presence, and a confidence that everything we shall ever need is within. This is the point where the human merges with the Divine.

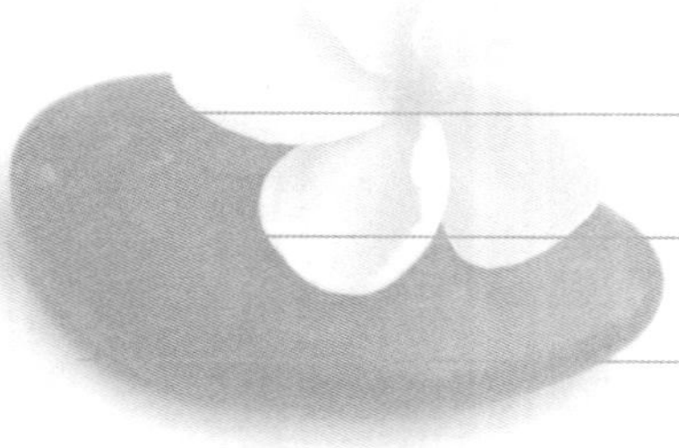

March 6

All the great things are simple, and many can be expressed in a single word: freedom; justice; honor; duty; mercy; hope.
Winston Churchill

DUTY

In our Western culture, the concept of duty is less understood than in other cultures where it is integrated into the spiritual teaching. Westerners tend to be more concerned with the concepts of human rights and the individual's freedom to choose, think, and live as each wishes. We are more likely to understand the concept of duty when considering what is required or expected of us in a job. However, in spiritual terms, duty is a trait that emerges from within ourselves, and denying it results in stressful living.

When it comes to living a spiritual life, two nurturing questions to ask yourself are: Do I have a duty to perform? Is there something that I am required to do, be, or express because it would be the "right thing" for my soul?

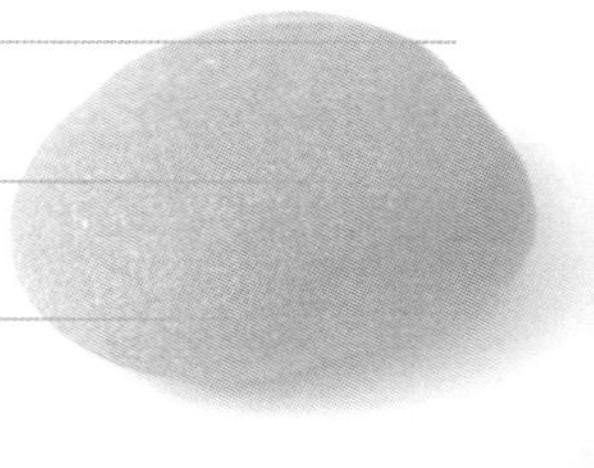

March 7

Don't back down just to keep the peace. Standing up for your beliefs builds self-confidence and self-esteem.
Oprah Winfrey

ESTEEM

To think well of yourself is not a selfish act. It is an awareness of the Presence of God within you. To love yourself is an acknowledgement of the value of that Presence.

Self-loathing is not healthy, nor does it come to us naturally. Hate must be taught. We don't come into the world with hatred in our hearts. We learn it from the people around us. Remove the tarnish of the world's ignorance and see the glory of God beneath it. Stand up for yourself. God has made you to stand upright. Feel the confidence rising from within. Trust that whatever God has given you is enough.

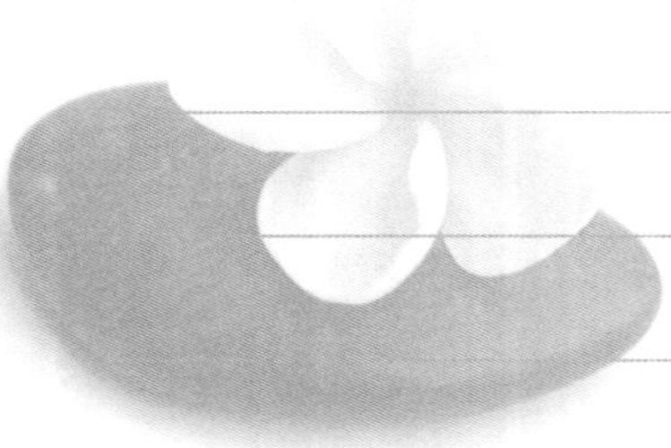

March 8

I know of no more encouraging fact than the unquestioning ability of man to evaluate his life by a conscious endeavor.
Henry David Thoreau

EVALUATING

When you compare yourself to others, do you do so in love or by harsh criticism? Do you use age, status, or gender in your comparisons? What determines the final outcome? Are you generally well-pleased by the results?

When making comparisons, it is best to look down your own path before you look down others'. No one has your challenges. No one has your gifts. Life is not a game of competition. We all die in the end. It's the journey that is important, definitely not the destination. Resist the temptation to judge yourself today. See if you can make it through an entire day without comparing yourself to someone else.

March 9

Good judgment comes from experience. Experience comes from bad judgment.
Bob Packwood

GOOD JUDGMENT

Many people learn through trial and error. By making mistakes, they learn how *not* to do things. By watching others fail, they learn of the pitfalls to avoid in their own lives. They judge the value of their lives on their ratio of successes to failures. Life experiences are categorized as either good or bad—win or lose.

The problem with this model is its concept of dualism. There is actually only one Presence in the universe. It is the Presence of a perfect, unconditional Lover. And in this Presence, there is no good or bad, no right or wrong. There is only love and acceptance.

Practice self-acceptance today. Practice not judging.

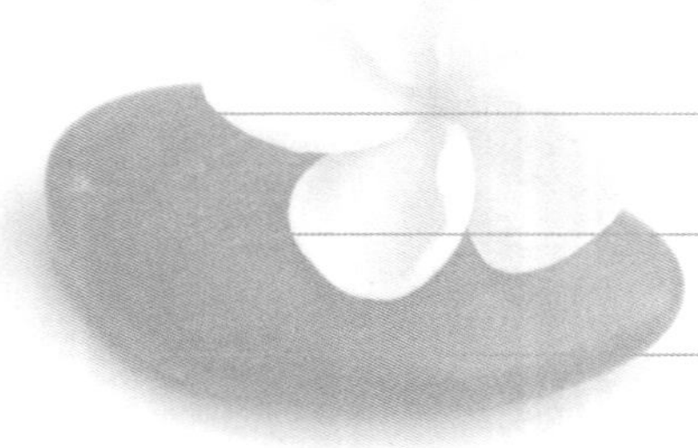

MARCH 10

There is no greatness where there is not simplicity, goodness, and truth.
Tolstoy

GOODNESS

Whenever something would surprise her, my grandmother would remark, "Well, for goodness' sake!" She was a simple, discreet woman who rarely drew attention to herself. And yet, in this humble woman, there was greatness. Perhaps we become great not by chasing after our egos' agendas, but by pursuing life for the sake of goodness alone. "For goodness' sake" might be a good motto for us to adopt.

For the sake of goodness alone, how might you redirect your life? Are you working "for goodness' sake," or just for a paycheck? Do you spend time with people in whom you see the most good? What goodness can you bring to life today?

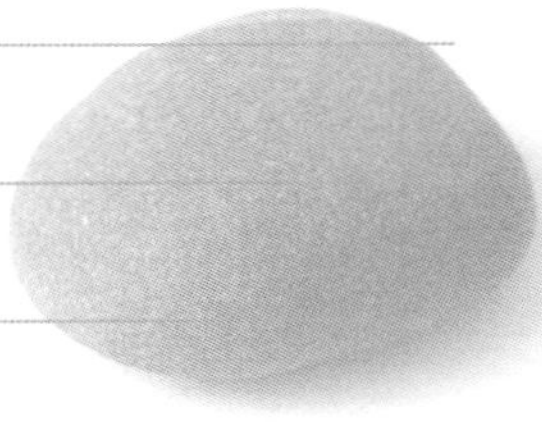

MARCH 11

What makes humility so desirable is the marvelous thing it does to us; it creates in us a capacity for the closest possible intimacy with God.
Monica Baldwin

HUMILITY

Being humble does not mean minimizing your value or contribution to life. It means recognizing who you really are in God's Presence. You do not have to put yourself down to lift God up. There is no hierarchy in heaven. There is only perfect love.

Do you have a close, personal relationship with your Creator? Can you feel the Presence of God in your home, in your life? Can you see the mystery and miracle of life?

See yourself as God sees you. Make that your goal. Look in the mirror today and resist the judgments you usually make there. Look past the physical to the metaphysical, and you will see your true self.

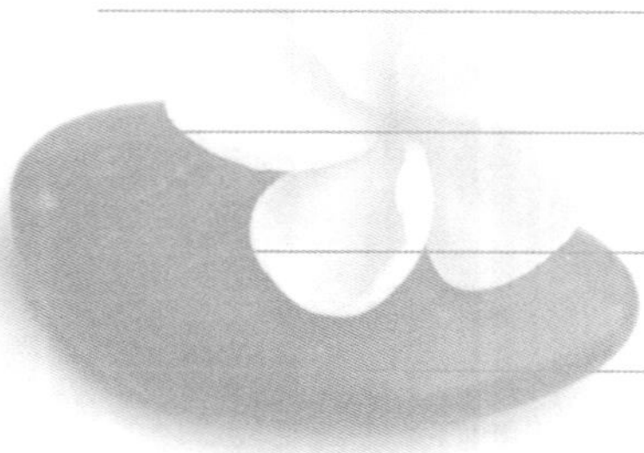

March 12

Pale death with impartial tread beats at the poor man's cottage door and at the palaces of kings.
Horace

IMPARTIALITY

Perhaps it is human nature to evaluate a situation as quickly as possible and pass judgment on it. We have to do this countless times each day. When making decisions about what to buy or where to go, we sometimes have to weigh the odds quickly. And though this may be practical on a human scale, it does not necessarily apply on the cosmic level.

God gives Itself away equally and impartially to all who will receive. Love is available to everyone. Peace and happiness are a here-and-now experience, if you so choose. The Universe has no favorites. The sun rises on the just and unjust alike. Every soul has the opportunity to redeem itself by making a new choice. What new choice would you like to make today?

March 13

Yes, if you want to say that I was a drum major, say that I was a drum major for justice; say that I was a drum major for peace; I was a drum major for righteousness.
Dr. Martin Luther King, Jr.

JUSTICE

If you judge by appearances alone, you will find no justice in life. Bad things happen to good people. People we love die. Children are abused. Thousands starve to death or suffer diseases that can easily be healed. Based on appearances alone, the world looks like a chaotic mess.

But if you stand back and take in the view of our world from space, all you see is a beautiful, blue planet, hanging there in the perfect balance of nature. Sometimes, justice requires the perspective of distance. In order to understand it, you may have to fly away from it and view it from a distance.

Concentrate on the life in front of you, and let God take care of the rest. In the end, everyone gets exactly what is coming to them.

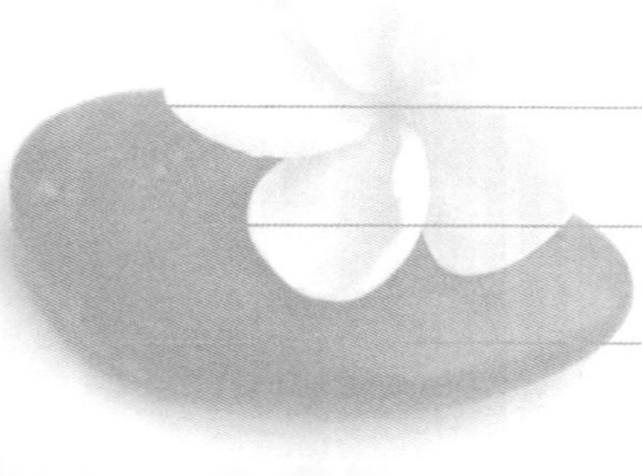

March 14

You have your way. I have my way. As for the right way,
the correct way, and the only way, it does not exist.
Friedrich Nietzsche

LENIENCY

Through my study of the world's religions, I learned that Islam, through its teaching of tolerance, instructs us to be lenient toward others and to understand their value systems. It made me think about the challenge of actually applying a value, such as leniency, rather than simply announcing it.

Aristotle said it was the mark of an educated mind to be able to entertain a thought without accepting it. This is the cornerstone of practicing leniency—allowing others to have their thoughts, their ways, and their customs, without feeling threatened or negated when yours are different. Leniency is an attitude toward life that is inclined toward gentleness and generosity.

March 15

The great secret, Eliza, is not having bad manners or good manners or any other particular sort of manners, but having the same manner for all human souls: in short, behaving as if you were in Heaven, where there are no third-class carriages, and one soul is as good as another.

George Bernard Shaw

MANNERS

To practice temperance as a pathway to experiencing the Presence means to exercise moderation in behavior and expression. This practice becomes particularly valuable when we start to investigate how our mannerisms shift, from interaction to interaction, when dealing with different types of people. For example, do we treat a person with greater prestige differently from one with less? As we become aware of this shift, we can begin to apply the remedy of treating each person equally, as if each was the embodiment of the Presence.

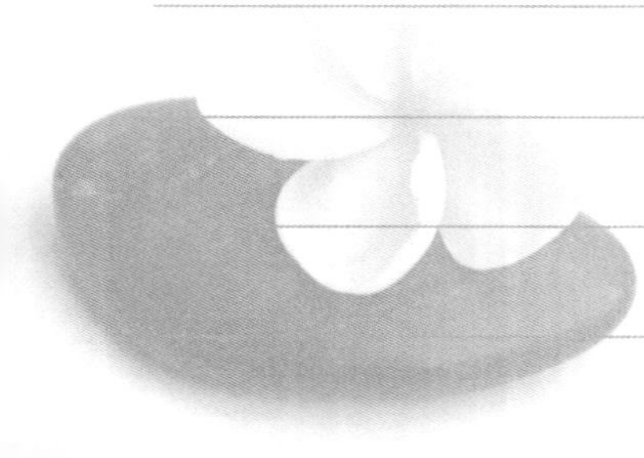

March 16

We may never be strong enough to be entirely
nonviolent in thought, word, and deed. But we must
keep nonviolence as our goal and make strong progress toward it.
Mahatma Gandhi

NONVIOLENCE

Justification for nonviolence as a way of life can be found in the *Tao,* which recommends effortless-effort; Christianity, in which Jesus exhorts his followers to love their enemies; Buddhism, where the instruction is to apply loving-kindness equally to all beings; and several other faiths, including Islam. In some forms of Hinduism, the concept is presented as *ahimsa.* This is a rule of conduct based on the belief that violence of any kind results in an accumulation of negative consequences. It means to *do no harm.*

In the West, nonviolence is also a movement for social change based on the rejection of physical violence. Mahatma Gandhi, Dr. Martin Luther King, Jr., and Cesar Chavez are examples of nonviolent leadership in recent history. Another form of nonviolence worthy of consideration when practicing the Presence is in our thought. Dr. King expressed it like this: "You not only refuse to shoot a man, but you refuse to hate him."

MARCH 17

Think about any attachments that are depleting your emotional reserves.
Consider letting them go.
Oprah Winfrey

NOT WANTING

Not wanting is another way of expressing the Buddhist axiom of non-attachment. With this concept, we examine an attitude toward life that can be a blessing or a curse. Wanting is invoked by the creative urge within us to be, do, and express more. There is a point past which wanting becomes a negative agent in our experience—the point at which it becomes attachment. In every moment of our lives, we encounter things, people, and experiences that attract us. To fill our days with these things appears to be the fulfillment of abundance. But it is a perilous path to travel on when we make the things more important to us than peace.

Not wanting, then, is the practice of balancing life in order to give us the space to be in the world, yet not controlled by it. The way to practice not wanting is to take time to be honest with yourself about which items, people, and experiences have you in their grip, so that you can begin the gentle task of disengaging from them.

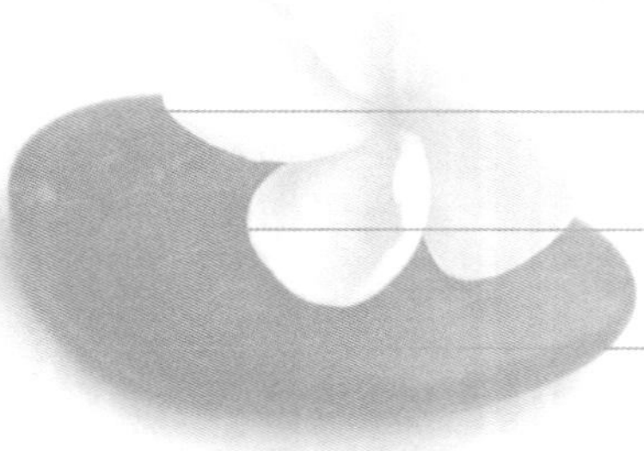

March 18

Your task is not to seek for love, but merely to seek and find all the barriers within yourself that you have built against it.
Jalal ad-Din Rumi

OPEN MINDEDNESS

Imagine moving through this world believing that everything in it exists for your highest good. It would most likely require a sober investigation into the nature of life and a willingness to look at difficulties with a mentality that can reframe them in terms of the benefits they contain.

I heard a speaker once refer to the benefits of challenges as "dark gifts." Thinking of challenges as "dark gifts" helps me be open-minded about what is going on in my life, because it opens me to be more willing to entertain the possibility that everything happening around me is part of a higher good.

March 19

Patience, persistence, and perspiration make an unbeatable combination for success.
Napoleon Hill

PATIENCE

Balancing patience with desire is part of practicing temperance. Ralph Waldo Emerson advised us to "Adopt the pace of nature; her secret is patience." A similar approach is to practice acceptance without surrendering hope. This is a shift in attitude, rather than in action.

When I accept the world around me, I am not giving up; I am shifting mental gears, so that I can become engaged in the world with a dynamic, yet relaxed, frame of mind. In this state of relaxed attentiveness, I begin to notice that all of life is about perfect timing, and that patience is necessary to truly witness what is going on. Without patience, we stand a very good chance of missing some perfect detail.

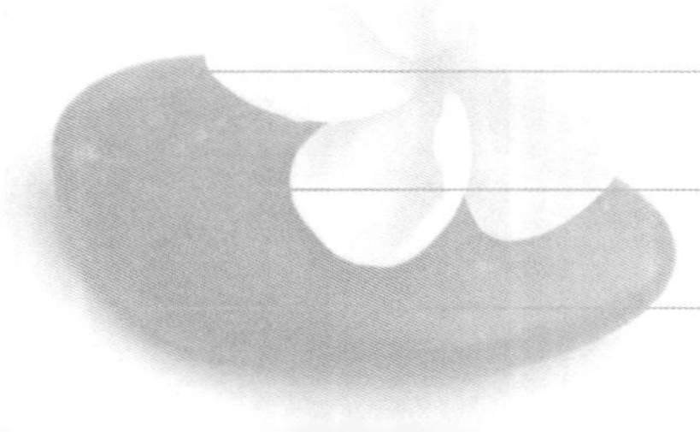

March 20

Politeness is the art of choosing among one's real thoughts.
Abel Stevens

POLITENESS

Temperance, restraint, and moderation are signs of maturity. Temperance in one's mind is the ability to observe the wide range of thoughts, feelings, and ideas that flow through, resisting the impulse to follow and express every one of them simply because they exist.

As we practice awareness of the Presence in our lives, we gradually become aware that the inner world is similar to watching a documentary on a screen—visually stimulating, emotionally rich, and sometimes boring. With practice, we see the screen for what it is and, less and less, confuse it with Reality. There comes a gradual awakening to the act of not being caught up in the events portrayed on the screen, nor losing any of the fascination and joy of observing them.

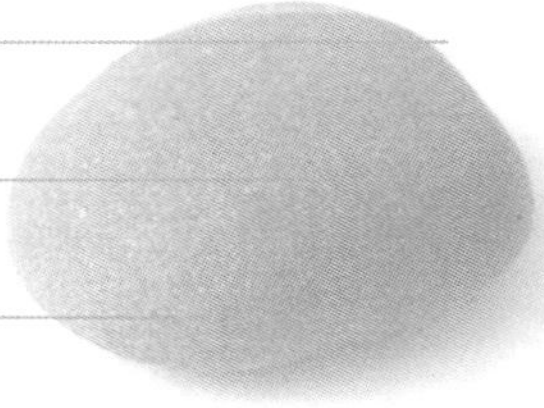

March 21

Wisely, and slow.
They stumble that run fast.
William Shakespeare

PRUDENCE

In our multi-tasking, fast-paced culture, we often find ourselves rushing about, trying to keep pace with others. We have over-scheduled days and sleep-deprived nights. How many times have you rushed to make a decision without first thinking clearly about it? What action did you take in haste? What was lost in this approach?

Do you think you would make better choices if you slowed down a bit and took time to gather strength and wisdom from within? What would be the benefit of those "wise and slow" choices in your life?

Take one challenge you face today, and give slow thought to its solution. Marinate it in the ancient and sacred wisdom you have within. When you go to sleep tonight, ask Spirit for guidance. As you awaken tomorrow morning, bring to mind your dreams. Within their mysteries are the solutions to your challenges.

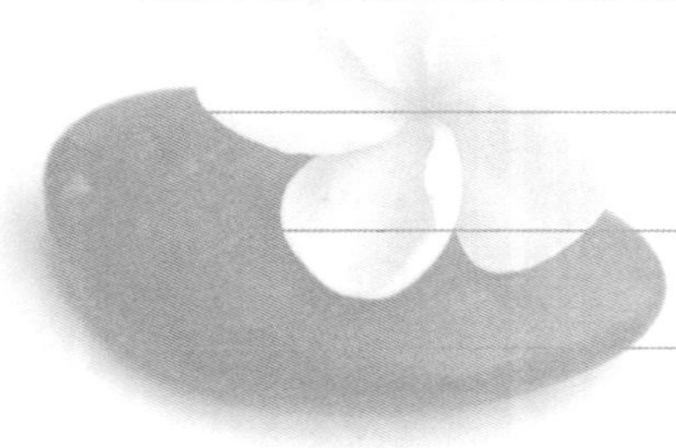

March 22

Purity and simplicity are the two wings with which man soars above the earth and all temporary nature.
Thomas Kempis

PURITY

In today's world, it's hard to find anything truly pure. Most foods have additives. Iodine is added to salt, and chlorine to water. Sugar is bleached, and food coloring is added to meat. Everything seems to have something else in it besides its original content. All of these additives are thought to contribute to the quality of the product, or at least make it more visually appealing.

However, there is a big movement toward local, organic foods. People are realizing the health benefits of a more holistic diet. Purity is making a comeback. Not only is this true of our food, it's also true of our lives. Simplicity is becoming popular again. We are getting back to basics.

What additives have made their way into your life? What would happen if you removed them? How can you practice purity?

MARCH 23

All ballplayers should quit when it starts
to feel as if all the baselines run uphill.
Babe Ruth

QUITTING

For everything, there is a season: a time to win, a time to lose; a time to start and a time to quit. Life is full of beginnings and endings. Trouble sets in when we try to avoid the endings and attempt to continue something that we need to stop. We do this in fear. We are afraid that if we quit, nothing else will show up for us. But just the opposite is true. You have to stop doing what no longer serves you in order to create an opening for something new to come along.

When there's no joy left in what you're doing, it is time to quit. When it takes more energy than it's worth, it is time to stop. What do you need to quit?

March 24

The only guide to a man is his conscience; the only shield to his memory is the rectitude and sincerity of his actions.
Winston Churchill

RECTITUDE

One of the fundamental spiritual laws of life states that the inner must become the outer, meaning that what is inside a person's mind or heart eventually shows up on the outside of a person's life. As much as we try to avoid revealing ourselves to others, who we are screams at the world through nonverbal communication.

When we find what is good within ourselves, we naturally show good will toward others. When we touch the true nature of our inner being and discover our oneness with all life, greater compassion for others is the natural consequence.

Look within and see if God hasn't placed something wonderful inside you.

March 25

Stand up to crises. Don't let them throw you! Refuse to renounce your self-image. No matter what happens, you must keep your good opinion of yourself. No matter what happens, no matter what you lose, no matter what failures you must endure, you must keep faith in yourself.

Maxwell Maltz

RENOUNCING

You have more power than you think and more resources than you are aware of. You are stronger than you realize. Never give up on yourself, even if you have to renounce the entire world. Nothing is more important to the value and quality of your life than keeping a good opinion of yourself.

Have faith in what God has given you. At the end of the day, other peoples' opinions don't matter. What matters most is what you think about yourself. You will know you have made the right choices if you can live with yourself in integrity and honor.

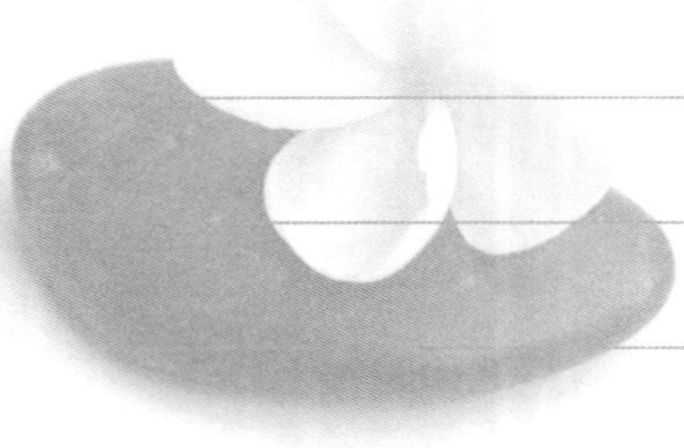

March 26

True religion is real living; living with all one's soul,
with all one's goodness and righteousness.
Albert Einstein

RIGHTEOUSNESS

To live a righteous life means to live in harmony with Spirit. It means listening to that inner voice that says, "Go forward today and know that you are loved." Righteousness is living in accordance with spiritual law.

Practice treating others as you wish to be treated. Practice giving to others what you want to receive. Practice sending out only that which you want to return into your life.

March 27

Only those who have learned the power of sincere and selfless contribution experience life's deepest joy: true fulfillment.
Tony Robbins

SINCERITY

Sincerely yours are words that end many written correspondences. These words speak the writer's intention to convey an open and honest communication. Every time your words or actions match the honesty of your heart, you enrich your life by being truly authentic.

To be true to your heart in all of your conveyances is also a gift you give to others. It honors their integrity and invites their virtue. Speak directly to the people around you. Look closely into their eyes, and let one soul see another through the veil of human matter. Be sincere in all of your communications and others will be so with you.

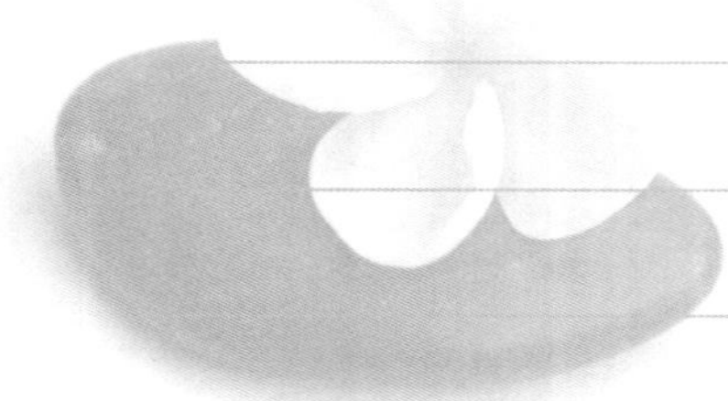

March 28

I keep telling people: Don't make me the poster boy for AA because I don't know a lot about sobriety, but I do know a lot about drinking.
Billy Joel

SOBRIETY

Today, the word *sobriety* refers to moderation in or abstinence from drinking alcohol or using drugs, largely in part to the excellent work of Alcoholics Anonymous. The word *sober* is also used to describe the personal characteristic of one who avoids excesses and tends toward seriousness.

In this month of practicing temperance, it is worthwhile to meditate on the word *sober* and to ask yourself if there are any areas in your life that, through inattention, have fallen into excess. It could be an excess of inaction, an excess of worry, an excess of negative self-talk, or an excess of the kind that is physically self-damaging. Is there some area of your life in which you are intoxicated by excess, and is there an action you need to take to adjust?

March 29

Tis plain that there is not in nature a point of stability to be found: everything either ascends or declines. When wars are ended abroad, sedition begins at home, and when men are freed from fighting for necessity, they quarrel through ambition.
Sir Walter Scott

STABILITY

The word *temperance* makes me think of balance; and balance requires stability. I remember watching a tightrope walker use a balancing bar to navigate her way across a rope. I was amazed at how stable she seemed, even though she was constantly in motion, making little adjustments every moment to bring her into balance.

Stability is not being static or stuck. It is the constant self-regulating action in which life is engaged all the time. Perhaps we can practice a type of conscious self-regulation by taking time daily to reflect and evaluate where there is a need to make subtle adjustments to keep our balance.

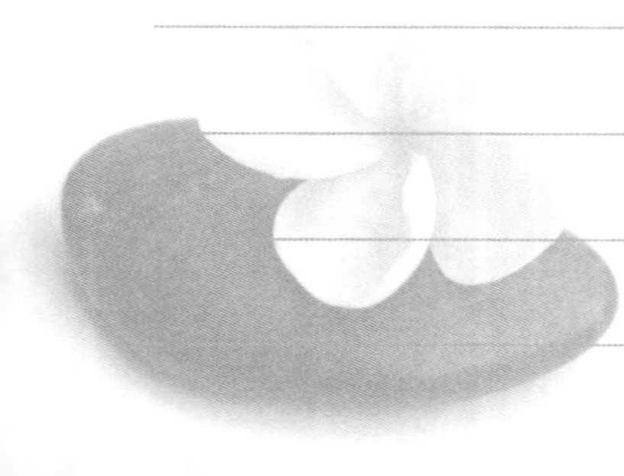

March 30

Blessed are the meek
for they shall inherit the earth.
King James Bible, Matthew 5:5

MEEKNESS

I remember attending a lecture by a Bible scholar who introduced to me a new way of thinking about the word *meek*. He explained that many people associate the word with weakness and cowardly behavior. However, in the stories of the Bible, those mentioned as meek tend to be strong leaders who have one thing in common: the ability to learn and follow intuition (or divine inspiration). They tend to be people of great power who have their power in check. They represent well-managed strength.

Meekness (not to be confused with weakness) can be thought of as the power it takes to live according to your values when the urges and pressures of life around you seem to strongly guide you in other directions. It is a way of not resisting what your highest mind knows is true of you, even though it seems you are being tossed about by the storms of desires and worldly influences.

March 31

Your greatness is measured by your kindness; your education and intellect by your modesty; your ignorance is betrayed by your suspicions and prejudices, and your real caliber is measured by the consideration and tolerance you have for others.
William J. H. Boetcker

MODESTY

A philosopher once said that one's modesty generally increases with one's beauty. It is a reminder that having a healthy relationship with yourself is an initial step toward spiritual awakening. Modesty cannot be faked with the hope that it will lead to emotional maturity and a spiritual life.

Become aware of the Presence that lives within you. Follow its guidance and choose to participate in life consciously as a self-reliant being. Then, as self-esteem grows, modesty will not be something to be turned on for certain occasions. Instead, it will be naturally present inside as you confidently embody the Presence.

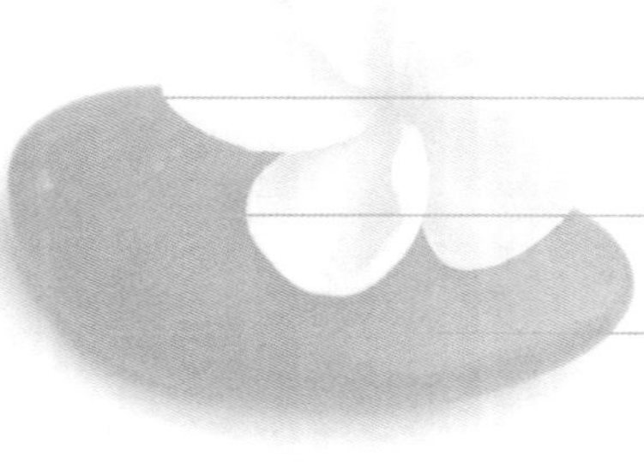

APRIL

Practice *the* Presence *through* Community

The way you get meaning into your life is to devote yourself to loving others, devote yourself to your community around you, and devote yourself to creating something that gives you purpose and meaning.
Mitch Albom

ANSWERING

We are all part of one human family, even though our independent and solitary lifestyles sometimes minimize the powerful connection of community. I believe that if we sit quietly and think about what community means, we will feel a deep, soulful call to step out of our self-imposed walls of isolated living. We belong to each other and have the capacity to love and care for each other. However, when we act as if we are separate and refuse to answer the call to connect, we support the illusion that we are separate and, for a while, mistakenly believe that we are safe in our separation.

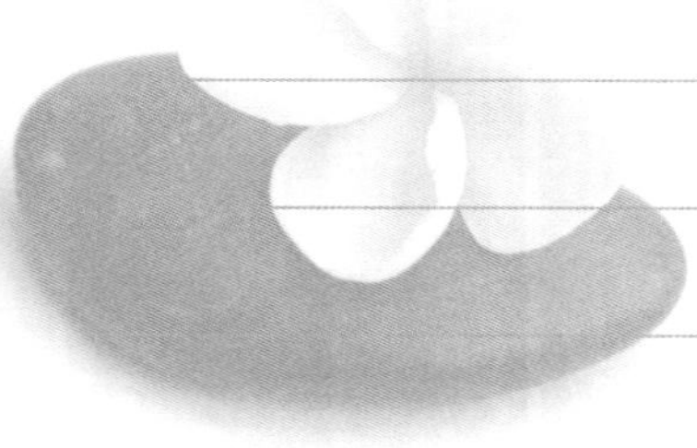

April 2

Don't approach a goat from the front,
a horse from the back, or a fool from any side.
Yiddish Proverb

APPROACHING

The proverb quoted above light-heartedly reminds us that the manner in which we answer the call to be in community is as important as the act of joining it. To understand this principle better, ask yourself: "How do I show up? What walks into a room with me? How does my personality contribute to the personality of the group?" If you make the choice to avoid community, you won't have the groundwork for exploring these questions.

April 3

First ask yourself: What is the worst that can happen?
Then prepare to accept it. Then proceed to improve on the worst.
Dale Carnegie

ASKING

Communities are groups of people united by a common interest. You can enrich the experience of community by asking people what interests them. You might already have a community of one or two people in your very own circle of acquaintances with whom you share an interest that you have not yet discovered. For some people, stepping through the fear of asking is the first step of taking down the walls that separate us.

One dynamic type of community is a group of two or more people who support each other in prayer. It is satisfying to go through life knowing that others support you in prayer as you likewise support them. Asking someone to be your prayer partner can be an act of vulnerability, though. You may be refused. And if you are refused, asking someone else becomes an even greater act of courage. In the end, it is worth it. Praying for someone's highest good on a weekly basis, and being prayed for in return, is like taking a spiritual vitamin. I can't imagine life without it.

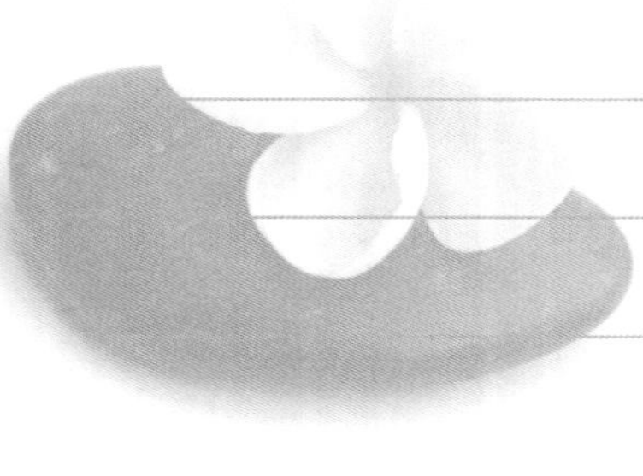

APRIL 4

A man is truly ethical only when he obeys the compulsion to help all life which he is able to assist, and shrinks from injuring anything that lives.
Albert Schweitzer

ASSISTING

More than any other species, we human beings require many years of guidance and nurturing before we can independently make it on our own in the world. From the cradle through our late teens, we require great amounts of assistance. Even into early adulthood, we still depend on friends and family for wisdom and clarity. This part of human nature speaks volumes. It reminds us that we are all here to help each other.

You were never meant to make it on your own. That's why there are so many people in the world who can assist you. Don't be afraid or ashamed to ask for help when you need it. What assistance do you need today?

April 5

The major block to compassion is the judgment in our minds.
Judgment is the mind's primary tool of separation.
Diane Berke

COMPASSION

It's easy to see what other people need to do to improve their lives. Their mistakes seem so obvious. Their limitations seem so ridiculous. Why can't they see what we see? Why can't they take our advice to fix their problems?

Everyone has blind spots—limitations to overcome and challenges to go through that are not outwardly visible. You have yours, too. You have areas in your life that need improvement. Knowing this allows us to show compassion for each other, even as we face our unique challenges in our own time and sequence. We have been created as individuals, so we must each walk our own path toward enlightenment.

How can you release judgment and practice compassion today?

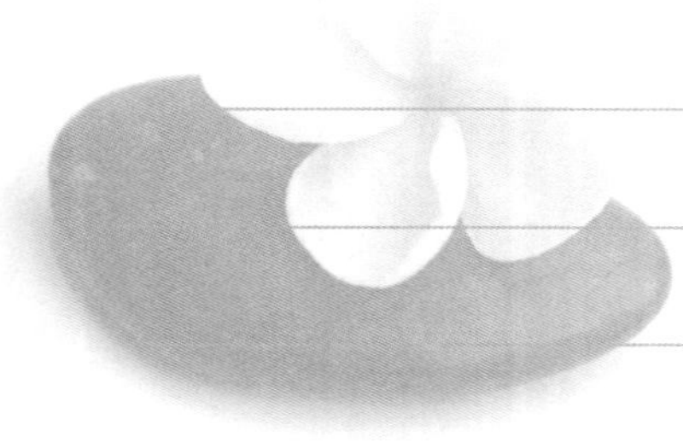

April 6

Better to bend
than break.
Scottish Proverb

COMPROMISING

Rigidity makes you age quickly. Uncompromising people become increasingly bitter and angry as they get older. They frequently end up alone, because their behavior tends to alienate other people, including their own family members. Self-righteousness is their only companion, and a cold one at that.

It is beneficial to remain flexible in life, bending in the wind, going with the flow, rather than insisting that life yield to your stern demands. This doesn't mean you sacrifice your integrity or authenticity. Some values must remain intact. However, there are things in life that just aren't worth fighting for.

Choose your battles wisely. Don't waste energy on things that don't really matter. When you take a stand, be sure it is on an issue of great importance to you. What have you been vehemently resisting? How can you be better served by compromising?

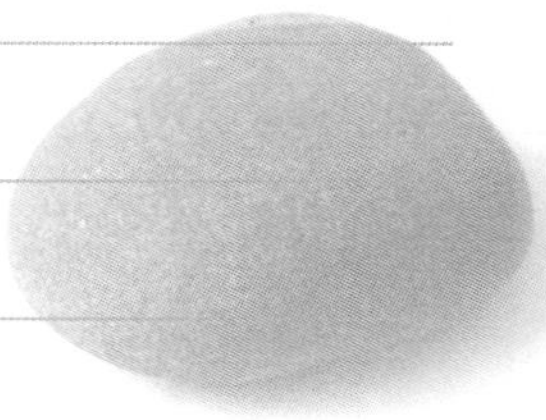

APRIL 7

Great discoveries and improvements invariably involve the cooperation of many minds.
Alexander Graham Bell

COOPERATION

Do you try to do too much on your own? Is it hard for you to ask for help when you need it? Are you getting tired of playing the Lone Ranger? Are you growing resentful that other people aren't helping—even though you haven't asked for their assistance? You may be one of the millions of people who believe they are alone and without resources in the world.

The truth is: No one accomplishes anything of real value on their own. Every great achievement thrives on the input and cooperation of many people. Behind every successful woman are many others who have supported her along the way. No man gets to the top by his own effort. Lifting him up were a thousand others.

Look to cooperate with others today. See what you can do to support their success. Practice asking for help. Enlist the cooperation of others in your dreams, and see what you can create together.

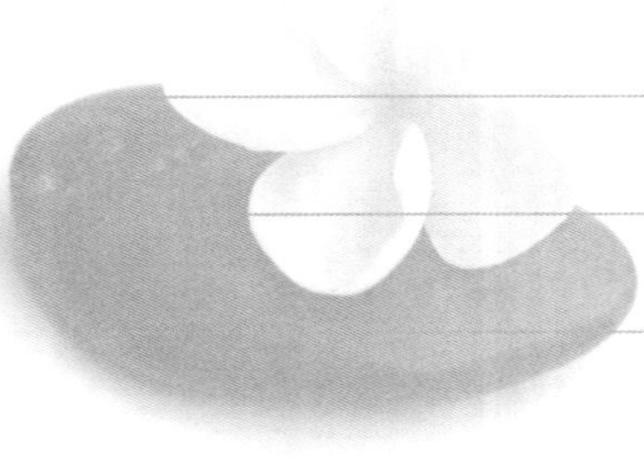

April 8

Preservation of one's own culture does not require contempt or disrespect for other cultures.
Cesar Chavez

CULTURE

The global society in which we live exposes each of us to a host of ethnicities and cultures. This is a good thing. Isolation within one group or tribe causes stagnation and self-righteousness. Exposure to others who think, act, and behave differently forces us to rethink our own commonly accepted behaviors. It invites change and growth.

The goal of a multicultural environment should not be to absorb each other into a melting pot where individuals lose their heritages and identities. It should be to embrace the differences and incorporate them into a new and better way to live for everyone.

Do you have a tribe? Are you a member of a subculture? How can you honor your heritage and, at the same time, respect others?

April 9

I would believe only in a God
that knows how to dance.
Friedrich Nietzsche

DANCING

Surely, the God that gives us the desire for self-expression must also desire that we fully exercise it. Surely, the God who causes us to feel rhythm must delight in our dancing.

Spirituality is a dance with the Creator. Sometimes you get to lead, and other times you are required to follow. Each day is a new opportunity to dance. Each day the rhythm changes. One day it is a salsa, and the next a slow dance. The purpose in variation is to prevent boredom and ignite passion.

Dance today! Feel the rhythm of your soul. Even if you are alone, play your favorite music and dance.

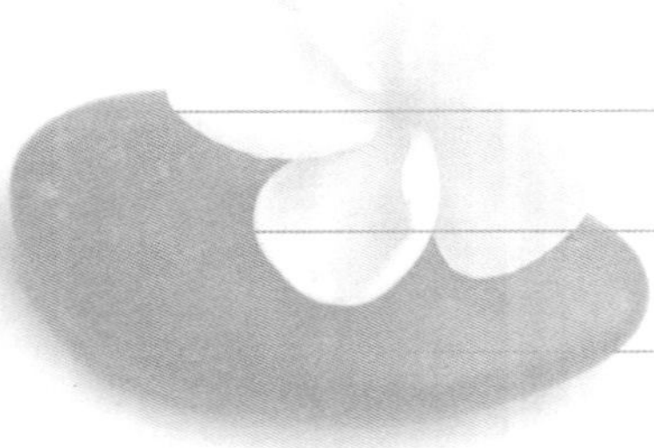

April 10

Be trustworthy. Be the person who can keep a secret, isn't a gossip, and can be counted on in all situations.
Larry Winget

DEPENDABILITY

Do you have a twenty-four-hour friend—someone you can call at any time of night or day, make any request, and have it fulfilled? Is there someone in your life who will grant your favor without question—someone who will stand up for you, no matter what? If so, then you understand the value of that type of dependability. Very few people offer it. Be one of them. Be the person others can count on in times of need. Give all of yourself to someone, being loyal to the end.

April 11

We all should know that diversity makes for a rich tapestry, and we must understand that all the threads of the tapestry are equal in value no matter what their color.
Maya Angelou

DIVERSITY

Once, in a diversity workshop I attended, the facilitator introduced us to the practice of listening deeply to the minority voice in our group. We learned that even though people will affirm their love and support of diversity, they can easily slip into the habit of minimizing the minority voice in a discussion or in a group. Through exercises, we began to notice how easily we assumed that the majority voice adequately represented everyone in the group. After carefully listening to those with the minority opinion, though, we began to understand that it is in the voice of the minority that we often found the cutting edge of our upward evolution. While we were engrossed in what seemed like universal agreement, we were missing the powerful contribution of the dissenting voice.

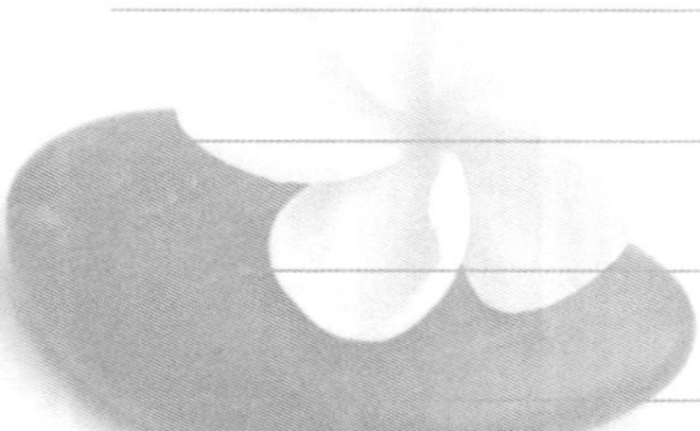

April 12

You don't have to accept the invitation to get angry. Instead, practice forgiveness, empathy, and encouragement.

Dan Fallon

EMPATHY

To someone interested in experiencing the Presence through community, the skill of empathy becomes invaluable. The ability to identify with or understand another person's situation is powerful. When we add to that the openness to truly recognize what other people are feeling and what might fuel their motives, we become more likely to have a wholesome experience of being in community.

A well-known strategy for practicing empathy is to put yourself in the other one's shoes, or in some way to try to experience the other person's point of view. Fully developed empathy requires practice and patience, and goes beyond simply resonating with another person's state of mind. It includes the willingness to look deeply inside and see how that person's life is part of your own.

April 13

The most important environmental issue is one that is rarely mentioned, and that is the lack of a conservation ethic in our culture.
Gaylord Nelson

ENVIRONMENTALISM

Any seekers of truth and students of the Presence can no more avoid becoming conscious of the life force in nature than they can stop breathing. At some point, passion for practicing the Presence requires us to be in the natural world and experience the majesty of what the Presence has created. Frequent time spent in nature gives rise to a curiosity about the balance between people and the planet, and our roles as stewards of the place we call home. For too long, we have thought of ourselves merely as temporary inhabitants on this planet; that it is here for our use and domination; that we are assured some future life elsewhere, if we can just get through this obstacle course called Earth.

Today, people everywhere are questioning the wisdom of thinking that the planet is something separate from the Power that created it. As you sit daily with the questions and thoughts posed in this journal, becoming more aware that you move and live and have your being inside the Presence, allow yourself to gradually awaken a more powerful conservation ethic.

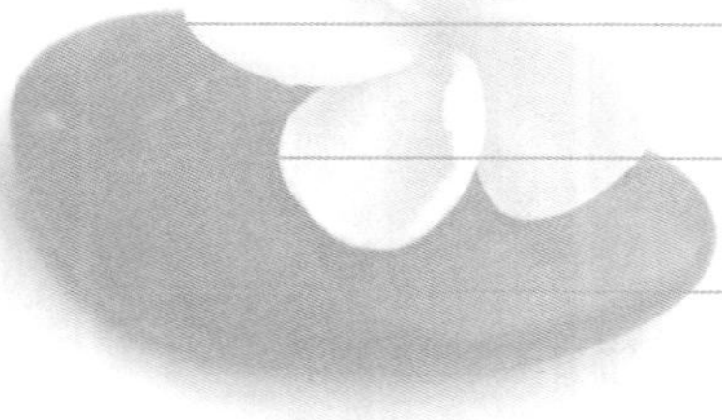

APRIL 14

It is not fair to ask of others
what you are unwilling to do yourself.
Eleanor Roosevelt

FAIRNESS

The power and value of community is that not only are we stronger together than we are apart, but that when we are together, we learn how to be stronger individually. Community develops our strengths, because, in community, we quickly discover that every person is a reflection of our own aspirations and flaws.

When looking at the faults in others, it becomes useful to examine whether we would be willing to change and grow in the way that we hope others would. Asking "Where am I the same as them?" is a wiser approach to practicing community than saying, "If only they would change."

April 15

If money is your hope for independence, you will never have it. The only real security that a man will have in this world is a reserve of knowledge, experience, and ability.
Henry Ford

INDEPENDENCE

Powerful independence can be found when we learn about and begin to appreciate how deeply interdependent we are. Strong communities possess a lot of room for diversity and individuality. Community builds character and strength. It connects us to one another and holds us accountable for our choices. It can be a place to share the joys of life and a place of sanctuary when we are hurting. In politics, *independence* refers to self-governance, as opposed to being ruled or subjugated by another power.

As you consider the role you play in your community, ask yourself how your community contributes to your ability to govern yourself.

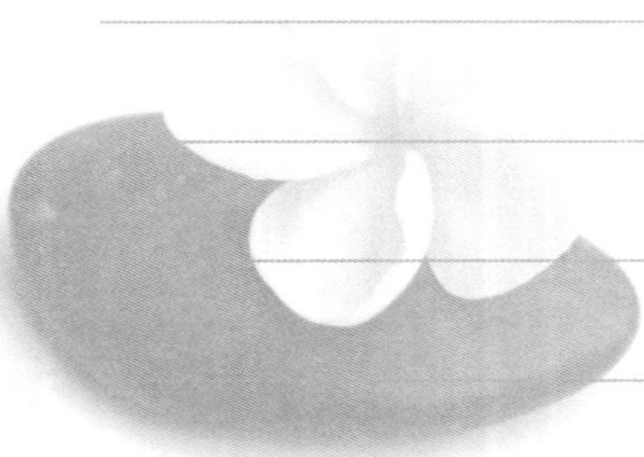

April 16

Most people are other people. Their thoughts are someone else's opinions, their lives a mimicry, their passions a quotation.

Oscar Wilde

INDIVIDUALITY

American actor Ethan Embry is quoted as saying, "You just have to do your own thing, no matter what anyone says. It's your life." This advice is worthy of reflection as we consider the spiritual growth potential of being in community. The strength of a community lies in the strength of its individuals and how well they maintain their individuality within the group identity. There is a fine balance to be struck in yielding to the greater good and knowing when it is time to stand alone.

A pastoral counseling teacher once advised that, to be effective in our communities, we would do well to remember that we have to know when to roar like a tiger and when to bleat like a lamb.

April 17

If you limit your choices only to what seems possible or reasonable, you disconnect yourself from what you truly want, and all that is left is compromise.
Robert Fritz

LIMITS

Community is a powerful sanctuary. It is said that Buddha advised us to take refuge in the community of faith. This is a beautiful and true thought. To turn to our community of fellow seekers in times of challenge can be mind-expanding and soul-healing.

However, there is the potential challenge for the person practicing the Presence: being swept up by the "average" thought that is inevitably present in any crowd. This "average" thought is known as *group mind* and represents a real limitation for one who stays within the possibilities that the group has heretofore experienced. It is both a contribution and a blessing to the community when members reach beyond their histories and previously achieved gains.

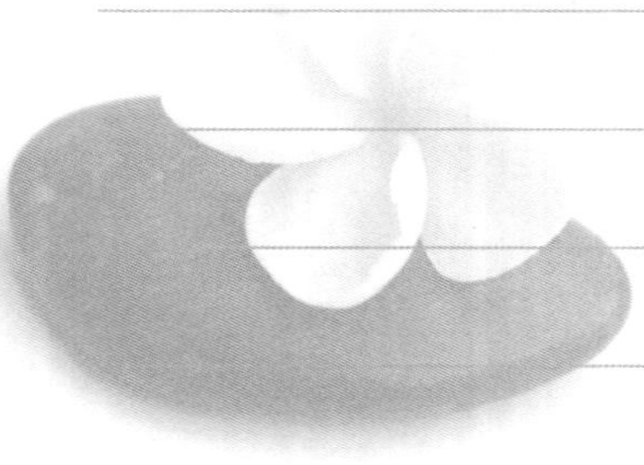

April 18

Many of us grow up to be people pleasers. The word "no" drops out of our vocabulary, and we substitute lots of ways to be agreeable and keep the other person happy.
Linda D. Tillman, Ph.D.

NO

Practice saying "no." Use the word as often as necessary. Use it when someone asks you to do something in which you have no heartfelt desire to participate. Use it when others invade your personal boundaries of self-care and replenishment. Use it when you are tempted to accept less than what you truly want. Use it when you are asked to sacrifice your integrity or honor.

Just say, "No!" Say it once and mean it. If you want to add a bit of kindness to it, then you could say, "No, thank you."

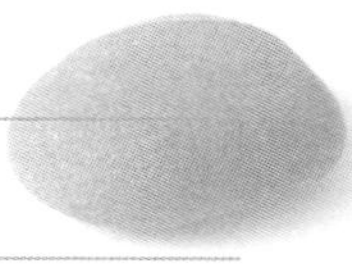

April 19

One of the penalties for refusing to participate in politics is that you end up being governed by your inferiors.
Plato

PARTICIPATING

It's easy to sit on the sidelines and let someone else make decisions for you. Many people are complacent and avoid getting actively involved. By choosing not to use their power, they hand it over to others. This isn't always the best decision, because it makes them victim to someone else's choices.

To be lived well, life requires participation. If you want to be happy, you must participate in activity that brings you joy and surround yourself with joyful people. If you want to be healthy, you must participate in your own well-being, taking time to address your physical, spiritual, and emotional needs.

Practice participating in life today. Find something that captures your interest and passion. Get involved.

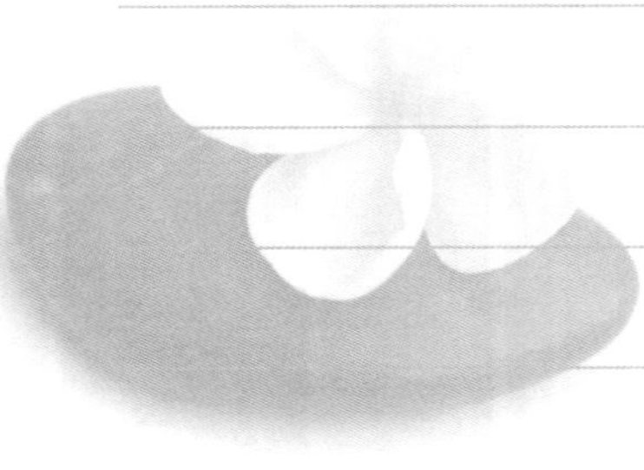

April 20

That's kind of like how jazz is sometimes. You're out there predicting the future, and no one believes you.
Branford Marsalis

PREDICTING

One of the fundamental laws of metaphysics states that every cause sets into motion an effect. Every action creates a reaction in your experience. Every thought in your mind produces some kind of experience in your body and affairs. If you want a prediction of your future, you don't have to visit a psychic. All you have to do is listen to your thoughts and pay close attention to your actions. They are creating your future experience.

What goes around, comes around. That which you send out returns to bless or haunt your life. Be sure that you are sending out what you want to receive. In so doing, you create a future that fulfills your dreams.

April 21

Oh, my dear friends,—you are letting miserable misunderstandings run on from year to year, meaning to clear them up some day,— if you only could see that the time is short...you would go instantly and do the thing which you might never have another chance to do!
Phillips Brooks

RECONCILIATION

We live in denial of our own demise, thinking we will have plenty of time to reconcile our differences with each other. We act as if we will live forever, ignoring our heart's longing for peace and forgiveness.

What if today was your last day on earth? What if April twenty-first is the date printed on your death certificate? This may be your last chance to say, "I love you." This may be your golden day to reconcile with someone you have harmed or misunderstood.

Make today's spiritual practice one of reconciliation. Pick up the phone and make the call. Speak from your heart, and let go of any attachment to results.

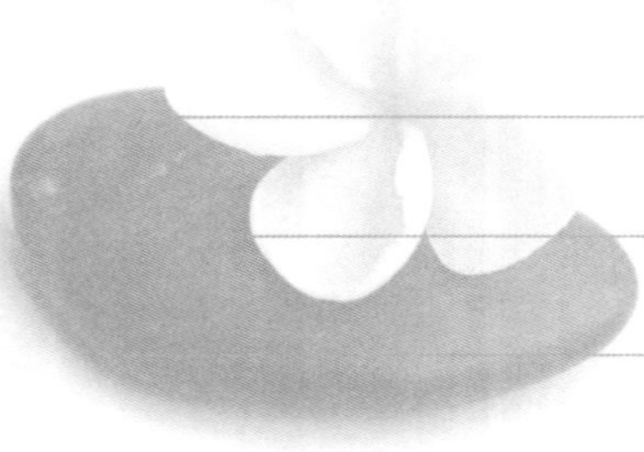

April 22

You can't stop loving or wanting to love because when it's right, it's the best thing in the world. When you're in a relationship and it's good, even if nothing else in your life is right, you feel like your whole world is complete.

Keith Sweat

RELATIONSHIPS

Personal relationships bring the greatest challenge to our lives. They are where we learn the most about our own character. We discover the perimeter of our patience and compassion. When we relate to others, we learn more about ourselves than we could ever learn from a book or class.

Dive in—don't tiptoe! Get completely soaked, not just damp. Allow yourself to feel the ecstasy of success and the agony of defeat. Only then will you discover how to really love someone. And when you do, you will have found your true destiny on earth.

April 23

Set your expectations high, find men and women whose integrity and values you respect, get their agreement on a course of action; and give them your ultimate trust.

John Akers

RESPECT

Rodney Dangerfield—the king of "no respect"—once recounted: "I went to see my doctor and told him, 'Doctor, every morning when I get up and look in the mirror, I feel like throwing up. What's wrong with me?' The doctor said, 'I don't know, but your eyesight is perfect.'" Mr. Dangerfield made a respectable living telling those jokes—no pun intended.

Regardless of one's position in life, we all deserve the respect of other human beings. From the homeless person on the street to the President of the United States, everyone is entitled to respect.

By surrounding yourself with people whom you respect, you create a life of honor and integrity. Do you respect your boss? Do you respect your parents or children? Do you respect your spouse or partner? Do you respect yourself?

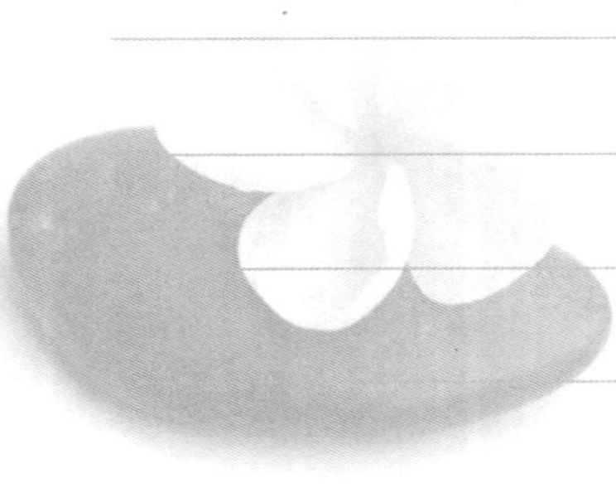

April 24

Our loyalties must transcend our race, our tribe, our class, and our nation; and this means we must develop a world perspective.
Dr. Martin Luther King, Jr.

SHIFTING PERSPECTIVE

The aptitude of great diplomats is their ability to shift perspective. Like gifted actors, they have the talent of putting aside their own personalities to take on another's. They are able to see life through someone else's eyes, even if it is for a short time.

The old wisdom not to judge other people until you have walked a few miles in their shoes is still relevant today. It is easy to be self-righteous in your own perspective. We all see our own positions quite clearly. The real gift is in being able to compassionately see someone else's perspective.

What person do you disagree with the most? Practice shifting your perspective to theirs. Try to see how they come to their conclusions. Try to understand how they feel.

April 25

We have to do the best we can.
This is our sacred human responsibility.
Albert Einstein

SOCIAL JUSTICE

Social justice is an idea of a society in which justice is prevalent in more than just the administration of law. It takes into consideration fair treatment of individuals, human rights, and the distribution of advantages and disadvantages within a society.

What would the role of a spiritually minded person be in a world in which justice prevailed? How do you see the role of justice in your own life? If it were up to you to create the definitive list of human rights, what would that list include?

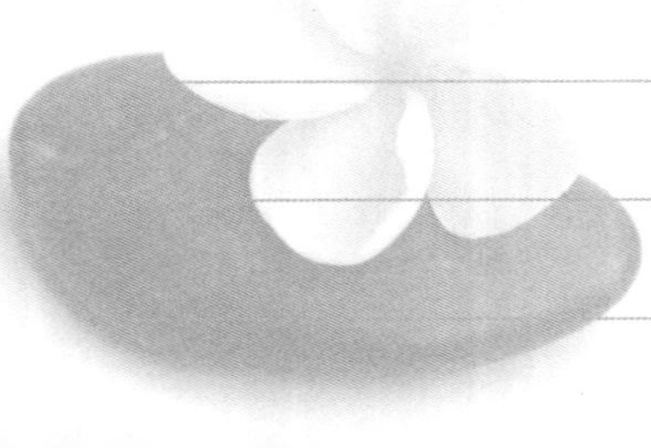

April 26

We are made wise not by the recollection of our past,
but by the responsibility for our future.
George Bernard Shaw

STANDING FOR SOMETHING

A philosopher once said that his philosophy encouraged people to stand for something and against nothing. Another way of putting this is, if you don't stand for something, you'll fall for anything.

Through practices such as inquiry, journaling, and prayer, we learn to become familiar with our values and dreams. As this familiarity deepens into certainty, we become less inclined to vacillate in times of challenge. We become more able to easily access that part of our mentality that knows what we stand for. What does your life stand for?

April 27

Be the change you want to see in the world.
Mahatma Gandhi

TAKING RESPONSIBILITY

Taking responsibility for that which you stand for inspires a powerful experience of maturity. Sometimes it seems that people in our culture do not emotionally or mentally mature past the teen years. Many people go through life making decisions on whims and minimizing the impact their choices have on the world and society. These people often look to others for direction and motivation, whereas those interested in developing spiritual awareness know that their direction and motivation must come from an inner awareness of the Presence.

April 28

Think before you speak. You might need to remember what you said.
Rain Bojangles

TEACHING

Whenever I meet someone I am attracted to or admire, my mouth seems to take on a life of its own. Out pours a train wreck of conversation that I later can hardly recall and that, when I do, embarrasses me. I have had to pay close attention to my tendency to speak without thinking, not because I want to remember everything I've said, but because, when I speak consciously, I don't have to remember anything.

Consciously speaking is consistent with my heart and mind. When speaking this way, my mouth comes out with the details and meanings I intend, no matter to whom I am talking. Now, when I meet someone, I breathe, smile, and pay attention to what they say. And I try not to speak for as long as possible.

April 29

No snowflake in an avalanche ever feels responsible.
Voltaire

TAKING CARE

Isolated living can promote a false sense of being cut off from the world. In community, when people watch over each other, they also learn from each other through example. At home, I am less inclined to recycle, because no one is watching; but at my place of work, my recycling ethic is beyond reproach. It has taken a conscious decision to bring my personal discipline into harmony with my public one. I had to remind myself that, whether or not anyone sees, every action of mine adds something to the whole, and I want to be able to look back at my day and see clearly how my values affect my actions.

Stay committed to your decisions, but stay flexible in your approach.
Tom Robbins

TRYING

Trying to do something means making an effort toward accomplishment. When something is trying, it denotes difficulty, challengd, perhaps even frustration. Tom Robbins suggests flexibility: being open to accomplishing something using methods and strategies that may not have been part of your original plan. Another way to be flexible is to remain open to the possibility that your goal may change and shift as you move toward it.

A friend went to college to become an architect, but ended up graduating as a yoga teacher. Somewhere along the line, as each step toward his goal revealed something he hadn't considered before, his goal shifted. He remained committed, and his level of engagement remained constant; however, the shifting landscape of his studies took turns that he couldn't have predicted.

Is there a place in your life where you may be trying too hard?

MAY

Practice *the* Presence *through* Order

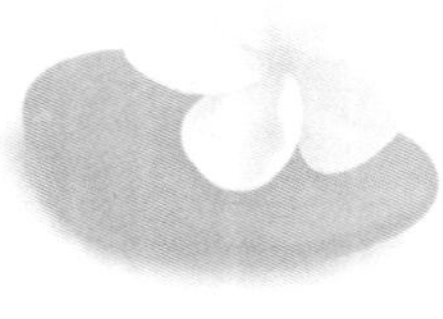

May 1

Fast is fine, but accuracy is everything.
Xenophon

ACCURACY

When reviewing a particularly difficult personnel matter, my human resources consultant advised that anything I said, wrote, or communicated regarding the matter should be something I'd not be ashamed to be broadcast on primetime television. She asked me to imagine that news cameras were running in every meeting and that my conduct would be broadcast around the country. As a result of this powerful advice, I learned to be accurate with my words and sincere in what I was expressing. The resulting meetings and communications took on a sober, but genuine, tone that I have attempted to maintain ever since.

May 2

The visible world is the invisible organization of energy.
Heinz Pagels

ARRANGING

The ancient art of *feng shui* is about arranging objects of the physical world in a way that allows the energy of the invisible to flow gently and evenly. Everything that is visible has been orderly arranged by an inherent Intelligence. From the design of each snowflake to the stars in the night-time sky, everything has an order and perfect arrangement.

To live simply and peacefully, things must be in their proper places. This is not only true of nature, it is also true of your life. Everything must be arranged neatly so that order may occur.

What is out of order in your life? What needs to be arranged properly? What steps can you take to get started today?

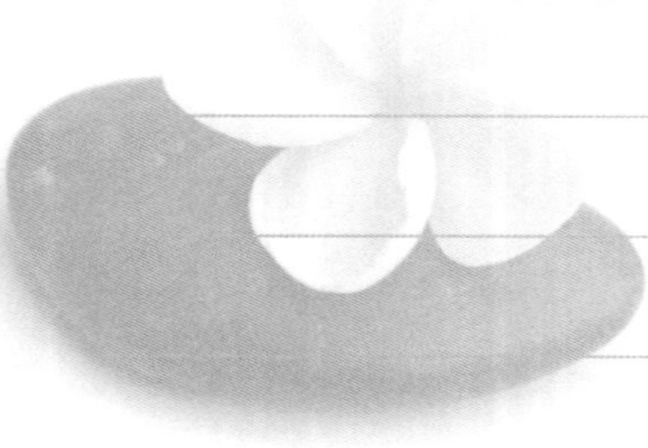

May 3

I'm not mad at you. I'm mad at the dirt.
Attributed to Joan Crawford

CLEANING

There's something therapeutic about cleaning, as long as you're not obsessive about it. Giving things to charity and throwing out useless items can be metaphors for doing the same thing in your life. When you occasionally take time to rid yourself of that which no longer serves you, you clear the way for new opportunities. Cleaning out the old makes way for the new. It's a spiritual principle.

Sometimes the cleaning job seems so overwhelming that we avoid getting started. But remember: You don't have to do it all today. You can start with just one area.

May 4

It does not require money to be
neat, clean, and dignified.
Mahatma Gandhi

CLEANLINESS

It has been said that cleanliness is next to godliness. Perhaps that is a way to say that a clean and simple life is the most spiritual.

Human life can be messy. It doesn't take much to get dirty. All you have to do is go outside and, before you know it, you need a shower. Regular, daily maintenance is necessary to live a clean life in this world.

How can you live more simply? What do you need to do to clean up your life?

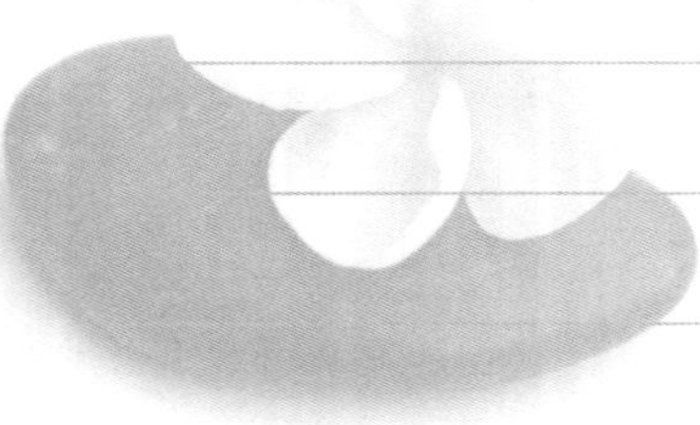

Everything you need you already have. You are complete right now, you are a whole, total person, not an apprentice person on the way to someplace else. Your completeness must be understood by you and experienced in your thoughts as your own personal reality.

Beverly Sills

COMPLETING

Many people see themselves as incomplete—needing something or someone to be whole. They wake up each day in search of the thing that's going to finally fulfill them. They have been conditioned to believe that alone, by themselves, they have no merit or value. Nothing could be further from the truth.

You are complete right now. Your Creator has made you unbroken and whole. You are not damaged goods. No matter what has hurt you, the greater part of your spirit is still intact and well. Realize the power and greatness you hold within. Stand tall, and act like you know who you are.

May 6

A certain harmony should be kept between actions and ideas if we want to fully develop the effects they can produce.
François de La Rochefoucauld

CONGRUENCY

There is nothing more frustrating than interacting with a person who says one thing and does another. This incongruence infects everything. You probably know someone just like this. And if you have ever been unfortunate enough to have one of them as a supervisor, you know just what poor leaders they make.

Be a person whose actions match your words. Be the example to others of a reliable person whose speech is in harmony with his or her efforts. Practice congruency. Make sure your actions are in alignment with your best ideas. Doing so will earn you the respect of your peers and admiration of your friends.

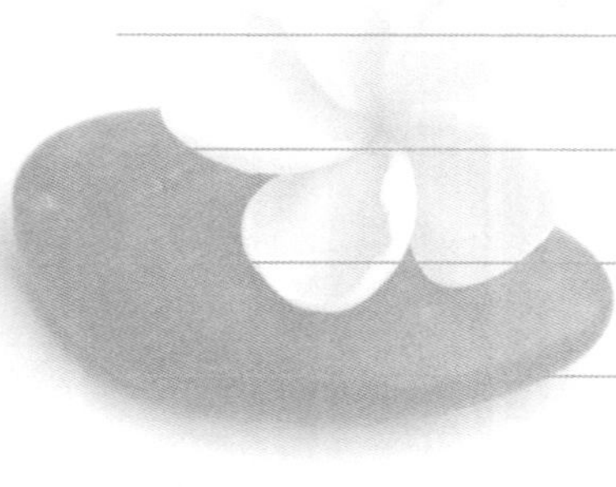

May 7

Our moral responsibility is not to stop the future, but to shape it...to channel our destiny in humane directions and to try to ease the trauma of transition.
Alvin Toffler

DEVELOPING

In the television series *Star Trek*, Spock ended his communication with others by saying, "Live long and prosper." In effect, he was saying, "Continue to live well and evolve." This is a profound wish for each other: that we may never cease to foster our highest dreams, develop our greatest talents, and advance toward the destiny God has in store for our lives.

Decide what is good within you. Give thought to your greatest talent, and then develop it. Continue down this road—never veering off to give a fool's attention to the things that are not so good—and you will arrive at your dream life. Keep developing each day. Keep polishing the diamond that you are. Concentrate on your own effort without comparing yourself to others.

May 8

I don't like a man to be too efficient. He's likely to be not human enough.
Felix Frankfurter

EFFICIENCY

There is a huge difference between being efficient and being effective. Doing everything that needs to be done in a precise and timely manner makes you efficient. If, on the other hand, you ignore the needs and feelings of other people in the process of that efficiency, you are actually quite ineffective.

Don't try to be too efficient. People won't care what gets accomplished if they don't feel cared for in the process. Don't practice efficiency. Practice compassion and empathy.

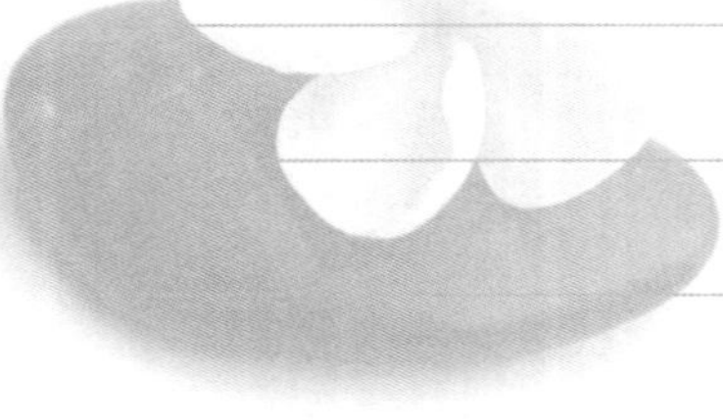

May 9

Excellence is not a skill. It is an attitude.
Ralph Marston

EXCELLENCE

In Don Miguel Ruiz's book *The Four Agreements*, the fourth agreement is to always do your best. Reading this book in a number of different group settings, I noticed that this agreement generates a tremendous amount of discussion about what your best is, and how, under different circumstances, "best" might have different interpretations.

Our personal best changes from moment to moment, depending on mood, health, and other influencing factors. Nevertheless, there is an attitude that we can adopt, no matter the time of day or situation in which we find ourselves, that leads to a deeply satisfying engagement. The attitude is one of simply trying to do your best by being present. Excellence is the state of being exceptionally good. In my experience, I excel in ways I couldn't predict whenever my attention is on doing my best.

May 10

Perfection is not attainable, but if we chase perfection we can catch excellence.
Vince Lombardi

IMPLEMENTATION

Putting the words "doing your best" into action requires a gentle approach and a willingness to suspend comparison to other people's standard of "best." Your best effort is more in your attitude than in your actions or results. Doing your best teaches you to accept yourself on the deepest level, as you become aware that the best part of the doing is being present for it, not what comes of it.

Some people struggle with the idea of doing their best, either because they are perfectionists who can see better ways to do whatever they have done, or because they have been too frequently criticized for their efforts in the past. What does "doing your best" mean to you, and how can you begin to introduce it as an attitude to whatever you do today?

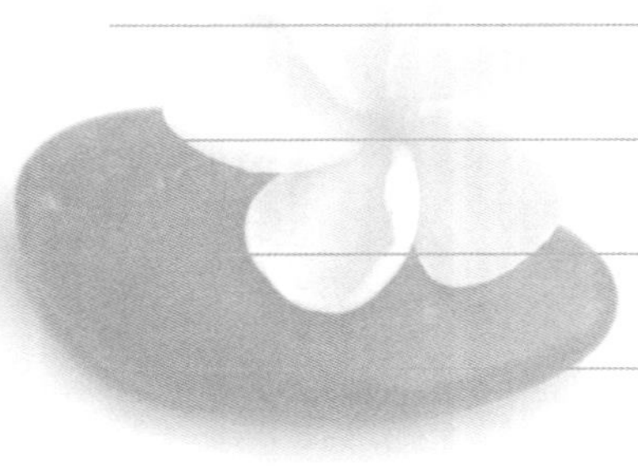

May 11

We are what we repeatedly do. Excellence, then, is not an act, but a habit.
Aristotle

LOOKING

Over time, the practice of doing your personal best becomes habit-forming. It is similar to opening a doorway that can never be closed again. Once you look at the result of applying yourself and the accumulated effect of doing so consistently, you will easily notice those times when you do not. It does not mean that you will never do a less-than-perfect job. It doesn't even mean that there is anything wrong with imperfect work. It simply means that now you know the difference.

Look for examples of where you are committed to excellence in your life.

May 12

We never stop investigating. We are never satisfied that we know enough to get by. Every question we answer leads on to another question. This has become the greatest survival trick of our species.
Desmond Morris

INVESTIGATING

Both in personal spiritual development and social responsibility, it is important to investigate what we take for granted and to inquire if the thoughts we regularly believe are actually true. A mind-expanding exercise is to watch television advertisements and silently ask yourself what statements in the advertisements you take as true without question.

We are more inclined to believe ideas when they are presented to us frequently, and we are prone to believe thoughts that we think often. The simple act of slowing down to ask "Is this true?" is a powerful way of growing in awareness of Reality.

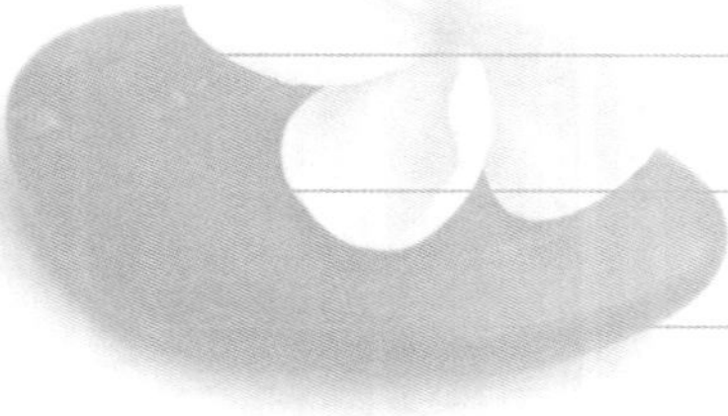

MAY 13

Don't agonize,
organize.
Florynce R. Kennedy

ORDER

Sometimes, when I face the overwhelming pressure of too many tasks or responsibilities, I become paralyzed and withdrawn. I have found a simple remedy that is very effective in addressing the overwhelm: I tidy up one drawer, one closet, or one room. I do it single-mindedly, avoiding the temptation to move on to other tasks. The straightforward action of bringing order to one place in my world has the effect of restoring my sense of well-being, even in the midst of tremendous pressure.

Another helpful act of creating order is to write down everything I have to do by the end of the day. Seeing the tasks on one piece of paper is often clarifying and helpful.

May 14

When dealing with people, remember you are not dealing with creatures of logic, but creatures of emotion.
Dale Carnegie

DISORDER

I noticed a bumper sticker recently: "Chaos is my friend!" It reminded me of the powerful creativity that comes from chaos. I sometimes forget that I live in a universe that works for me, and I inadvertently make disorder my enemy. When I remember to pause, breathe, and stop resisting the way things are, I allow a softness to come into my awareness that lets me see the patterns and potential in the disorder around me.

I also try to remember the wisdom of knowing what is mine to change and what is not. I remember that, even though my environment influences me, there is something within me that is untouched by the energy and sway of my environment.

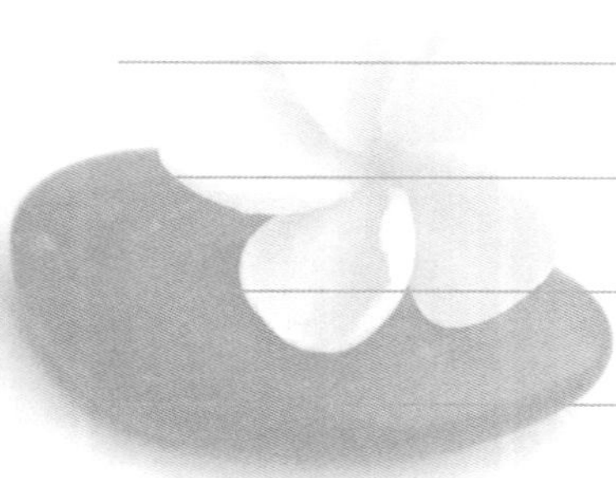

May 15

Elbow grease is
the best polish.
English Proverb

POLISH

The verb *polish* means to make smooth and shiny through rubbing or by friction. It also describes the state of being refined or properly finished. People described as *polished* are those who handles themselves well. We become polished in life by rubbing up against each other's differences or by the stressful events we learn to navigate. This illustrates how order and beauty can come out of stress and disorder.

Gem stones are polished by abrasion, using fine grits of harder substances. In order to become a fine gem, a stone must encounter gritty stuff that is harder that itself. This analogy helps me better maintain my peace of mind when I am in the Presence of stressful circumstances. I try to imagine that I am being refined.

May 16

An ounce of practice is worth more than tons of preaching.
Mahatma Gandhi

PRACTICING

Like a counselor, doctor, or lawyer, you are in private practice. Your practice is the daily discipline of your life. This shows up in the priorities you set each day. The quality of your life is dependent on the actions you take each day to pursue those priorities.

Like everything else in life, practice makes perfect. If you practice love, you will become loving. If you practice joy, you will become joyful. If you practice wholeness, you will be healthy.

Give all of your effort to the best practices you have, and let somebody else do the preaching.

May 17

The quality, not the longevity, of one's life is what is important.
Dr. Martin Luther King, Jr.

QUALITY

If you ask most people how long they wish to live, they will say, "I want to live to be a hundred years old." Then they usually quickly add, "…as long as I have a good quality of life." It is the quality of our lives that matters most, not the quantity.

The best way to ensure a high-quality life is to follow the formula that says, "Plan like you're going to live forever, but live like you're going to die tonight." In other words, be smart about your finances. Make plans for your future health. But don't sacrifice the quality of today's experience too much for it.

Take care of your body. You may need it to be in good shape for several decades. Eat right. Exercise and do whatever you can to ensure continued health in your future. Then go ahead and have some ice cream tonight.

May 18

The shifts of fortune test the reliability of friends.
Cicero

RELIABILITY

It's been said that if you want to find out how reliable your friends are, all you have to do is ask them to help you move. The people who show up on moving day are usually your best friends. They can be depended on for almost anything.

There's great comfort in that reliability. Knowing that someone "has your back" is empowering. And don't forget: The bonds of sisterhood or brotherhood don't always come from our biological families.

On whom do you rely? Who relies on you?

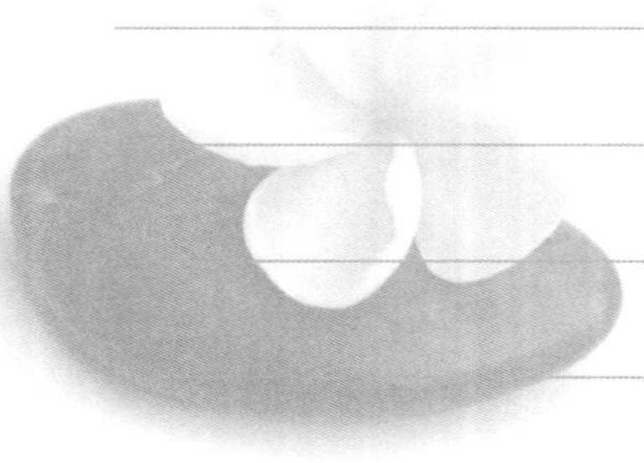

MAY 19

Organize priorities so that God is first in our lives.
John H. Groberg

REORGANIZING

The first of the Ten Commandments says, "I am the Lord thy God. Thou shalt have no other gods before me." Contrary to popular belief, this wasn't commanded because God is jealous and needs our total attention. God is not an arrogant, distant deity issuing demands from on high. God is a Living Presence in our lives.

Because the nature of God is love, putting God first in your life means to make loving your top priority. Love-making should always take precedence over money-making. Because God is also joy, joyfulness should be a priority as well. To be close to God, you must be joyful and loving. How can your reorganize your life so that love and joy are your first priorities?

May 20

Tenderness and kindness are not signs of weakness and despair,
but manifestations of strength and resolution.
Kahlil Gibran

RESOLUTION

What is seeking resolution in your life? If you don't know, there's an easy way to find out. Unresolved issues are the things you lie awake worrying about at night. They show up in the conversations you replay over and over again in your mind. They get stuck on a loop, repeating themselves until you resolve them.

Usually, resolution involves some level of forgiveness, whether it is for you or someone else. People are reluctant to offer forgiveness because they have so many reasons not to, some of which might be very compelling. But hanging on to your reasons still doesn't change the effect it has on your life. The unresolved issues will continue to keep you stuck right where you are, unable to move forward.

Make today the day of resolution. Lay these issues to rest, once and for all.

May 21

There cannot be a crisis today;
my schedule is already full.
Dr. Henry Kissinger

SCHEDULING

The interesting thing about scheduling is that whatever you make accommodations for will usually show up in your life. If you make room for love, love will enter. If you make plans to have fun, a joyful life will be yours.

Be careful, though. Don't make too many accommodations for the negatives in life, because they too will begin to take up space. You are the creator. Don't be a victim of your own schedule. The majority of your time is under your own control; choose wisely what to do with it.

What is on your schedule today? Have you scheduled time to be with family and friends? Are you going to have fun today?

May 22

When love and skill work together,
expect a masterpiece.
John Ruskin

SKILL

When I asked the vocalist at my church how she got to be so good, she replied, "God gave me skills, baby." Each of us has some God-given skill—bestowed upon us at inception—that is a unique gift from our Creator.

Whether you are consciously aware of it or whether it remains a hidden talent, there is something you can do like no one else. When you blend that skill with love and passion, you will not only find your true destiny, but you will have also found the quickest path to prosperity.

What are your skills? How can you match them with love and passion?

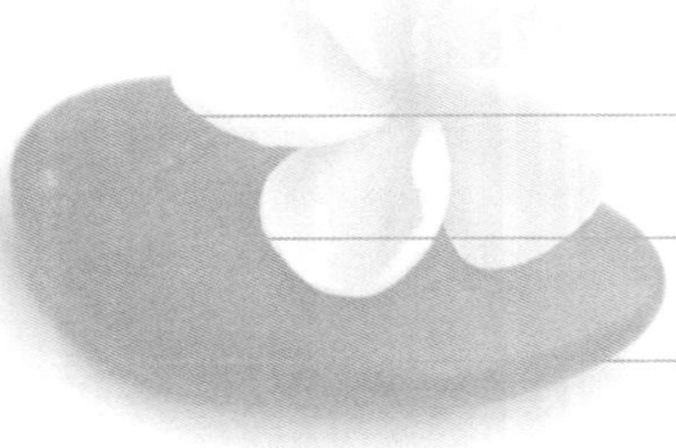

May 23

The ultimate value of life depends upon awareness
and the power of contemplation, rather than upon mere survival.
Aristotle

THINKING

Thinking is a powerful capacity that, when left unattended, can cause mischief. The way you attend to thinking is to examine it periodically and inquire if it is accurate, helpful, and true. Without this kind of contemplation, it is easy for thoughts to become rote or go off-track.

A helpful practice is to think about some phrase or passage that did not originate in your own mind. Taking the time to slowly read an inspiring passage—thinking about each part of it and what it means—can help open awareness and refresh your approach to life. For example, take the following phrase from Buddha with you through the day: "Make a proper investigation first. Proper investigation is good for a well-known person like yourself." Pause from time to time to consider how it applies to your life.

May 24

One who wants to keep their yard tidy
does not reserve a plot for the weeds.
Proverb

TIDINESS

Tidiness is easy for some people, while others are challenged by it. While it may not be important for everyone, each of us has to find out for ourselves if tidiness is something we should consider in our practice. Perhaps those who say tidiness is not important for them simply haven't yet learned to apply it and don't have an experience of the benefits that come with it. When people say they don't have the time for tidiness, I venture to say that tidiness is the very thing that will produce more time for them. Yet, some people truly flourish more in an environment that would seem chaotic to others.

When my home is tidy, I can find the things I need more easily. For this reason, I try to declutter my home and workspace on a regular basis. But, also, I find that tidiness contributes to a peaceful mind.

May 25

The two most important requirements for major success are: first, being in the right place at the right time, and second, doing something about it.
Ray Kroc

TIMING

I read a statement in a book of affirmations that inspired me to think about the idea of perfect timing: "Everyone is in the right place at the right time, successfully engaged in the right activity." In the past, this has helped me consider whether it is possible to miss an opportunity. Now, I am more inclined to think it is all about quality of awareness.

There are no missed opportunities when everything is working together in seamless perfection. However, when my awareness is distracted or crowded with worrisome thoughts, I have the experience of being in the wrong place, missing opportunities, and becoming frustrated.

May 26

Experience is the name everyone gives to their mistakes.
Oscar Wilde

TESTING

Testing refers to, among other things, the process by which you prove something to be genuine. Some people believe that life is constantly testing them or that God has devised a learning environment through which they must successfully navigate. I prefer to think that life is available to us to test ourselves, to discover if what we say we stand for is genuine.

Make a list of your highest values—the qualities in yourself that your life stands for. For example, I believe that my most important value is kindness. Then, ask your friends if they see that quality in you, and, if you're willing, ask them to comment on where you are not like that. Or, if you prefer, come up with a list of three examples of where you exhibit your most valued quality, and three examples of where you do not.

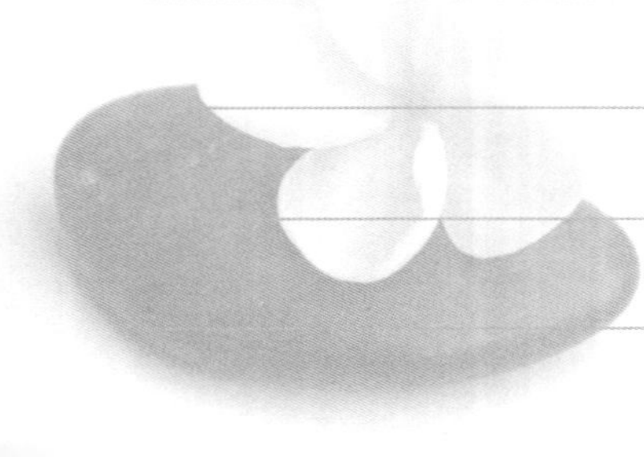

May 27

There are no failures—just experiences and your reactions to them.
Tom Krause

TRYING

American philosopher Ernest Holmes wrote, "If a man believes himself to be a failure and that it is useless for him to try to be anything else, he carries with him the mental equivalent of failure. So he succeeds in being a failure according to law." In other words, the mindset I nurture related to success and failure becomes a powerful determining factor in my reaction to these experiences.

If I am expecting to fail or to be rejected, I may be less inclined to try something new. I may not experiment with a new enterprise because, in my mind, I have already settled my fate. In this way, the range of my possibilities extends only as far as my concept of what is possible.

May 28

I know that the twelve notes in each octave and the variety of rhythm offer me opportunities that all of human genius will never exhaust.
Igor Stravinsky

VARIETY

Igor Stravinsky was named by *Time* magazine as one of the top one hundred most influential people of the twentieth century, in part for the impact he had on modern classical music. He introduced sounds and ways of understanding sound sequences that were completely new. He was fascinated with the relationships among notes and how, from a limited number of tones, an infinite number of compositions could be produced.

Life might be thought of in the same way: drawing unlimited variety from one source. You are like that—reenacting variety in your thinking and actions, never coming to the end of what is possible.

May 29

The idea that seeing life means going from place to place and doing a great variety of obvious things is an illusion natural to dull minds.
Charles Horton Cooley

VIEWING

Wherever you are and whatever you are doing, imagine that you are at the center of life and that there is no more interesting spot or exciting moment in which to be. If the idea of Divinity as infinite is true, then this imagined scenario is not unreasonable.

In infinity, every spot is the center. This reminds me that, whether I am at the Grand Canyon or in Grand Central Station, I have equal access to life. This allows me to feel awe and wonder at whatever occupies my view, and inspires me to absorb the view and really see what the Presence has produced.

May 30

When love beckons to you, follow him, though his ways are hard and steep. And when his wings enfold you, yield to him, though the sword hidden among his pinions may wound you.
Kahlil Gibran

YIELDING

We each set our own course through life and make our own plans. We move in the direction most appropriate to the destination we desire. However, the best things that come into our lives are usually the unplanned surprises that show up on the path.

To yield means to make way or to allow room for something else on your path. In the course of your daily plans, don't forget to yield. There may be something wonderful trying to get into your life that just needs a little wiggle room.

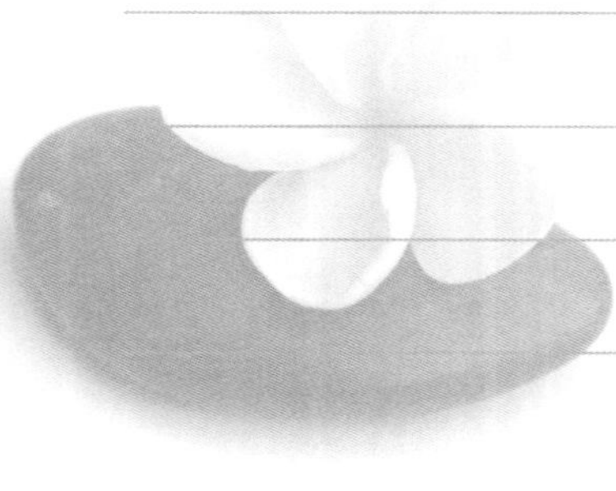

May 31

Every choice moves us closer to or farther away from something. Where are your choices taking your life? What do your behaviors demonstrate that you are saying yes or no to in life?
Eric Allenbaugh

YES

Yes is the most powerfully affirmative word in your language. That to which you say "yes" will expand in your life. If you say "yes" to prosperity, you will become rich. If you say "yes" to love, your life will be filled with adoration. If you say "yes" to joy, you will live a happy life.

But be cautious; the opposite is true as well. Don't say "yes" to disease or lack. Don't say "yes" to being a victim or living an unhappy life. Don't accept less than what you really want. Starting today, say "yes" to every good thing!

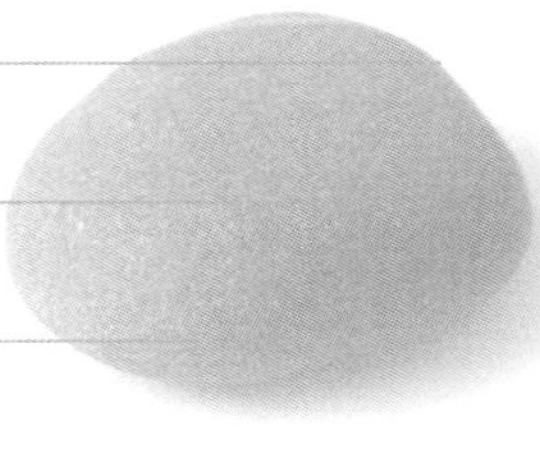

JUNE

Practice *the* Presence *through* Contemplation

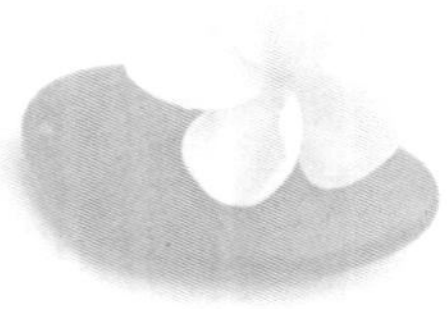

June 1

To chant is the most sublime and exalted activity in this world.
Sri Guru Granth Sahib

CHANTING

Chanting is a spiritual practice that has been used for thousands of years by many different cultures around the world. It is not mere mindless chatter. When the conscious mind is kept busy with a repetitive activity, the subconscious is allowed to open and receive. The power to change your life rests in your ability to change your thinking. For this, chanting can be quite useful.

Repeating affirmative words over and over again can yield positive results, particularly if your mind is often occupied with fear or negativity. When you stop the fearful thoughts and replace them with a positive chant, you immediately shift the focus of your mind and affect your experience in a more affirmative way. For instance, if your body is not well, you may try a chant that repeats: "I am whole, I am perfect. I am well." Or, if you are fearful, you might try: "I am safe. I am under God's care, and all is well."

June 2

You can't do anything about the length of your life,
but you can do something about its width and depth.
Henry Louis Mencken

DEPTH

Swimming pools are excellent metaphors for people: both have shallow ends and deep ends. Some people live pretty shallow lives, focusing only on their own narcissistic desires, and never investing time or interest in anyone else. In the end, they are left alone, because no one can tolerate being around them for long.

And then there are those people who live deep, meaningful lives. They are rich, because they have the spiritual maturity to understand that we are all one. They realize that investment in compassion and care for others is the same as worshipping God.

Go to the deep end. There are greater risks, but there are also richer rewards. Invest your heart in others. Make a contribution to someone's life. Live a deep, meaningful life.

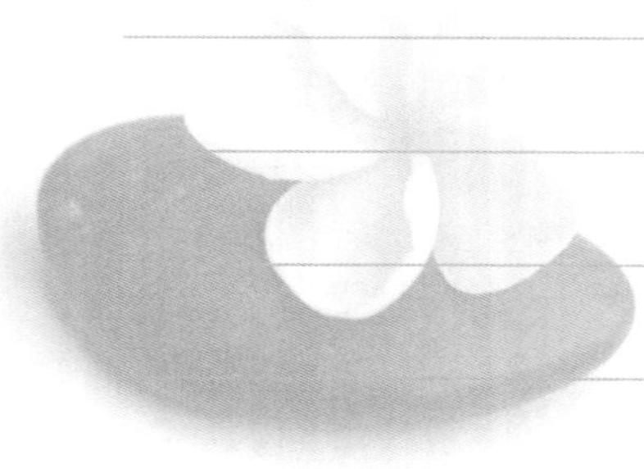

June 3

It makes no difference how deeply seated may be the trouble, how hopeless the outlook, how muddled the tangle, how great the mistake. A sufficient realization of love will dissolve it all.
Emmet Fox

DISSOLVING

Hardening of the arteries occurs when plaque builds up inside the artery walls. The arteries become so clogged that blood cannot flow through them on its way to or from the heart. Before the development of stints and bypass surgery, hardening of the arteries inevitably led to death.

It's not just a poor diet or genetic predisposition that can harden the pathways to our hearts. They can become hardened by the dwindling flow of love we allow into our lives, or by the hurts that never get healed. The body then responds to these emotional and spiritual obstacles by creating blockages of its own.

Whatever the case, love is the healer. As Emmet Fox says, "A sufficient realization of love will dissolve it all." Apply love to every area of your life that is blocked or hardened. Start dissolving everything that stands in its way.

June 4

Real elation is when you feel you could touch a star without standing on tiptoe.

Doug Larson

ELATION

Do you remember the last time you were really happy? When did you last feel elation? Bring to mind the very best day of your life. What was going on around you? Who was present? What were you doing?

These memories are priceless. They help us make it through times that are difficult and challenging. Not every day is going to be perfect. There will be trials and tribulations in human life. That's why it is so important to make time for joyful activity.

What can you do for fun today?

JUNE 5

Allowing the truth of who you are—your spiritual self—to rule your life means you stop the struggle and learn to move with the flow of your life.
Oprah Winfrey

FLOWING

Water flows downstream for a reason. Gravity is a natural law; ease is water's natural expression. Water does not fight or struggle for its own expression. It simply follows the law and flows.

There is a natural order to your life—a sequence that must unfold in its own time. Your Higher Self has a destiny to realize that includes your enlightenment and fulfillment. You may sometimes be consciously aware of this activity, but not always. Appearances can fool you, and the twists and turns that your life takes may seem chaotic and unstructured.

Trust the natural flow of life. Your destiny is guaranteed. You will find love, be happy, and know what it's like to never be afraid or hurt again. Take Oprah's advice and move with the flow of your life today.

June 6

Music is perpetual, and only the hearing is intermittent.
Henry David Thoreau

HEARING

You are surrounded by and infused with the Presence. This must be so if the Presence is truly infinite and everywhere present. There is never a moment in which you are separate from it. Only when you let yourself be distracted do you waver from listening to its perpetual guidance.

Here is a wonderfully playful exercise to enhance your practice of the Presence. Imagine that the Presence is delivering to you a secret message tailored to your exact need. This message will be delivered to you through something you hear today, either in an overheard conversation or on the radio. Spend the day listening for the meaning, connection, and relevance that comes from unexpected places. Then, note in your journal what you received through your hearing.

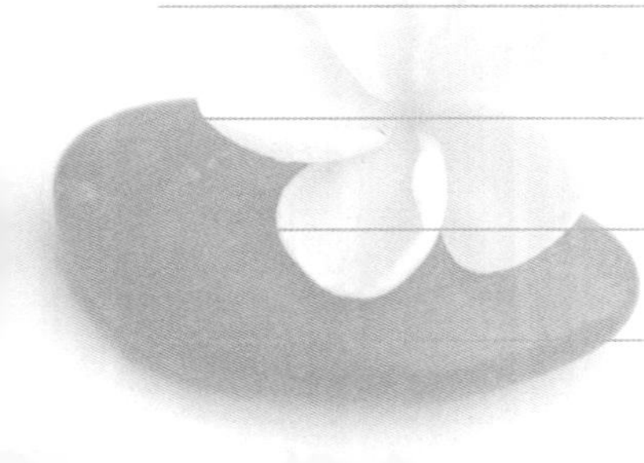

June 7

It is a shameful thing to be weary of inquiry when what we search for is excellent.
Marcus Tullius Cicero

INQUIRY

Contemplative practices lead to deep peace and personal understanding. Even so, our minds can grow weary of the meditative process and turn our thoughts to more active engagements. Sometimes, the mind seems to flee from moments of introspection, almost as if it fears what it will discover there. This is why our minds appreciate it when we choose to move as busily as we can through life.

Journaling is a way of slowing the mind down to the "speed of write," giving you the time to look at your thoughts as they appear on paper and inquire into their solidity, value, and accuracy.

JUNE 8

Intuition is a spiritual faculty and does not explain, but simply points the way.
Florence Scovel Shinn

INTUITION

Intuition is one of those faculties that becomes increasingly available to us the more we engage in contemplative practices such as meditation, prayer, and journaling. These practices create the inner environment where intuition has the opportunity to enjoy itself—a place unavailable to an overly busy mind. Sitting still with a question and allowing answers to rise up from within you is a powerful practice of accessing intuition, which is the activity of the Presence within you.

Intuition requires patience and gentleness. It is not accomplished by trying to hush the mind or stop thoughts, or even change them. It is to be approached with serenity and a willingness to sift through the myriad thoughts until, at last, a stress-free and beautiful voice emerges from within.

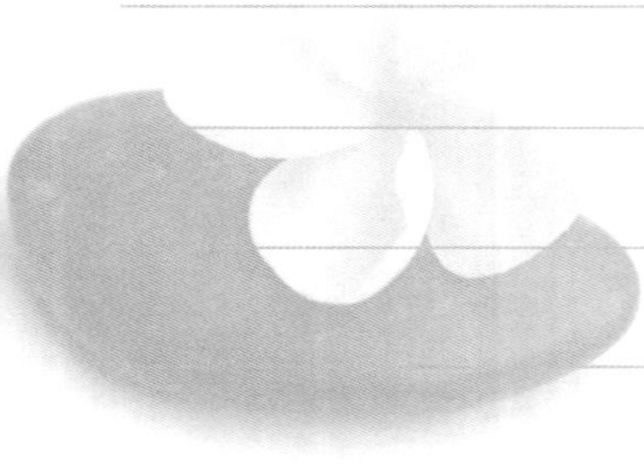

JUNE 9

Learn to let your intuition—gut instinct—tell you when the food, the relationship, the job isn't good for you (and conversely, when what you're doing is just right).
Oprah Winfrey

LEARNING

It is possible to access an instinctual wisdom within you that is untroubled by anything, yet has deep respect for the power of your emotions, urges, and attachments. This gut instinct may be neither precise nor communicate through any specific language; yet, when nurtured, it can ring like an alarm when something is *not* right, or sing like a choir in a distant cathedral when something *is* quite right. It is that voice within you that understands without obvious effort, always in possession of the complete picture and able to know you and guide you through your urges with precision.

What has your gut feeling been telling you, and have you been listening?

June 10

Trusting our intuition
often saves us from disaster.
Anne Wilson Schaef

LOOKING

To truly know what your intuition is guiding you to do requires purposeful time spent in its company. In other words, when your mind is overly engaged in problem solving, using the strategies and experiences it is accustomed to using, it may not have room to access a more powerful instructor—the Presence within you.

Use your journal to practice looking with intuition. You may not be adept at this right away; however, over time, you will find the right responses when you invite them in. Try answering the following question with whatever unedited thoughts come to you. Don't worry if the outcome makes no sense at first; just begin the practice of asking this question: What is my gut feeling telling me?

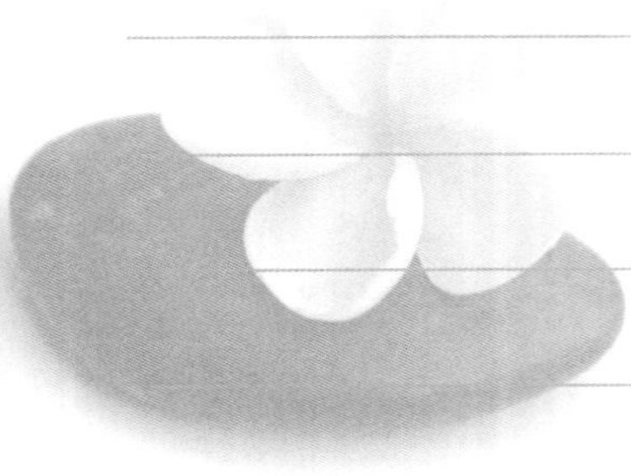

June 11

The more I read, the more I meditate; and the more I acquire,
the more I am enabled to affirm that I know nothing.
Voltaire

MEDITATION

Contemplative practices, such as meditation and inquiry, assist us in the awareness of our connection to the Presence. Out of that awareness, intuition arises and direction comes. But these practices should have no other purpose to us than the act of practicing them. Meditation itself is the purpose.

Meditation is often mistaken as a tool for achieving goals. Indeed, it is effective for moving us forward in life with projects or dreams, as are the practices of visualization, willpower, and goal-setting. However, the primary benefit of meditation is inner peace and intuition. And intuition is the Presence active in us, revealing to us the nature of being.

Meditate without a purpose. Afterward, notice if your awareness has shifted.

June 12

No great work has ever been produced except
after a long interval of still and musing meditation.
Walter Bagehot

MUSING

To sit and let your mind wander is a wonderfully creative practice, especially if you have a serene place in which to do it, such as a garden or park. In the end, though, it is less about the location than it is about the time taken to allow the mind to run free, noticing when it gets hooked on a particular thought for too long, and then gently setting it loose to run again.

The Muses of ancient Greece were spirits who inspired artists and performers. They were traditionally invoked at the beginning of the recitation of a poem, hymn, or play. Before diving into your next activity, take a moment to "muse"—not to appeal to an external deity, but to let your mind "space out," allowing the Presence of inspiration to have room to be active.

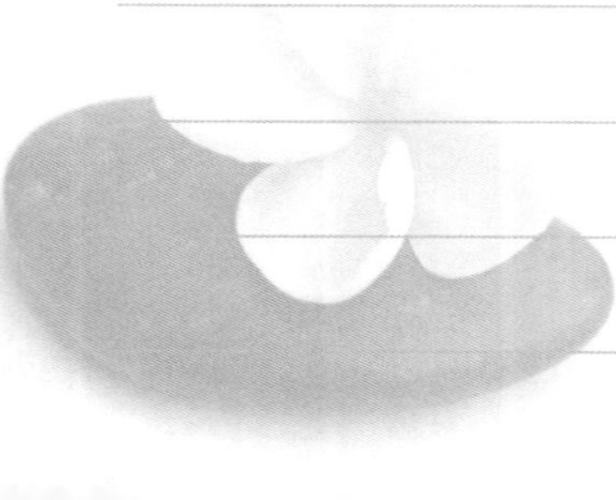

June 13

I am turned into a sort of machine for
observing facts and grinding out conclusions.
Charles Darwin

OBSERVING

Most of what happens during our day goes unnoticed. Very little of what is going on around us is actually captured by our minds. Early on, we learned to tune out most of the world's noise and chaos. This is probably a good thing. However, if you want to be a good leader or a good partner to your spouse, it might help to develop keener observation skills.

Pay close attention when people speak to you. Don't plan what you are going to say next. Look into their eyes and observe their body language. Give them your full attention. You will immediately notice the difference in their behavior.

Open your eyes. Observe what goes on around you. Take time today to observe the beauty of nature and enjoy God's Presence.

June 14

The highest happiness of man is to have probed what is knowable and quietly to revere what is unknowable.
Johann Wolfgang von Goethe

PROBING

God created us to wonder. We were designed by nature to probe deeper into reality in our quest for knowledge. That is why we went to the Moon and sent robots to Mars, and why, someday, we will go even further, beyond our own galaxy, to explore the universe.

To probe is to observe things more acutely, to look more thoroughly into the nature of Reality. Jesus advised us not to judge by appearances alone, implying that there is a deeper meaning to things just below the surface of what can be seen.

What do you need to look more closely at today? Practice looking beyond the surface level.

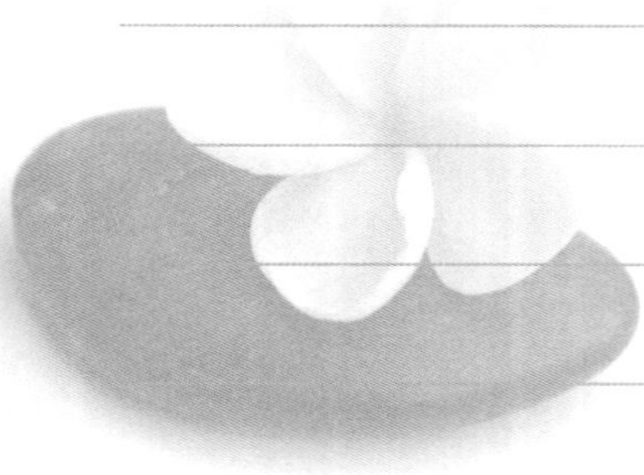

June 15

Quality questions create a quality life. Successful people ask better questions, and as a result, they get better answers.
Anthony Robbins

QUESTIONING

There are no dumb questions. Knowledge begins with questions. All questions lead to answers, which lead to more questions, and so on.

Don't be afraid to ask questions, even if the answers already seem apparent to others. Sometimes people nod their heads in agreement even when they don't really understand what is going on. The true test of intelligence isn't in how many answers you have; it's in how many questions you ask.

Children are naturally inquisitive. They ask a lot of questions—so many, in fact, that it can be annoying to adults. The Bible says, "Become as little children." Perhaps our lives would improve if we were more inquiring and childlike. Make a point of asking more questions today.

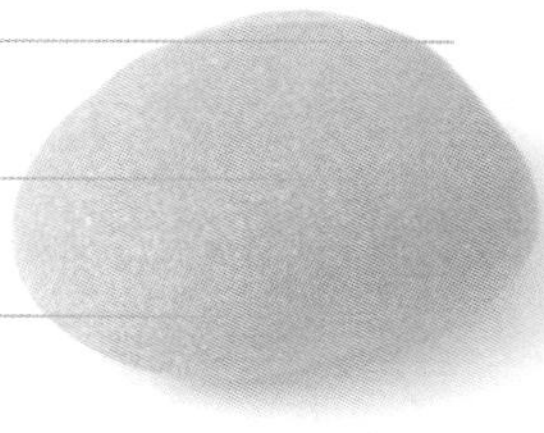

June 16

It is what you read when you don't have to
that determines what you will be when you can't help it.
Oscar Wilde

READING

Americans read fewer books today than they did in the past. A poll released in 2007 by The Associated Press and Ipsos found that the typical American read only four books the previous year. One in four adults read no books at all. If this trend continues, an increasing number of bookstores and newspapers will be going out of business soon.

In addition to this journal, what books are you reading? Do you read for inspiration, information, or pleasure? Find something to read that is outside your comfort zone, something that you wouldn't ordinarily choose. Expand your horizons.

JUNE 17

You will know that forgiveness has begun when you recall those who hurt you and feel the power to wish them well.
Lewis B. Smedes

RECALLING

Memory was not designed to be used in a destructive or harmful manner. It is not to be used to relive the painful memories of past negative events. Your mind's ability to retain knowledge is one of God's gifts, allowing you to recall the smell of spring in the dark, cold days of winter, or loved ones who have passed away. It is to be used to gather wisdom and learning, not to torture yourself daily with regurgitated pain.

The key to letting go of negative memories is to forgive. Take whatever value you received from a negative experience, claim the wisdom learned from it, and move on with your life. Let the past stay where it belongs—in the past. Live for today. Your body is here, now. Why not bring your mind with it?

June 18

A moral being is one who is capable of reflecting
on his past actions and their motives.
Charles Darwin

REFLECTING

Life moves quickly in modern culture. Most people are so busy they hardly have time to stop and eat. As soon as one thing is accomplished, we hurry on to the next. Rarely, if ever, is there time to stop and reflect on the day's journey.

One of my favorite Bible quotes is, "Be still and know that I am God." It reminds me to stop my crazy pace and just get quiet for a minute. It's amazing how many things get resolved when you let go and let God take over. There really is a Power beyond our egos.

Use this journal for reflection. Make it a place to gather your thoughts and ponder what lessons you learned from your day's experiences. Write down your dreams and create affirmative statements for tomorrow. Be still!

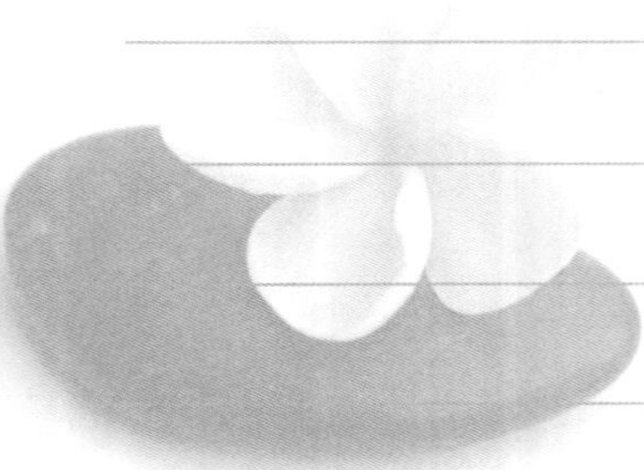

June 19

May you never forget what is worth remembering,
nor ever remember what is best forgotten.
Irish Blessings

REMEMBERING

We have already forgotten much of what has happened in our lives. We may have a few pleasant or poignant memories from childhood, but most of the details have been dissolved by now. Even the powerful truths that we intended to remember from one day to the next must be frequently reentered into our minds so that we don't completely lose the original inspiration of their wisdom. We are in a constant state of flux, remembering and forgetting and then remembering again.

What truth do you need to remember today?

June 20

Passion is in all great searches and
is necessary to all creative endeavors.
W. Eugene Smith

SEARCHING

Searching your own consciousness to discover what is there is a powerful way to grow spiritually. To look carefully inward in order to find what is concealed in your awareness is to begin to liberate yourself from unexamined concepts and belief in ideas that may have been inherited, installed through advertising, or adopted by accident. To search for them, you must look directly at or beneath the habitual thoughts that occupy your mind. You must search for stressful feelings or ideas that inevitably point the way to something that does not deserve to have residence in your mind.

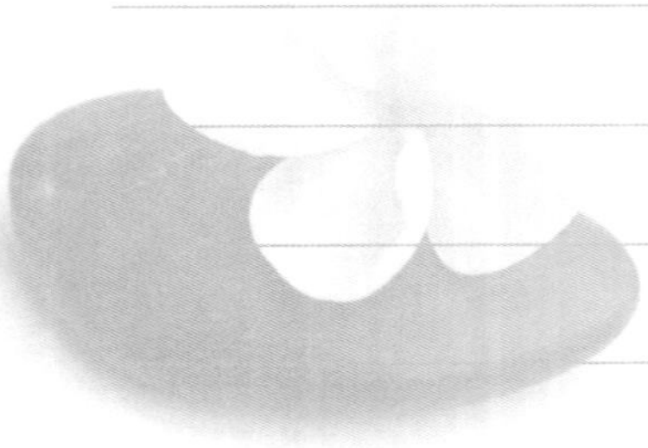

June 21

The person who seeks all their applause from outside
has their happiness in another's keeping.
Dale Carnegie

SEEKING

Some people turn their search for meaning and value outward. It is a risky proposition to think that your purpose and happiness come from something or someone outside of you. When you hinge your happiness on temporal things, it will always be subject to the rules of temporality. It will come and go with the things and people with which it associates.

Make a list of the people and things in your life to which your happiness is attached. You do not have to do anything with the list; just writing it down is a powerful step in evaluating yourself and uncovering the freedom that comes from this kind of inward seeking.

June 22

I know of no more encouraging fact than the unquestioning ability of man to evaluate his life by a conscious endeavor.
Henry David Thoreau

SELF-EVALUATING

An interesting spiritual practice is a method frequently employed in the work place—writing a self-evaluation as part of a job review. Imagine you are being asked to do a self-evaluation of the last six months of your life. You might begin by looking at the projects you have been working on, listing those that are complete, those that were successful, that were fun, and so on. Assign a value to each project based on how you experienced it. Then, follow up with a summary of what you learned from these projects, being as specific as you can both with tangible skills and intangible experiences. Finally, take a moment to describe what seems to be your next step in life.

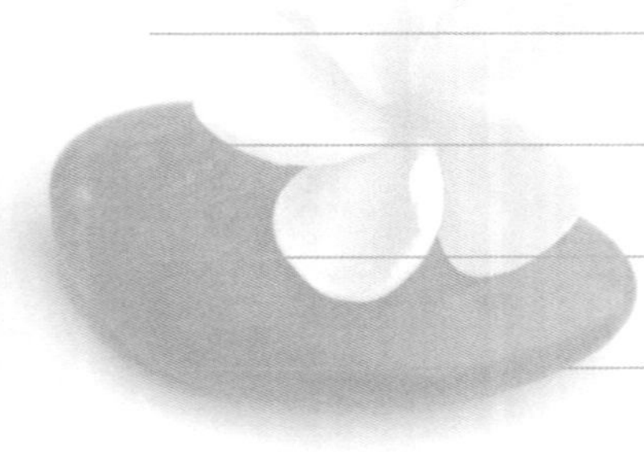

June 23

One must be entirely sensitive to the structure of the material that one is handling. One must yield to it in tiny details of execution, perhaps the handling of the surface or grain, and one must master it as a whole.

Barbara Hepworth

SENSITIVITY

British artist Dame Barbara Hepworth was one of the most significant sculptors of the twentieth century. After studying with an Italian master, Ardini, she became aware of the nature of sensitivity in creating art, saying that "it was not dominance which one had to obtain over material, but an understanding, almost a kind of persuasion, and above all a kind of coordination between head and hand."

Spiritual living is like that. Progress and creation are not achieved through dominance and coercion. Only after becoming sensitive to the nature of Reality can we slip easily into a powerful collaborative relationship with life. Through understanding, we become less inclined to wrestle something out of life that it is not able to yield, and less interested in shaping it into something that it is not intended to be.

June 24

A pessimist sees the difficulty in every opportunity;
an optimist sees the opportunity in every difficulty.
Winston Churchill

SUSPENDING

Contemplative practices are well-suited for suspending your ordinary view of the world. Beyond the normal assessment of what things mean, and beyond the automatic categories we tend to assign to everything, there is a world of possibilities. For example, select two very different items in your home and place them next to each other. Sit for a while and look at them. Begin to let yourself see the connections and similarities between them. The more different the items, the more creativity is required.

This practice fosters flexibility in how we view the world. We can generally detect where in our world we are strongly attached to a rigid point of view by using stress as a guide. What is causing you stress right now? Take that situation and, in your mind, place it alongside another situation that causes you joy. Then, practice looking for similarities between the two.

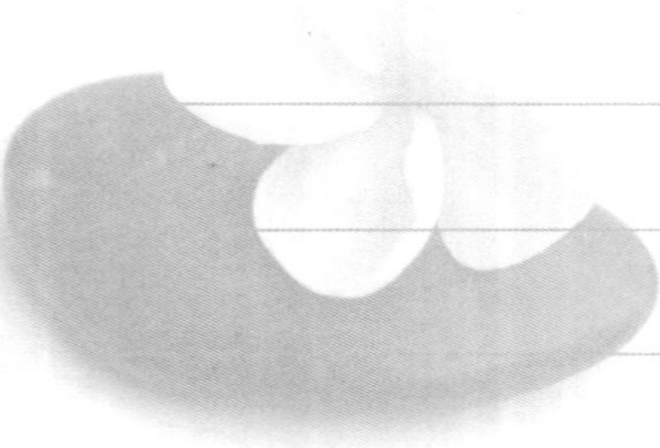

JUNE 25

For the one who is moderate in eating, recreation, working, sleeping, and waking, this yoga [of meditation] destroys [all] sorrow.
Bhagavad Gita

TAKING A VACATION

It is a symptom of our culture that people often drive themselves at top speed. Whether it is in work or recreation, relationship or solitude, they create an atmosphere of intensity that reveals a belief in urgency: "I have to do this and get as much as I can from it, and then hurry on to the next thing." There is nothing wrong with intense engagement or the purposeful pursuit of a favorite pastime, especially when balanced with other experiences where this intensity is absent.

Sometimes we drive ourselves so hard that, when it is time for us to take a vacation, the vacation becomes a period of recovery instead of recreation. We are so empty that the vacation is empty, too. Perhaps if the advice offered in the Bhagavad Gita could be incorporated into our routines, we might find a way of living in balance, so that, by the time it is vacation time, we are poised and ready to use that time for something wonderful.

June 26

A man is but the product of his thoughts; what he thinks, he becomes.
Mahatma Gandhi

THINKING

Author James Allen was inspired by a Bible verse, Proverbs 23:7, when writing his classic book, *As a Man Thinketh*. In it, he explores the freedom we have to think and, through thinking, become what we are meant to be. Allen says that we are the complete sum of all our thoughts. In other words, it is not so much the isolated or random thought that powerfully shapes us; it is the accumulated and habitual thoughts stored in our psyche. It is this collected tendency of all our thinking that can be described as our "belief system."

The good news is that this accumulation is an ongoing process. When trained to investigate our thinking, we gradually become adept at noticing which thoughts to believe and which are not worth believing. Allen advises us to cherish our visions and ideals, and to value the beauty that forms in our minds, because our soul attracts that which it harbors.

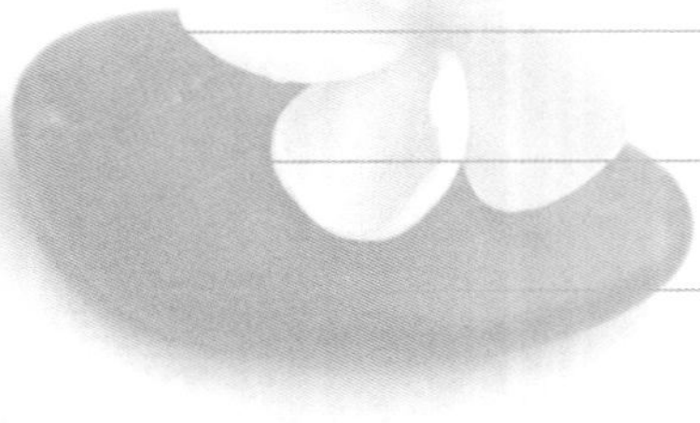

June 27

The universe is full of magical things, patiently waiting for our wits to grow sharper.
Eden Phillpotts

WAITING

Nobody likes waiting. Even if you consider yourself to be a patient person, you'd probably still like to see your desires fulfilled more quickly. But time is a necessary ingredient in your spiritual advancement. It gives you the opportunity to gather the wisdom you need, while the Universe works at manifesting your dream.

God is at work right now, doing whatever is needed to give you the good you desire. It is making arrangements on your behalf and planning glorious things for your future. Knowing this will make it easier to wait.

June 28

I know not how I may seem to others, but to myself I am but a small child wandering upon the vast shores of knowledge, every now and then finding a small, bright pebble to content myself with.

Plato

WANDERING

At times, your spiritual journey may seem to be an aimless meandering from one experience to another. It may appear that you are simply wandering through life, randomly moving hither and yon. While involved in the daily minutiae, you may not be able to see the clear path that you are on. Viewed from a distance, though, it all makes perfect sense. Each choice you made led you to where you are today, and the path that you are on is perfect for your soul's evolution.

You are not wandering through life, aimlessly slipping along. You are on the right path. Stay on it and keep your eyes open. You will see exactly what you need to see to get where you want to go.

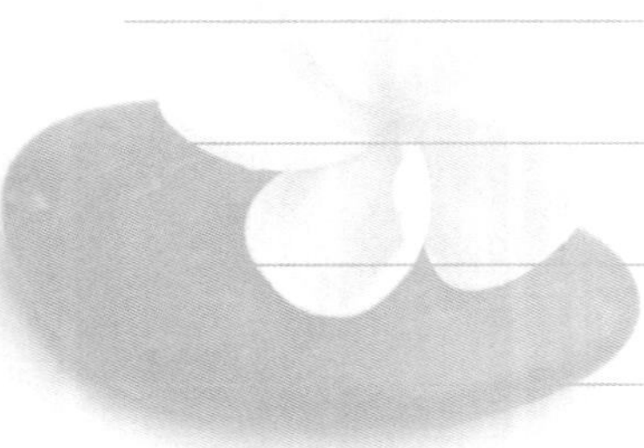

June 29

He who can no longer pause to wonder and stand rapt in awe, is as good as dead; his eyes are closed.
Albert Einstein

WONDERING

The word *wonderful* means to be full of wonder and astonishment. To live a wonderful life, you must have a fascination and an awe of Life Itself. You must be passionately engaged in living and loving.

Life is good and people are awesome. Take time to sit in wonder today, and remind yourself of all that's good.

June 30

There are no holy places and no holy people,
only holy moments, only moments of wisdom.
Unknown

WISDOM

Education does not necessarily bring greater wisdom. Neither does experience. There are many highly educated people who lack basic wisdom. And there are many people with decades of experience who still have no understanding of how or why any of it happened.

True wisdom can't be taught in a classroom, nor does it come from repeating negative experiences over and over again. Wisdom has only one Source—God. You do not have to visit a holy place or find a holy person to obtain God's wisdom. You can access it anytime you like, because God is a Presence that lives inside of you.

Go within. Seek God's Presence. Claim Its wisdom, and you will know what to do next.

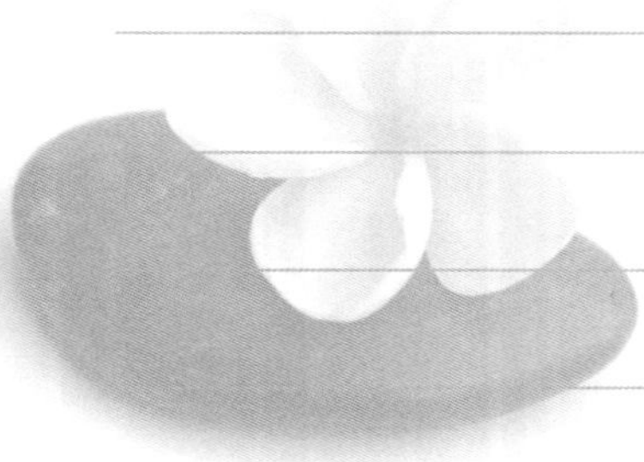

JULY

Practice *the* Presence *through* Charity

July 1

If you have come to help me, you are wasting your time. But if you have come because your liberation is bound with mine, then let us work together.
Aboriginal Activists Group

SERVICE

Service imparts the highest recognition that we are all one. Living in service to others is an act of spiritual maturity, and it can only be practiced by those who have left the false dream of duality behind. These people have surpassed the "win/lose" paradigm and realized that "win/win" is the only sane solution to the world's problems.

It has been said that if you want to succeed in life, help someone else succeed. By helping others get what they want from life, you really help yourself, because, ultimately, what goes out from you must return to you.

How can you practice service today?

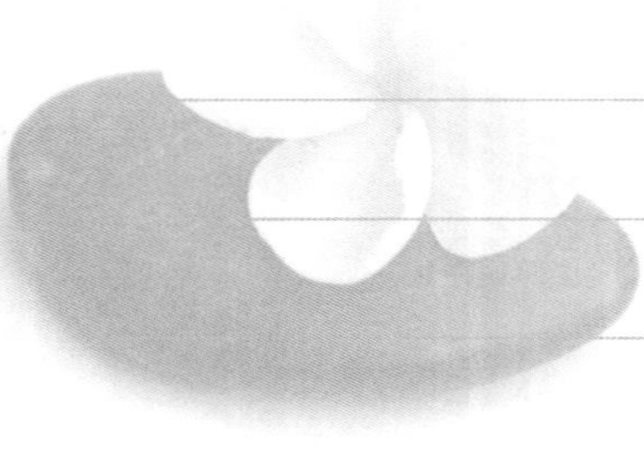

July 2

People can be more forgiving than you can imagine. But you have to forgive yourself. Let go of what's bitter and move on.
Bill Cosby

FORGIVING

Your body is not designed to live in pain; neither is your spirit. You can't make it through life holding on to the pain of the past. It will ruin everything.

If you are holding resentment or guilt over your past behaviors, today is the day to begin releasing it. Give yourself the gift, before you give it to others. Forgive yourself first, and then extend the same courtesy to others who have harmed you. If you don't know how to forgive yourself, just start by being willing to do it. Practice saying, "I am willing to forgive now."

July 3

Only the weak are cruel. Gentleness can only be expected from the strong.
Leo Buscaglia

GENTLENESS

Don't marry a man who slams doors or throws things around in an abrupt manner. Don't go out on a second date with a woman who curses and shows anger toward her family. These things are signs of weakness. They are the behaviors of the poor in spirit.

Gentleness is a sign of a loving consciousness. Being gentle with inanimate objects shows respect for the energy of Life in all things. Being gentle with other people honors the sacredness of their being. It acknowledges their virtue and godliness.

Practice setting things down gently. Don't slam doors or throw things around. Be gentle and kind to others today, and watch what happens. They will return your kindness in measure.

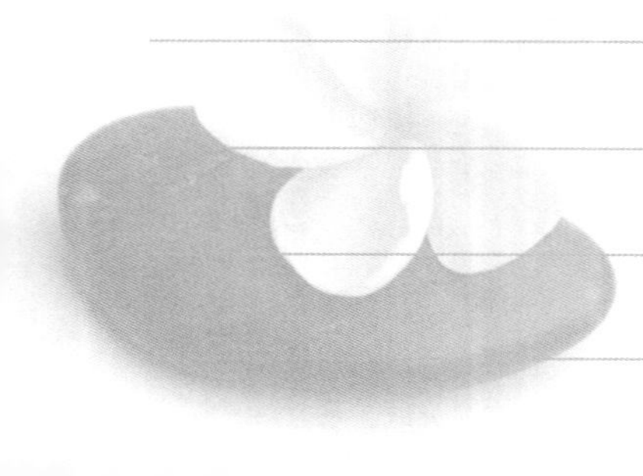

July 4

Charity sees the need, not the cause.
German Proverb

GIVING

Giving is the most powerful method of practice that leads to an experience of the Presence. The manner in which giving is practiced can either lead deeper into the experience of the Presence or further out of it. Giving is sometimes control thinly disguised as kindness; as such, it tends to create distance and resistance. This kind of giving quickly reveals itself because it is filled with expectation. It expects the receiver to accept the gift. It expects the receiver to appreciate the gift. The true practice of giving has no expectations.

The practice of giving to benefit the poor, to nurture virtue, or simply to help others is prescribed in a number of faith traditions. What role does giving play in your life?

July 5

With malice toward none, with charity for all, with firmness in the right as God gives us to see the right, let us finish the work we are in.
Abraham Lincoln

HEART

Sometimes, people follow their hearts' instructions when deciding where to contribute. They seek out people or organizations that have "heart value." This is a wonderful practice, because each of us has different heart connections to the world.

There are two other ways to look at giving from the heart: to give to the person or organization that causes you to be spiritually inspired; and to give randomly, whether need exists or not. Realize that giving does not necessarily have to be attached to need. It is wonderful when good people see a need and meet it. And it is wonderful when good people give simply because they realize it is their nature to do so.

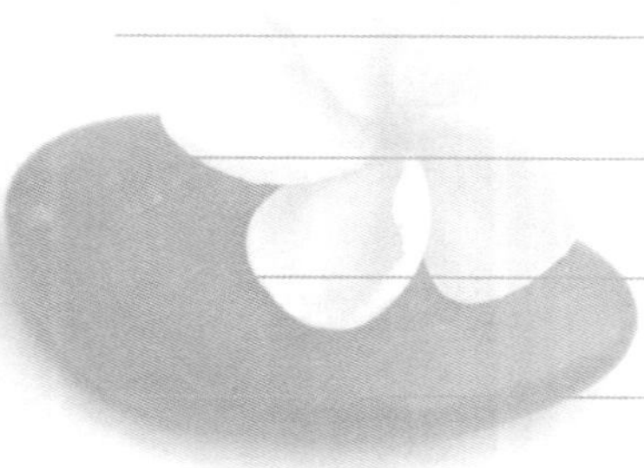

July 6

He who wished to secure the good
of others, has already secured his own.
Confucius

HEROISM

In ancient Greek folklore, a hero was the offspring of a blended parentage—a human and a god. The resulting demigod had power and skill above that of the ordinary humans, but not quite that of the gods. The hero tended to come to the rescue in times of need and was necessary to tip the balance toward victory in unfavorable situations.

Today's heroes are ordinary people who, although born of mortal parents, have found a way to blend their humanity and spirituality so that they appear to have more courage and valor than the ordinary person. I believe we all have the capacity to be heroes and to display great courage or noble qualities. We can practice being heroic by looking out for others and caring about the people closest to us. Think about a time you did something kind or thoughtful for someone, and journal about the effect it had on you and those around you.

July 7

Charity begins at home, but should not end there.
Proverb

INVOLVEMENT

Practicing charity with the people closest to us is a wonderful way to get involved. You most likely have a foundation of love in your nuclear or extended family or circle of friends that will allow you to access your charitable nature easily.

Once you have made a habit of contributing to the well-being of those closest to you, you can begin to expand the circle of your giving to include your neighborhood or town. It is likely that, with a little bit of research, you will discover that there are endless opportunities to volunteer, contribute, and participate in your area. Following your heart, you can select something to participate in that matches your schedule and availability. In this way, you open yourself to an ever-growing influence of love and circulation.

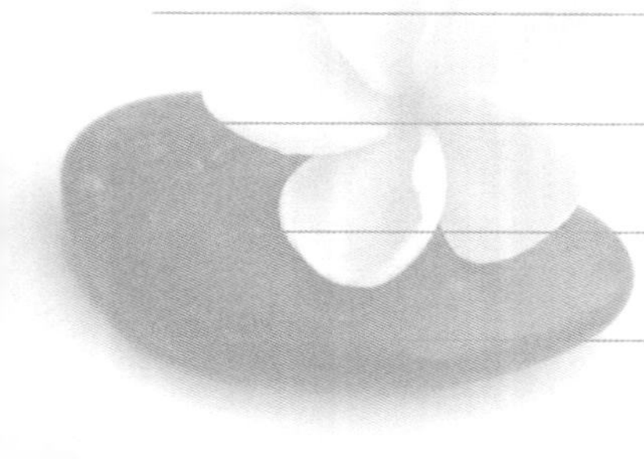

July 8

Real charity doesn't care if it's tax-deductible or not.
Dan Bennett

JOY

Joy is more than a deep form of happiness. It is more than an emotion that results from an event or circumstance. It is more than the opposite of sadness or the absence of depression. Joy is the natural state of one who has learned to take delight in Reality.

Try to think of joy as having no cause. Try to think of joy as being always present and available. Imagine that you don't have to do anything to cause it and that you can't create it because it exists already. This thinking puts you in the best frame of mind to serve and be generous, because everything you see and everyone you encounter is an opportunity to experience the natural joy of being.

Can you recall a time when you felt joyfulness that had no particular cause attached to it? If so, describe it in detail. If not, try to imagine what that would be like.

July 9

Kindness in words creates confidence. Kindness in thinking creates profoundness. Kindness in giving creates love.

Lao Tzu

KINDNESS

I am committed to spreading joy in the world. I want everything I do, say, and think to result in more happiness. I value kindness and try to let it govern me. Still, I notice that some of my duties are difficult.

When I was a music teacher, I had to tell an aspiring young pianist that she wasn't going to be able to participate in a concert because she could not manage the part. I told her with as much kindness as I could. As I saw the painful disappointment on her face, I felt such love for her. I also noticed that I was powerless to control her experience.

Years later, I came to realize that it was my attachment to immediate results that made it difficult for me to see the long-range effects of giving bad news kindly. I have been lucky to receive both unkind bad news and kind bad news, and I now understand the power of giving bad news with kindness. It is a sobering thought to understand that I cannot control anyone, but that I can be kind.

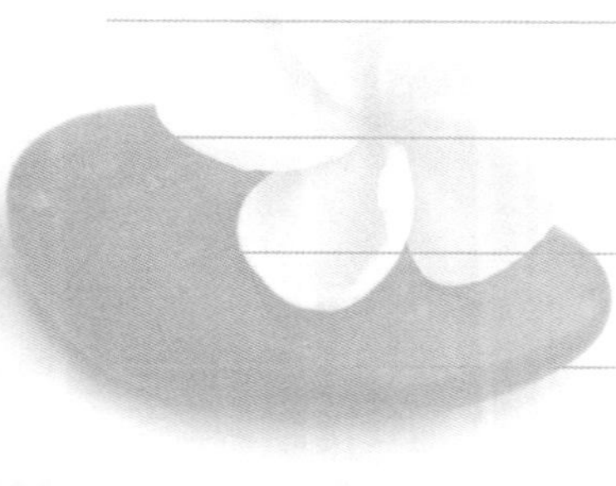

July 10

A society that has more justice
is a society that needs less charity.
Ralph Nader

LEADING

I wonder if Ralph Nader's quote is upside-down. Maybe a society that has more charity is a society that needs less justice. Maybe it is neither. Maybe charity has nothing to do with justice, and justice nothing to do with charity.

Do you see a relationship between justice and charity? Do you think the absence of one affects the presence of the other?

July 11

Learn from yesterday, live
for today, hope for tomorrow.
Albert Einstein

LEARNING

There are only two ways to learn: with intuition or with tuition. To acquire much of what you know today, you have paid the price of tuition, either through direct experience or through someone else's. Experience, as they say, is a good teacher.

However, you can also learn through intuition—by tapping into the One Knower within you. This infinite resource of wisdom is accessible to you anytime you seek it. By using intuition, you can save a lot of time and wasted energy.

Practice learning the easy way. Take your challenges and questions to the Source of all knowing. Go within and ask. You will find your answers.

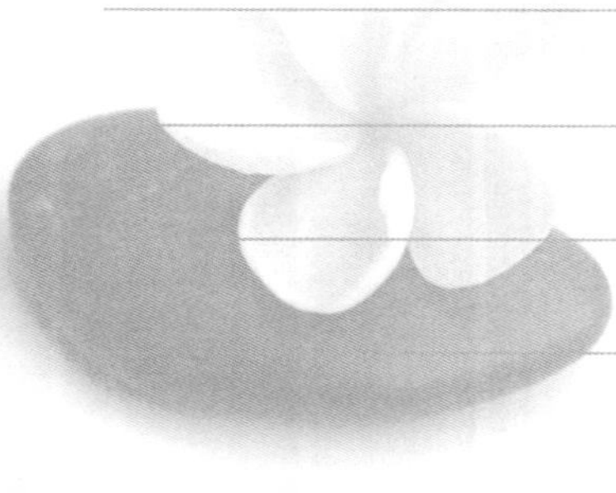

JULY 12

We must not, in trying to think about how we can make a big difference, ignore the small daily differences we can make which, over time, add up to big differences that we often cannot foresee.
Marian Wright Edelman

MAKING A DIFFERENCE

You make a difference in the world simply by living your life. It is impossible not to! Someone is always listening to what you have to say and then deciding how to respond. Someone is always watching what you do and then choosing what they are going to do. We affect each other; we can't help it.

Most of us want to leave the world better than we found it. We want to make a difference and leave a positive impression. We want to contribute something worthwhile and valuable. But we forget that every time we choose love over fear, or forgiveness instead of resentment, we create ripples in consciousness that affect everyone on the planet.

July 13

I have always found that mercy
bears richer fruits than strict justice.
Abraham Lincoln

MERCY

Nature is always seeking balance. That's why the nature of God is both Love and Law. The Spiritual Laws of Nature are immutable. They are the same for everyone. Each of us must either accept the blessings or suffer the consequences of our own thoughts, choices, and actions. However, to balance this cold, hard fact, God is also unconditional love.

Even though you may break many spiritual laws, there is always mercy. No matter what crime you have committed or sin you have incurred, Spirit cannot and will not alter Its love for you. The love It has for you is perfect, ever-forgiving, and eternal. Why not begin to accept it today?

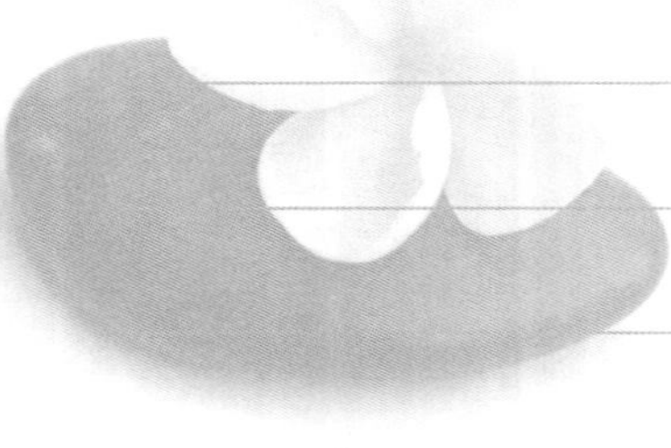

July 14

Imagine for yourself a character, a model personality,
whose example you determine to follow, in private as well as in public.
Epictetus

MODELING

We all need role models, people who exemplify the attributes that we seek to embody. We need to be around people who mirror the qualities we wish to develop within ourselves. Think of the people whose lives you would like to emulate. How are their choices different from yours? What is their attitude toward life? Are they positive and affirmative? Do they operate with integrity? Do they have a healthy lifestyle and good sense of humor? Do you respect them?

Here is your assignment for the day: Bring to mind a person who is a role model for your life. Then, try to think as this person does, or make the choices you think he or she might make. Model this person's character until it becomes your own. Don't try to mimic. Just take the good things from his or her life and add it to yours.

July 15

The results of philanthropy
are always beyond calculation.
Miriam Beard

PHILANTHROPY

Make a contribution to someone in need or to some organization that is doing good in the world. Do it anonymously. Feel what it is like to be part of someone else's blessing, without having to be noticed or recognized for your gift.

You have much to give. It's not just your financial support that is needed; it is also your time and talent. Volunteer. Get involved. Pray.

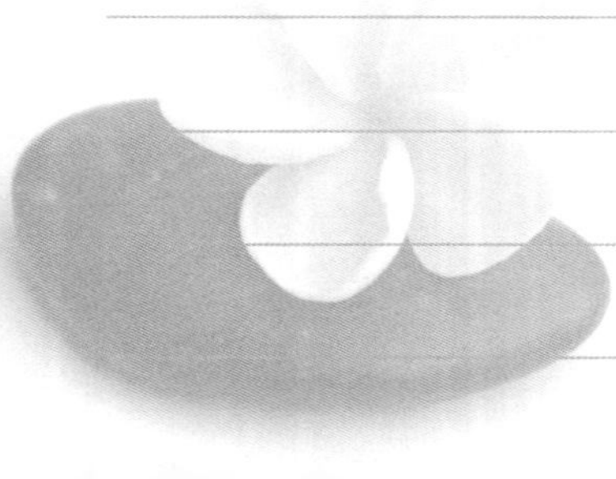

July 16

I have the consolation of having added nothing to my private fortune during my public service, and of retiring with hands clean as they are empty.
Thomas Jefferson

PUBLIC SERVICE

The people in my neighborhood allot one day a year to clean up our local park. It is a public service in which we all love to participate. We turn it into a social event. Everyone brings their pets, and we all get to know each other a little better. Parents also bring their children, to teach them the need to give something back to their community.

At the end of the day, the park is cleaner. But more important, our sense of community has been enriched, and the bond between neighbors has become stronger.

Practice public service. Schedule a block party. Teach someone to read. Volunteer your time at a homeless shelter. Give something to the betterment of humankind.

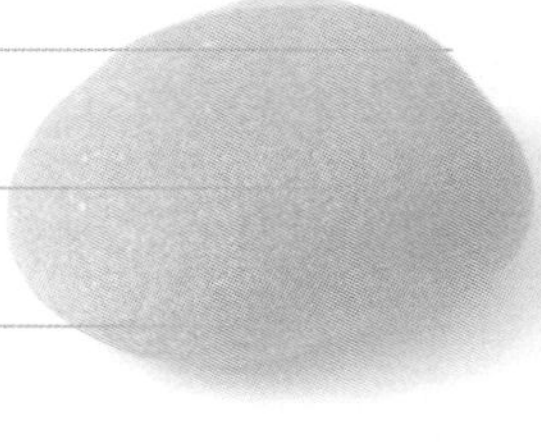

July 17

To achieve true sustainability, we must reduce our "garbage index"—that which we permanently throw away into the environment that will not be naturally recycled for reuse—to near zero.

David Korten

RECYCLING

We are running out of places to throw things away. Landfills are becoming mountains of garbage. Old warships are being sunk into the ocean. Our technology is changing so rapidly that last year's computer monitors and hard drives are quickly becoming tomorrow's trash.

There are millions of people living on the planet with much to discard. The only answer to this problem is to recycle. For the sake of our future, and so that our children can inherit a cleaner earth, be more conscious of what you throw away.

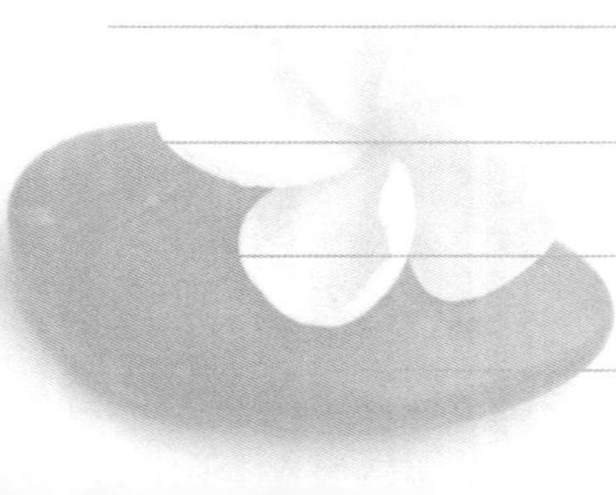

July 18

A bone to the dog is not charity. Charity is the bone shared with the dog, when you are just as hungry as the dog.
Jack London

REDISTRIBUTION

I grew up poor. When food was scarce, my mother taught me how to share. We would take delight in seeing who could share the most. It created a sense of mutual love and support. Being dissatisfied with a meal didn't seem as bothersome as it does now, because we knew the power of giving.

This teaching instilled in me an ability to give the better portion away, not out of duty, but out of the happiness that comes with sharing. Nevertheless, there are still things in my life I don't want to share; still times when I give a pittance when I could give more; and still times when I don't look, because I am afraid to see a need to which I don't want to contribute. I wonder if it is exactly in these moments that I am blocking the flow of good into my own life.

July 19

Simplicity is the ultimate sophistication.
Leonardo da Vinci

REDUCING

I overheard a conversation in a restaurant in which two friends discussed the idea of listing every item they possessed as a way of becoming aware of their tendency toward excess, and to inspire them to really think about what each item was useful for, what it meant, and whether or not they needed it. One of the friends said she thought it would be better to just sell everything and start all over, with an upper limit of how many items could be owned at any one time.

That comment really got me thinking about what I would acquire if, for some reason, I had the freedom to start fresh. I confess, I am somewhat of a hoarder when it comes to my favorite things, and this conversation caused me to think strongly about whether I could do things differently. Now, I look around my environment and think about who might want some of the items I have—and wonder if I should give some of my things away.

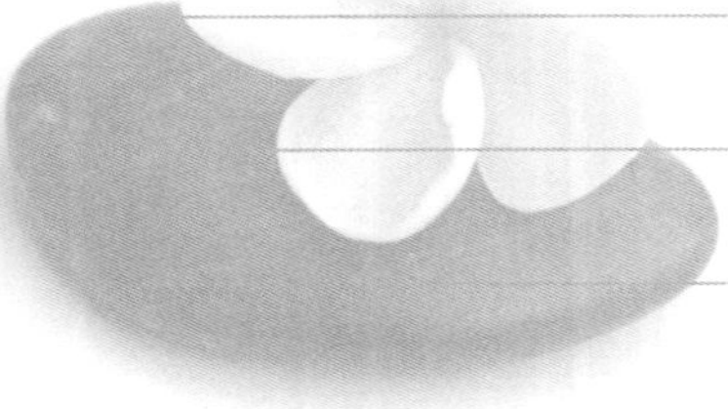

July 20

Always and in everything let there be reverence.
Confucius

REVERENCE

Practicing reverence for that which is greater than we are leads to kindness, respect, and a giving nature. Reverence is the art of being awe-inspired and is easily dismissed in a culture where the personal self is raised up in importance over all things. To practice reverence, we can begin with respect for the objects that we say belong to us.

Sometimes, I am sloppy in the way I treat my objects. I lose reverence for them when I don't maintain them or when I use them unconsciously. I notice I do that with people too, and that when I am out of reverence, I am into me. Being overly self-centered does not lead me to sharing and respect. So, I practice respect a little more every day by respecting the objects and people around me.

July 21

Don't wait until everything is just right. It will never be perfect. There will always be challenges, obstacles, and less than perfect conditions. So what? Get started now. With each step you take, you will grow stronger and stronger, more and more skilled, more and more self-confident, and more and more successful.

Mark Victor Hansen

RIGHT ACTION

Consider the idea that everything is in the right place at the right time and that you are engaged, at any moment, in the right activity. In other words, there is no time when you will be better suited to make your contribution to the world than today.

Imagine that you are the right person in the right place, and that you always have been and always will be. Can you see anything that might be different for you and your interaction with other people when you live from this perspective?

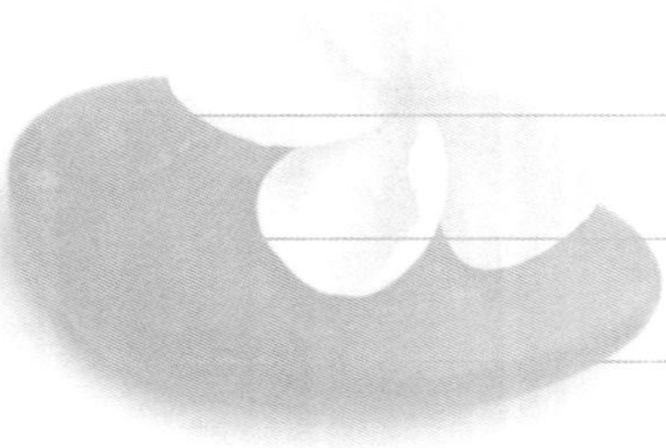

July 22

Learn and grow all you can; serve and befriend all you can; enrich and inspire all you can.
William Arthur Ward

SERVING

Life provides us with endlessly fascinating opportunities. An old adage says that the best things in life are free. Yet we are more inclined to pursue things that have a price tag. In truth, there is nothing wrong with that; however, there is so much more in life that, when pursued, will yield a more profound peace and joy. Chief among these freebies are activities that focus on other people. Of course, you can and should allow things into your life that make you comfortable and prosperous. But a person who views service, kindness, and philanthropy as priorities has accessed the special truth that the very best things in life are free.

July 23

There is no delight in
owning anything unshared.
Seneca

SHARING

A teacher once told me that sharing is natural and hoarding is unnatural. I took that to mean that my nature is to share, and, when I don't share, I'm going against that nature and produce friction and resistance. After thinking about it, that seems reasonable. After all, nature seems to be a radical example of lavish, unrestricted sharing. I am part of nature. So when I'm sharing, I am expanding my reach into my community and feel great doing so.

I also notice that I hoard the craziest things. Or, maybe I should say, I collect them. Regardless, the end result is the same. I collect things that I value, like handsome, blank journals. Then I don't write in them because I love to look at them. Recently, I started giving them away. I've been having fun with the internal process of letting go of something I love to hoard, and then noticing the happiness that comes from sharing what I have. Do you possess something that would bring joy to someone else? What would it be like to give that thing away?

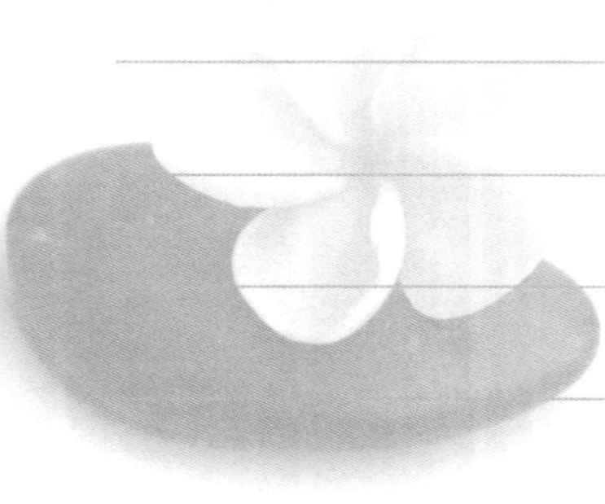

JULY 24

If you're not serving the customer,
you'd better be serving someone who is.
Karl Albrecht

SUPPORT

Giving support costs nothing. Support is one of those miraculous qualities that, once given, reaches out with its influence into places where you cannot go yourself. I remember the times when someone has been there for me, shoring up my self-esteem when I forgot it. When this happens, I try to imagine someone doing the same for the person who supported me. I then think about the beneficial impact on my life as a result of one, simple act of support that a friend or loved one extended to me.

Is there someone in your life right now who is going through a challenging time? Is there something you can do to support to this person?

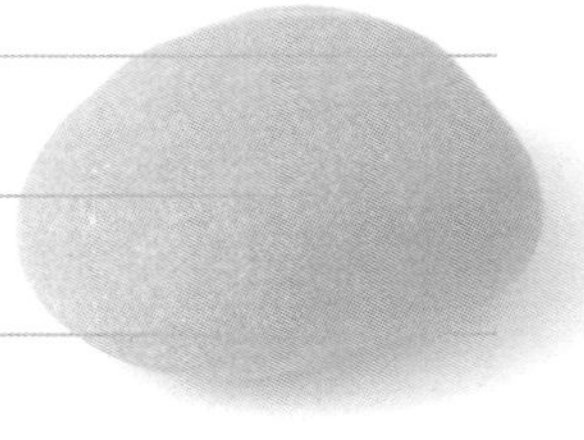

July 25

As citizens, we have to be more thoughtful and more educated and more informed. I turn on the TV and I see these grown people screaming at each other, and I think, well, if we don't get our civility back, we're in trouble.

Emmylou Harris

THOUGHTFULNESS

We don't need much from other people. We don't need others to overcome our challenges or solve our problems for us. We just need them to be thoughtful and considerate. A little kindness goes a long way.

An encouraging word from a boss instills loyalty and increases performance. A kind gesture from a partner or spouse opens your heart to love. A considerate act from a friend or family member incites joy.

All of these actions are healing. Each time you show consideration toward another human being through your actions or words, you are actually healing that person. You can play a role in the healing of our world simply by being thoughtful toward others. Start today.

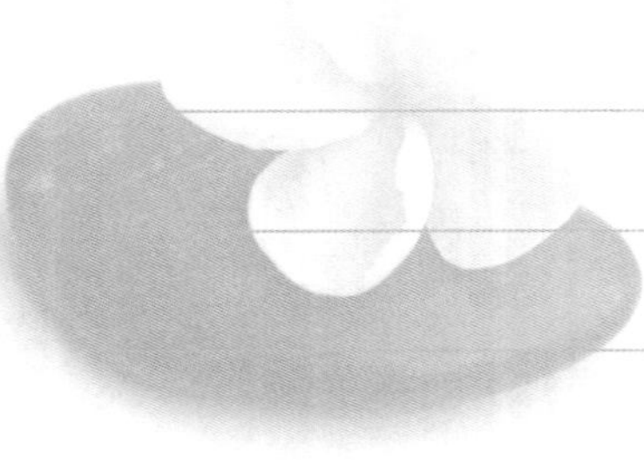

July 26

If you can't explain it simply,
you don't understand it well enough.
Albert Einstein

UNDERSTANDING

It is important for you to understand your faith and be able to communicate it to others in a respectful way. Study the principles of your faith. Practice using your own words to describe them. Rethink your core values and why they are important to your life. Now, try to explain them to others. When you are equipped with a clear understanding of what you believe, you are positioned to impact others in a positive way.

What faith do you practice? Can you describe your religious beliefs in simple terms? If someone asks, "What does your religion believe about Christ?", can you answer in a clear and understandable way? If you can't explain it simply, perhaps you don't understand your religion well enough.

July 27

Perfect valor is to behave, without witnesses,
as one would act were all the world watching.
François de la Rochefoucauld

VALOR

The world has always been desperate for heroes. Some women remain quiet and demure, unwilling to risk offending others even when they completely disagree with what they see around them. Some men have trouble mustering enough moxie to take a stand for their highest principles, especially if it means risking the approval of other men.

Act boldly today. Say publicly what you believe privately. Be courageous, but at the same time, kind. You do not have to be rude or brash to speak your mind or to stand for what you believe. Practice valor.

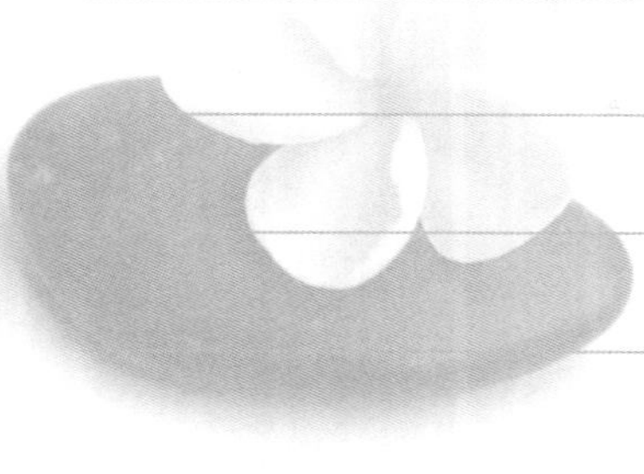

July 28

A high station in life is earned by the gallantry
with which appalling experiences are survived with grace.
Tennessee Williams

GALLANTRY

It's not what happens to you in life that matters; it's how you deal with it. With what attitude do you face your problems? Are you an optimist or pessimist? When you begin the day, do you expect good things to happen or wonder what horrible thing may happen next? When new problems arise, do you immediately succumb to them or do you start rallying your resources to overcome them? Do you think you are a brave person? What challenges have you faced bravely? What issues have you resolved with grace and elegance?

It is one thing to survive your challenges and quite another to be made a better person because of them. Don't merely survive. Be the person who rises valiantly above the challenge.

July 29

The only work that will ultimately bring any good to any of us is the work of contributing to the healing of the world.
Marianne Williamson

CONTRIBUTING

There is no such thing as a small gift from an infinite, ever-expanding Creator. Each gift is powerful and valuable, no matter how the world perceives it. Never underestimate the value of your uniqueness. Never discount yourself.

We have each been given a gift by our Creator. Each one of us has some unique quality or character that is our contribution to the world. Have you found yours yet? Do you know what your gift is?

If you don't know, go within and ask. Say something like this: "God, tell me why I am here. What contribution am I to make to the greater good of all? Show me. Lead me. Guide me." Keep asking and be patient. Your answer will be revealed.

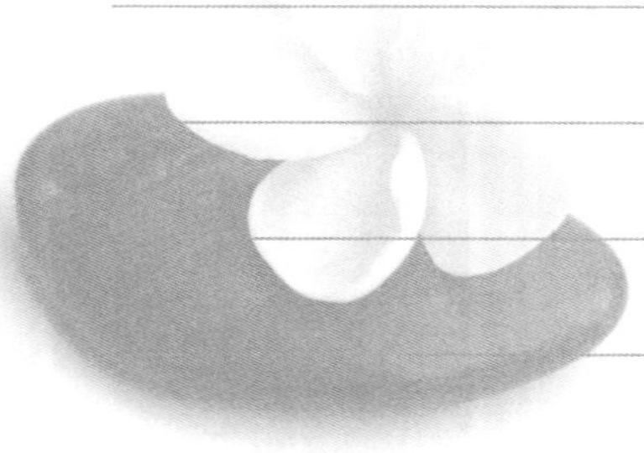

July 30

You know, there's a lot of talk in this country about the federal deficit. But I think we should talk more about our empathy deficit—the ability to put ourselves in someone else's shoes; to see the world through the eyes of those who are different from us.

President Barack Obama

COMPASSION

The ability to feel compassion toward another is a sign of emotional and spiritual maturity. To be able to look beyond your own needs and see another's is a view reserved only for those who truly know God.

Self-absorbed people are immature and childlike. They can't see beyond their own desires. They feel separated from their good and make demands on other people to provide it. Because of this disconnect from the oneness of all humanity, they often feel lonely and afraid.

Reach out to them. Show compassion. Resist the temptation to judge and condemn them. They are doing the best they can with the wisdom they currently possess.

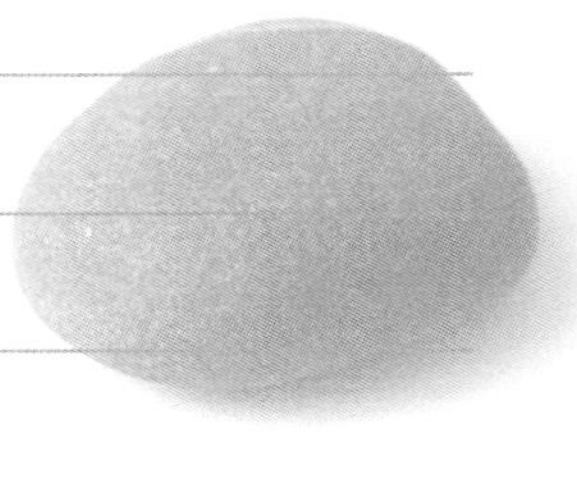

July 31

A little consideration, a little thought for others, makes all the difference.
Winnie the Pooh

CONSIDERATION

We are one. And because this is so, what you do to another, you also do to yourself. How you treat other people determines how you will be treated. What you give to others is evaluated and returned to you in like manner.

Give love, and love will return to you. Be generous, and others will be generous with you. Speak kindly of others, and they will speak kindly of you. Show respect, and you will be respected. Help others succeed in life, and they will help you.

Give what you wish to receive. Be the person you want others to be.

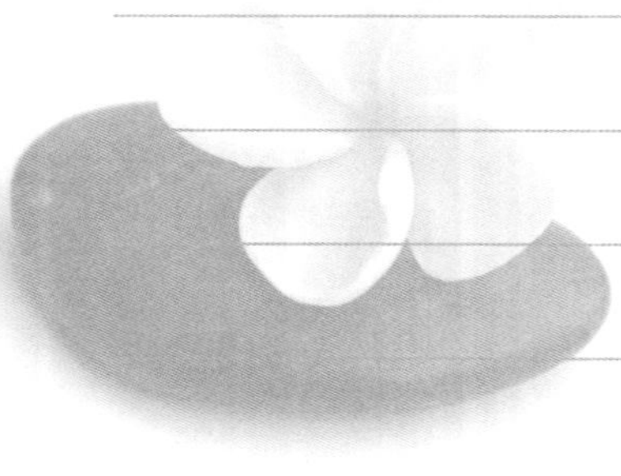

AUGUST

Practice *the* Presence *through* Being

August 1

For my part I know nothing with any certainty,
but the sight of the stars makes me dream.
Vincent van Gogh

CERTAINTY

There is an urge within us toward certainty and solid, dependable knowledge. We want to know what the weather is going to be like next week. We want to know what to expect from our friends. We want to know what we can depend on in the future.

I was telling a friend about how I'm sometimes caught up in the pursuit of future assurances. He asked me a powerful question: "How is that working for you?" I laughed out loud, because I realized that there is very little in life of which a person can be certain. Confident, yes; certain, I'm not so sure.

Of what in your life are you certain?

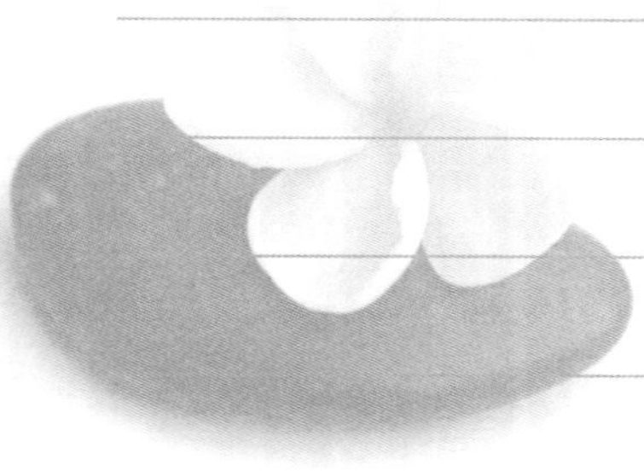

August 2

To believe with certainty,
we must begin with doubting.
King Stanislaus of Poland

UNCERTAINTY

Once I made friends with uncertainty, it seemed like the world became a friendlier place in which to live. It was as if I stopped trying to make the world conform to my need to have everything be predictable and reliable. It helped me free up some much-needed energy, energy that I had been using to plot out the way things should happen. With that liberated energy, I found a greater pleasure in just "being." In other words, my trust in the process of life increased, even though I had few assurances that things would work out the way I wanted them to.

Can you think of an example in your life where being uncertain led to peace of mind?

August 3

The greater our innocence, the greater our strength.
Mahatma Gandhi

BLAMELESSNESS

Practicing "being" means freeing yourself from the tendency to control events and experiences. You can practice this by adopting a childlike innocence toward an activity, such as a walk. As you walk, imagine that you have none of the responsibilities that have accumulated over the years, and that there is absolutely nothing you have to do at that time but walk. As you walk with this in mind, you will suddenly find you have more options available. You can pause to look at whatever appears before you and do as you feel appropriate.

I realize this may not be a wise approach to all areas of life; however, you will see how specific opportunities to just "be" in the world can make a tremendous contribution to your experience of the Presence.

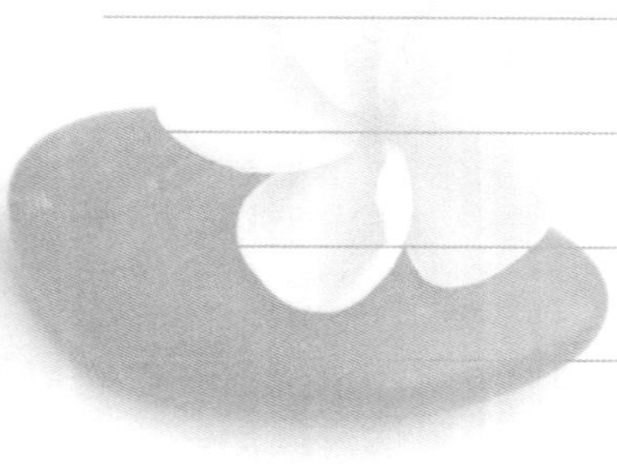

August 4

Whenever I feel blue, I start breathing again.
L. Frank Baum

BREATHING

I have a friend who gets quickly bored if he doesn't have something to do. When traveling to foreign cities, he is the type who will not be satisfied for very long if he's not going somewhere or seeing something new. I admire this quality. Left to my own devices, I might be content to sit on a bench and just breathe. But I tag along with him because he adds adventure to life. There is value in both our approaches. We must embrace life fully. And we must sit and breathe.

I notice over time, however, that my sit-and-breathe moments have become fewer and fewer. When I remember to practice sitting and breathing, I realize how beautiful it is to "be."

August 5

A mind once stretched by a new idea never regains its original dimension.
Oliver Wendell Holmes, Jr.

DEXTERITY

Physical dexterity is the result of flexibility and strength. Spiritual dexterity benefits from the same combination. Thinking outside of the box develops dexterity and allows you more options for "being." Breaking out of ordinary thought patterns requires purposefully testing new ideas.

There are many different and playful ways to practice dexterity. Think of a question in your life that you want answered in this moment. Now, grab the nearest book you can get your hands on (other than this journal) and flip through the pages, letting your finger find a page at random. Read the sentence your finger landed on, and ask yourself: "How is this sentence an answer to my question?"

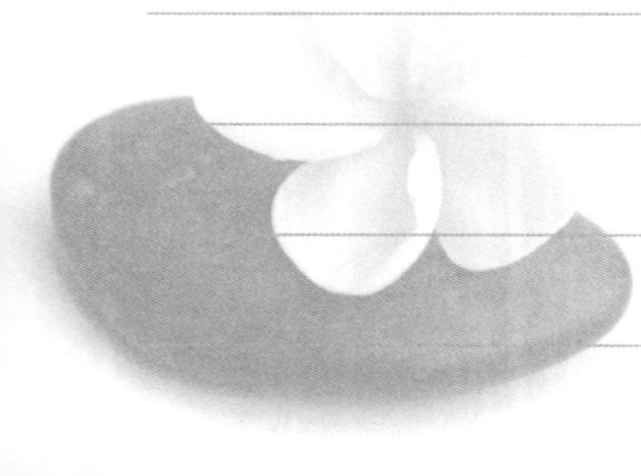

AUGUST 6

Music is the best means we have of digesting time.
W. H. Auden

DIGESTING

A professional musician once explained to me how music accesses specific brain functions. He told me about studies in which students taking exams were exposed to different types of music, and how peaceful, structured music had beneficial effects on their test scores. It reminded me that I need to take time to sit and absorb the experiences of my day and to integrate everything that has passed by and through me. If I sit for a while and listen to a favorite piece of music or song, and even maybe sing along, I begin to experience peace.

August 7

To accomplish great things, we must not only act,
but also dream; not only plan, but also believe.
Anatole France

DREAMING

There is a lot of emphasis on action and results in our culture. *Productivity* and *efficiency* are popular words in the workplace and our lives. However, I believe there should be more emphasis on *dreaming* and *imagination.*

I remember being admonished as a child because I was "such a daydreamer," usually by an adult after I'd related an idea I'd had. Fortunately, there were some adults in my life who understood the benefits of daydreams and encouraged me to create even more. As a result, I learned the power of balancing action with dreams. Anyway, daydreaming is just plain fun. Try it.

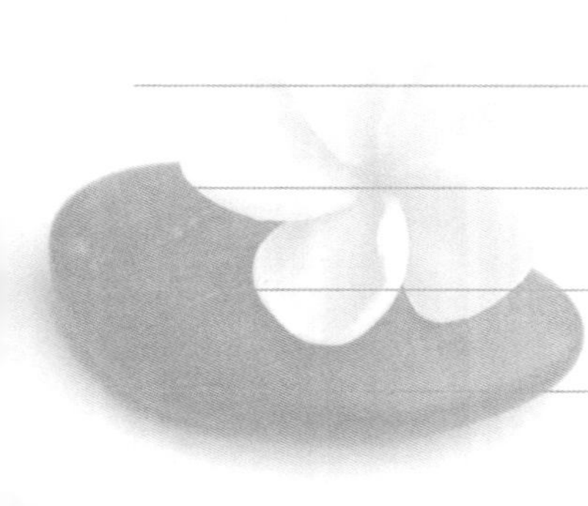

August 8

The really efficient laborer will be found not to crown his day with work, but will saunter to his task surrounded by a wide halo of ease and leisure.
Henry David Thoreau

EASE

Do you have too much to do today? Are you feeling the weight of adult responsibilities? Is your life overscheduled?

Perhaps you should take time for ease. What would ease your day? How about a massage or facial? Maybe lunch with a friend would be fun. And if there's no time for that, you could just take an afternoon "ease" break.

Leave the office sometime. Go outside and walk around. Enjoy the smell of summer and the warmth on your face. When you drive home tonight, play your favorite music in the car and sing out loud, even if you don't know the words.

August 9

Eat, drink, and be merry.
For tomorrow we die.
American Proverb

EATING

Portion control is necessary to maintain a proper weight. Your body does not process excessive amounts of calories quickly. It was never designed to handle the amount of food that is available to us in modern society.

However, that does not mean you should starve yourself or frantically shift from one fad diet to another. There are no quick and easy answers. Moderation in all things is the key.

Diets don't work because they are punitive—built on denial. To stay on the diet, you have to deny yourself the pleasurable part of eating—and that never works. Eat healthily. Make smart choices. But have dessert once in a while, too.

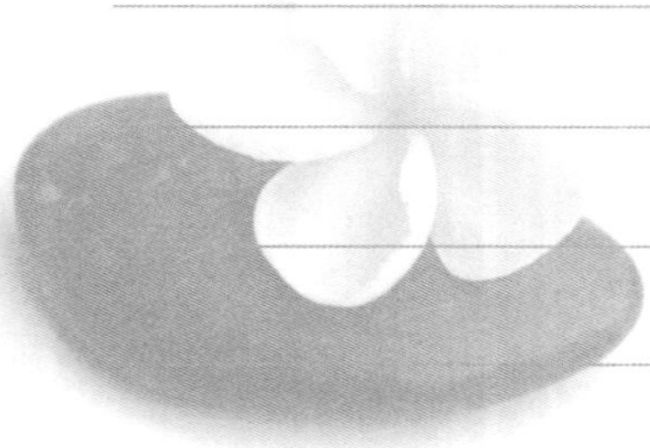

August 10

The highest education is that which does not merely give us information but makes our life in harmony with all existence.
Rabindranath Tagore

EDUCATION

Being able to memorize facts and figures does not mean you are educated. Just because you can effectively quote the wisdom of others does not mean you are wise. Exposure to mountains of information does not necessarily guarantee you will make better choices.

To educate means to draw outward that which is within. Education is not about cramming information and facts into someone's head; it is about encouraging the innate wisdom that exists within them.

The universe has given each of us special wisdom. You know something others don't. You see things in a way others can't. You have a unique perspective on life. Don't be afraid to offer your voice or speak your mind. It has value.

August 11

I think the thing to do is to
enjoy the ride while you're on it.
Johnny Depp

ENJOYING

Today is a great day to begin enjoying your life. Happiness is a choice you make every day. You don't have to respond to the challenges before you in a negative, self-defeating way. You can make a different choice.

Each day brings a new set of circumstances. Each day has its problems and worries. This is true for everyone. No one has a problem-free life. But that doesn't mean it has to get you down.

Practice enjoying your day. Enjoy riding in the car. Enjoy your work and coworkers. Enjoy your family and friends. Enjoy your lunch and dinner. Enjoy being yourself.

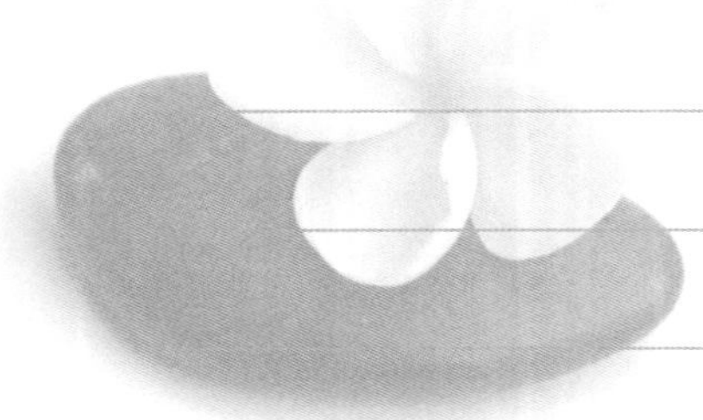

August 12

That's the difference between me and the rest of the world!
Happiness isn't good enough for me! I demand euphoria!
Bill Watterson

EUPHORIA

Have you ever gone parasailing or skydiving? If so, you understand the meaning of euphoria. It is an intense feeling of joy, mixed with a splash of fear or danger. Those are the moments you remember—the times you feel most alive.

Every day can't be euphoric; to expect it to be is unreasonable. Only addicts constantly search for euphoria, and we all know where that road leads.

You can practice euphoria by planning an exciting event in your life. Schedule a bungee jump, a tandem sky dive, a hot air balloon ride, anything that takes you beyond your comfort zone.

August 13

Take care of your body with steadfast fidelity. The soul must see through these eyes alone, and if they are dim, the whole world is clouded.

Goethe

FITNESS

Human bodies were designed to move regularly and frequently. We are not a stationary species. As time passes and the body ages, nature requires that you move it or lose it. Sedimentary lifestyles create havoc and disease in the body.

Create a daily fitness routine. Schedule some time each day for exercise. Take good care of the only body you've got, and it will reward you with a long and healthy life.

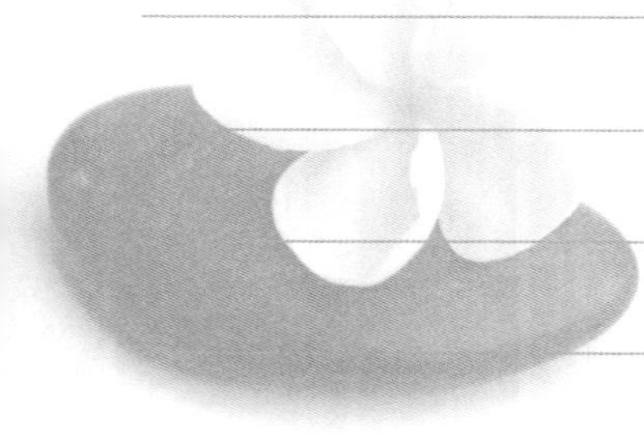

August 14

Grace isn't a little prayer you chant
before receiving a meal. It's a way to live.
Jackie Windspear

GRACE

In Greek mythology, the daughters of Zeus were called The Three Graces. Each one embodied an aspect of God's nature: Love, Beauty, and Prosperity.

Love is God's first gift. Without the ability to feel intimacy and experience love, life would not be worth living. Love brings meaning to our lives.

Beauty is a delightful gift from our Creator. We live in a beautiful world and are surrounded each day by God's elegant nature. Every sunrise is a masterpiece; each flower shows the artistry of a genius at work.

Prosperity is a beneficent gift of Spirit. We have been created to prosper. We have inherited an abundant universe. There is always more than enough of everything we need to live well in this world.

Practice the three graces. Make it a point to notice the gifts God has created.

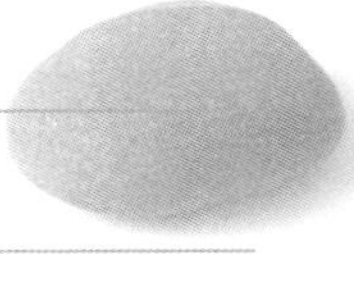

August 15

The secret of health for both mind and body is not to mourn for the past, worry about the future, or anticipate troubles, but to live in the present moment wisely and earnestly.
Buddha

HEALTH

The secret to practicing being in the Presence is to be right where you are and fully experience the present moment. You cannot practice it by dwelling in the past or reaching for the future. Simply being in the Presence is a spiritually satisfying practice that generates all kinds of inward peacefulness. And it has a beneficial influence on our health.

It is widely accepted that meditation has beneficial biological effects on the body, from reducing stress to coping with pain. Take some time today to do a survey of your entire body. Lie down comfortably at a time when you are not tired. Let your mind start at your toes and move slowly up the feet, pausing to mentally name as many parts of the body as you can, until you reach the top of your head. Say something affirming about each part of your body. For example, you might say to yourself, "I bless my feet."

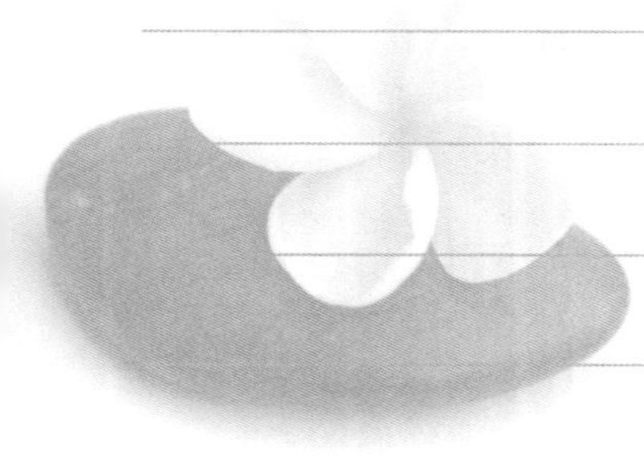

August 16

There is nothing as mysterious
as something clearly seen.
Robert Frost

HYGIENE

Some folks so thoroughly separate spirituality from the rest of their lives that they do not consider health or hygiene to be a part of their spiritual practice. Hygiene, as a spiritual practice that leads to good health and cleanliness, may be incorporated into your devotional practices.

Imagine that taking care of your body is equivalent to taking care of a most sacred temple, and that everything you do to contribute to its well-being is a holy task. What would change in your morning routine if you were to consider caring for your body in this way?

August 17

To the dull mind, nature is leaden. To the illumined mind, the whole world burns and sparkles with light.
Ralph Waldo Emerson

BEING IN NATURE

My grandmother taught me many things. Toward the end of her life, she became less mobile and, because of her arthritis, could not go outside much. When I would come into the house, she would ask me what I had seen while outside. Over time, I realized that I wasn't going to get away with the standard "not much" or "nothing" or "same old, same old." She wanted to know details, from the leaves on the tree to the chewing gum on the sidewalk.

This came in handy when I started visiting nature in my practice of the Presence. Trained by my grandmother, I now see the natural world as a symphony of colors and secrets that can entertain me for hours. Not only that, but I come out refreshed and alive. There is no better tonic for that which ails us than being in nature.

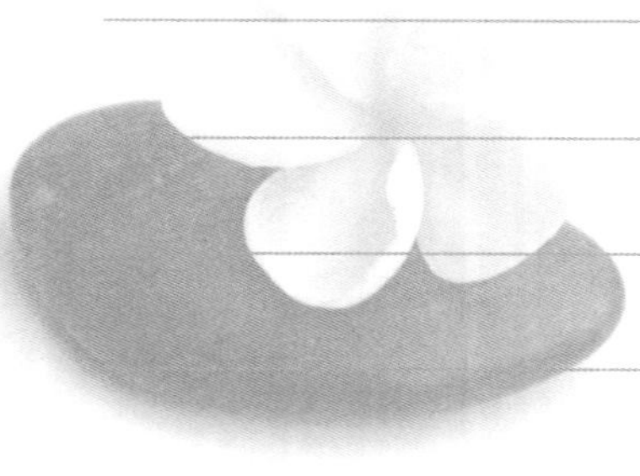

August 18

Adopt the pace of nature;
her secret is patience.
Ralph Waldo Emerson

LIVING

When the pace of life becomes too hectic, I visit a local redwood grove. A simple walk through the solid, majestic trunks slows down my mind. I have only to stand peacefully and look at one tree for a few moments before I notice something inside me adjusting itself to a different pace of life.

Some people experience a similar adjustment at the ocean or by going to the movies. There is no right way or wrong way; but there is a way tailored to your specific needs by which you can adjust the inner pace of living to something more reasonable than that which our speedy society seems to favor.

August 19

It is human nature to think wisely and act foolishly.
Anatole France

MEANING

Sometimes we act foolishly in life because of the significance we have attached to situations, people, and events. When we believe our thoughts without questioning them, we might easily create foolish situations. For example, think of a phone call that a friend didn't return, or the look on the face of a person in the car the next lane over on the freeway. These are instances in which it would be quite easy to add meaning that is not accurate.

Can you find an example in your life where you have given meaning to a situation without having verified if the meaning is correct?

August 20

Outside noisy, inside empty.
Chinese Proverbs

BEING OUTSIDE

Being outside is a stimulating way to practice peacefulness. Whether in a busy city or a quiet neighborhood, when we are outside, we have the opportunity to notice that our inner world is not determined by our outer location or events.

A meditation teacher once responded to my complaint about the traffic noise and its ability to distract me from my meditation by advising me to practice my meditation on a busy downtown street. She asked why I was giving my precious attention to the noise when something so beautiful was waiting inside.

August 21

Declare today "sacred time"—off-limits to everyone, unless invited by you. Take care of your personal wants and needs. Say no, graciously but firmly, to others' demands.
Oprah Winfrey

RECREATION

I have a friend who goes to a large mall when she wants recreation. She doesn't shop; she walks, observes, listens, and does whatever presents itself to her in the moment. She finds freedom in the anonymity of being in large crowds. I have another friend who can only experience recreation in nature, preferably in the sun.

It is a wonderful and healthful practice to take time to be completely self-centered, not in a mean-spirited or socially destructive way, but in a way that lets you focus specifically on your own re-creation. By practicing self-centered re-creation, you can put all distractions and responsibilities on hold, knowing that you can pick up where you left off afterwards.

If possible, get away from your regular surroundings today, with no agenda or goal in mind. What is your way of re-creating yourself, and when was the last time you did it?

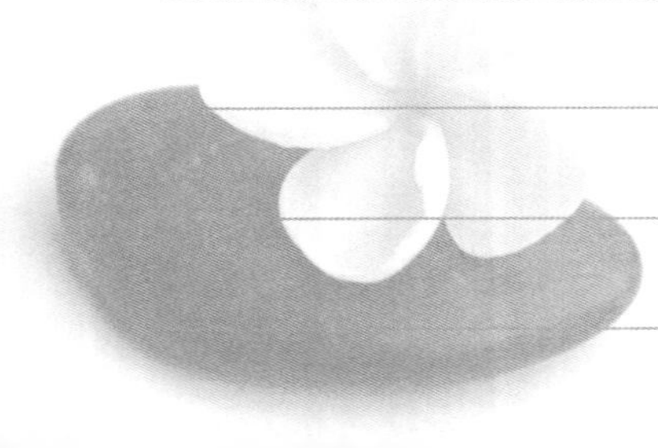

August 22

A good retreat is better
than a bad stand.
Irish Saying

RETREAT

Adult life is chaotic; it's full of activity. Much is asked of us in modern culture. We are supposed to be good at multitasking, juggling the responsibilities of work, family, and social life. Keeping pace with all of this activity in a sane manner requires a peaceful core. Without a place of serenity, you can quickly stress out.

You can't keep going at full speed. You will hit the wall. If you keep pushing ahead without a break, some circumstance will occur in your life to slow you down. Usually when this happens, it is not positive. That is why taking time for retreat is so important. Withdrawing from your activities and responsibilities, even just for an hour or two, will soothe your soul and add buoyancy to your spirit.

Take some time away from your everyday responsibilities and retreat.

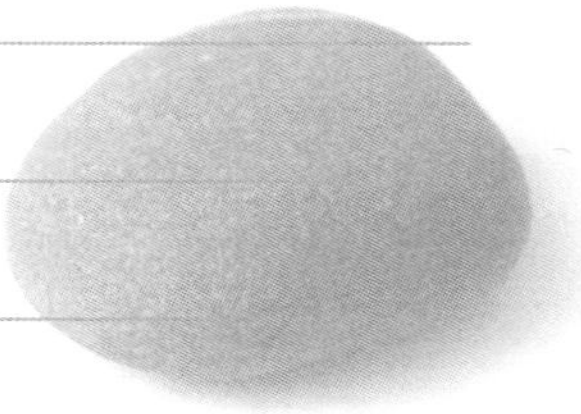

August 23

Serenity is not freedom from the storm,
but peace amid the storm.
Unknown

SERENITY

Do you remain calm when others are rattled? Are you the stable one when everyone around you begins to panic? If so, you have a serene nature. You are the person others seek when they are in trouble. You are their touchstone.

To maintain your peaceful nature, you must attend to your spiritual needs daily. It is imperative that you remain close to your source—God. Without an intimate connection to your Creator, you will not be able to weather the storms of life. You will be tossed around, as others are.

Practice serenity. Go within. Find your center of peace.

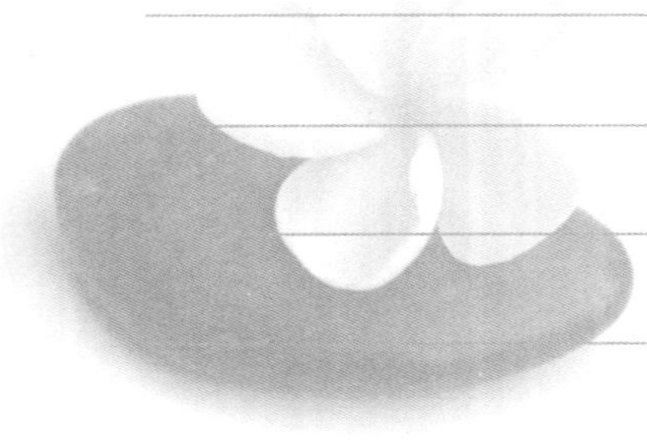

August 24

He is his own best friend, and takes delight in privacy; whereas the man of no virtue or ability is his own worst enemy and is afraid of solitude.
Aristotle

SOLITUDE

Some people don't enjoy solitude. They can't stand the pressure of being faced with their own thoughts. They busy themselves with social activities to avoid feeling lonely. They will do anything to avoid being alone, even if it means spending time with people they don't particularly like.

It is possible to be alone and happy. It is possible to be alone and not lonely. The truth is: You are never alone. Spirit is with you all of the time. You will never be abandoned by God. When your heart knows the Presence, you will never feel loneliness again.

Step away from the crowd for a few minutes today. Go somewhere by yourself and sit quietly. Practice feeling the Presence of God with you.

August 25

Spontaneity is the quality of being able to do something just because you feel like it at the moment, of trusting your instincts, of taking yourself by surprise and snatching from the clutches of your well-organized routine, a bit of unscheduled pleasure.

Unknown

SPONTANEITY

We all have our routines. We are creatures of habit. We like eating the same foods, going to the same restaurants, driving the same route to work each day. Routine brings a certain comfort and stability to our lives. However, the routine can easily become mundane. It can confine you to rigidity and get you stuck in a rut.

Spontaneity is the "free spirit" part of our nature. It is the childlike quality within us, the part that wants to play all of the time. Balance is the key to healthy living. Routines are important because they keep us on track. But sometimes we need to get off the track and explore. Today is the day for spontaneity. Go somewhere new. Do something you wouldn't ordinarily do. Practice being a free spirit.

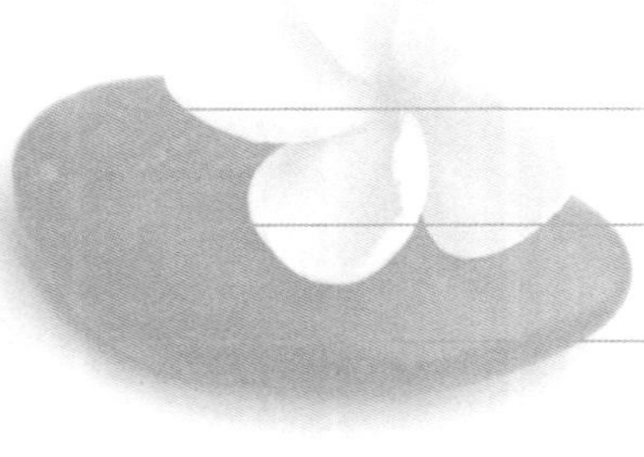

August 26

All these [seekers] are indeed noble, but I regard the wise as My very Self, because the one who is steadfast becomes one with the Supreme Being.
Bhagavad Gita

STEADFASTNESS

If you want to be close to God, you must remain steadfast in your pursuit. It is easy to get lost in the negativity of this world and forget the truth. The news reports only the most extreme circumstances and violent crimes. Without a spiritual screen to interpret the news, you will succumb to fear.

Stay on course toward your goal of unity with Spirit. Remain steadfast in your studies. Insist on the spiritual truths you know are universal and immutable. Remind yourself daily that God is in charge and all is well.

August 27

I have a real problem with stillness,
with just stopping and being quiet.
Gillian Anderson

STOPPING

God's universe has a rhythm. The Energy of life pulsates in nature and through your body. You are alive because God lives in you. Sometimes, this Divine rhythm moves quickly; sometimes, it moves slowly. Sometimes, it stops and then starts again.

The key is to follow the rhythm—to know when to move quickly, when to slow down, and when to stop. If you listen closely, the rhythm will guide you. If it says stop, you must stop. If you don't, it will find some way to stop you. It is best if you make that choice yourself.

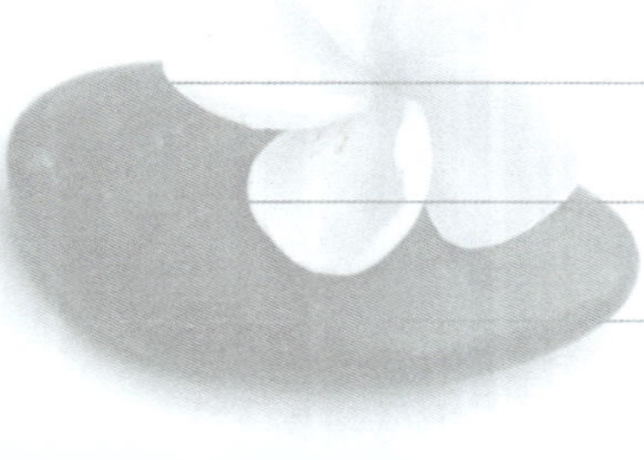

AUGUST 28

...by stretching yourself beyond your perceived level of confidence you accelerate your development of competence.
Michael J. Gelb

STRETCHING

Stretch your faith today. Ask for something you wouldn't ordinarily have the courage to ask for. Stretch beyond your comfort zone and go somewhere different. Talk to someone you don't usually speak to. Try something new to eat. Wear your hair differently or combine your clothing in a new way.

Stretch your body as soon as you wake up, and periodically throughout the day. Stretch your mind by entertaining new ideas. Practice stretching.

August 29

In nature we never see anything isolated, but everything in connection with something else which is before it, beside it, under it, and over it.
Johann Wolfgang von Goethe

SYNERGY

I grew up with a superstitious grandfather. To him, the world was filled with signs and omens. He taught me to watch for repetitive patterns. For example, if someone dropped something, he would carefully wait for the next time somebody dropped something. That would be a sign to him that a third similar event was about to happen. To me it was nothing more than a silly game. However, over time, I've noticed myself watching for repetitive events happening in close sequence. I don't think of it so much as superstition, yet I continue to be fascinated by the connections between people, events, and ideas.

Synergy is the interaction between two or more agents, with the combined effect being greater than the sum of the individual actions. What connections can you notice today?

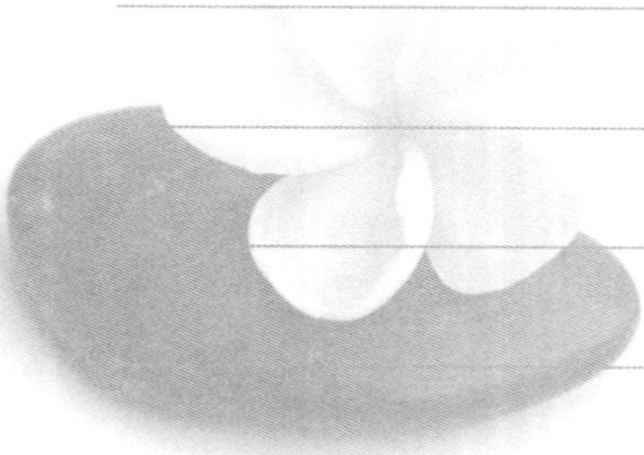

August 30

The vitality of thought is in adventure. Ideas won't keep.
Something must be done about them.
Alfred North Whitehead

VITALITY

The joy of practicing "being" comes through experiencing the Presence and becoming aware that the vitality of our thoughts lies in the endless supply of them. When a particularly interesting thought passes through your mind, notice it, follow it, and do something about it. Be cautious, though, of the thought that scares you into thinking that an idea and opportunity can be lost.

For today, practice noticing what thoughts pass through your mind. Notice which feel compelling, and see if you can let each one go as easily as it came. In this way, you may open up the door for even more thoughts to pass through. Practicing this results in a sense of calm that comes from the trust in the endless supply of ideas that are available to everyone.

August 31

All truly great thoughts are conceived while walking.
Friedrich Nietzsche

WALKING

I'm seldom conscious of walking. I frequently take for granted the fact that I know how to walk. I am here, and then I'm there. However, when I enjoy the act of walking, that awareness opens up a whole world of experience. So now, in addition to walking to move myself around, I also walk just to walk. This kind of walking is typically slower because there is nowhere to go. In this slower pace, I discover more of the world around me and notice a rich flow of creative thinking.

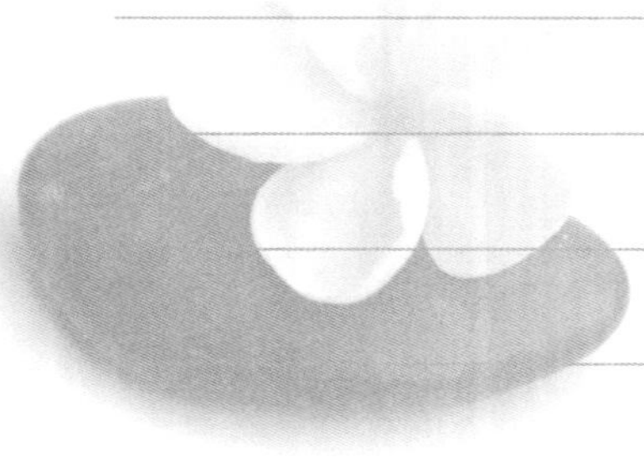

SEPTEMBER

Practice *the* Presence *through* Inner Peace

September 1

I walk slowly, but I never walk backward.
Abraham Lincoln

ACCEPTING

Acceptance is a powerful spiritual practice. It is not the same as acquiescence, nor is it the same as resignation. Acceptance is a powerful forward motion based on the deep realization that everything is in its right place, and that arguing with Reality is pointless and painful and has the effect of bringing progress to a standstill.

Inner tranquility is not achieved; it is realized. In other words, practice doesn't create inner peace as much as it brings into our consciousness the awareness that it is always present within us, like an old friend.

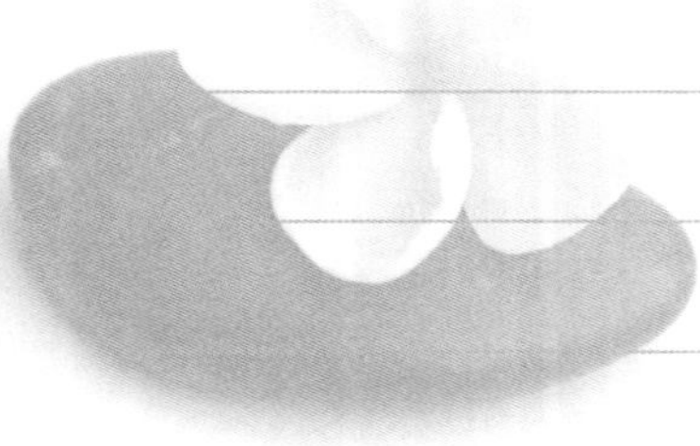

September 2

Walking with a friend in the dark is better than walking alone in the light.
Helen Keller

ASSURANCE

American philosopher Ernest Holmes describes the Presence you are practicing in this journal as an Inner Friend—a Presence of great peace and tranquility. He writes: "You have a Friend within you who is closer than your shadow. This Friend anticipates your every desire, knows your every need, and governs your every act. This Friend is the God within your own soul, the animating Presence. This Friend within you is Infinite, and since it is Infinite, it is not limited by previous experiences which you may have had, by present conditions nor passing situations."

How do you describe the Presence?

September 3

This moment contains all moments.
C.S. Lewis

CONTAINMENT

To contain something means to hold it within a specific space, like a box or room, thereby preventing it from spreading or expanding. In practicing inner peace, the ability to contain your awareness without struggle or aggression becomes a valuable skill.

Think of your mind as a glass and your awareness as the water in the glass. Eventually, the water will be poured out of the glass in some fashion; but for a short while, it is restricted to a specific space. When you practice gently bringing your awareness back to a single point, you are practicing containment. The skill is to do so without violence or disappointment when you notice your awareness spilling out and expanding to other things.

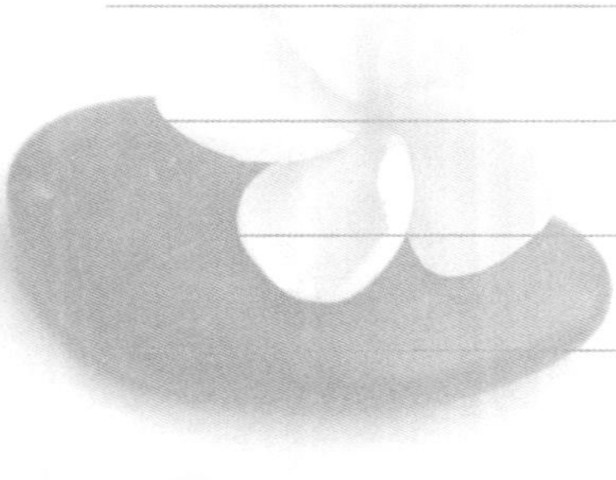

September 4

O Holy Spirit, descend plentifully into my heart.
Saint Augustine

DESCENDING

When practicing the art of gently bringing your awareness to a single point during meditation, you will begin to notice a sensation similar to the feeling of descending and coming to rest. It is as if your awareness is retiring from the generalities of the ordinary awakened state to something specific—an inner peace. Accompanying this is a feeling that defies description, yet is akin to slowing down without loss of vitality or focus.

September 5

He who would be serene and pure needs but one thing, detachment.
Meister Eckhart

DETACHMENT

Don't take things so personally. Much of what happens in life is not to be taken personally. The weather is neither good nor bad. It's just weather. The economic condition of the country is not your fault. It has always fluctuated. The shape and look of your body will change as it ages. It happens to everyone. You can't control someone's opinion of you. Some people will like you and others will not.

Practice detaching yourself from unimportant issues and concentrate on the only thing you really can control—your own thought.

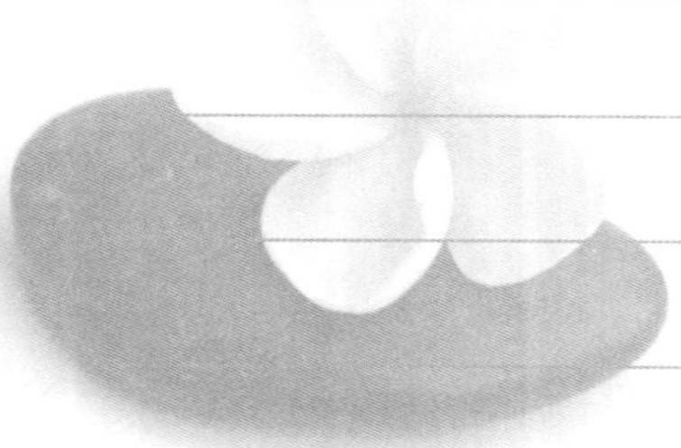

SEPTEMBER 6

There is no shame in not knowing; the shame is in not finding out.
Russian Proverb

FINDING

What do you wonder about? Do you want to know how many stars are in the galaxy? Do you want to know more about historical events? What special interests do you have?

Keep learning. Look for new things to know. Research your best ideas. Rekindle your sense of awe and wonder for life. It will keep you young, refreshed, and relevant.

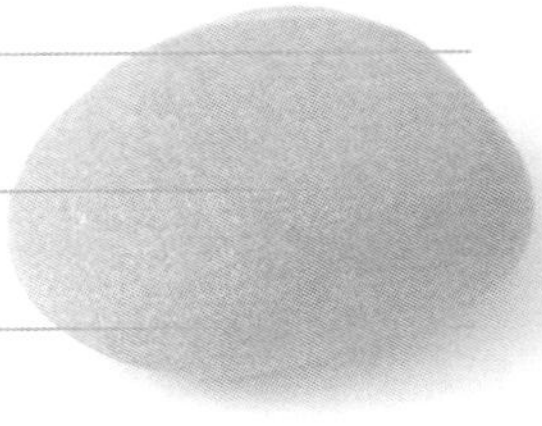

September 7

Focus on where you want to go, not on what you fear.
Anthony Robbins

FOCUS

That on which you focus your attention will be created in your life. Like a magnifying glass on a sunny day, your focus will heat up whatever it is you are looking at. That's why it is so important to notice, speak, and think only about that which you wish to see more of in your life.

If you want more love in your life, focus on what you love today. If you want greater prosperity, focus on what you have, not what you lack. If your desire is for higher self-esteem, focus on the things you like about yourself, not the things you disapprove of.

Keep focusing on what you want, and it will show up in your life.

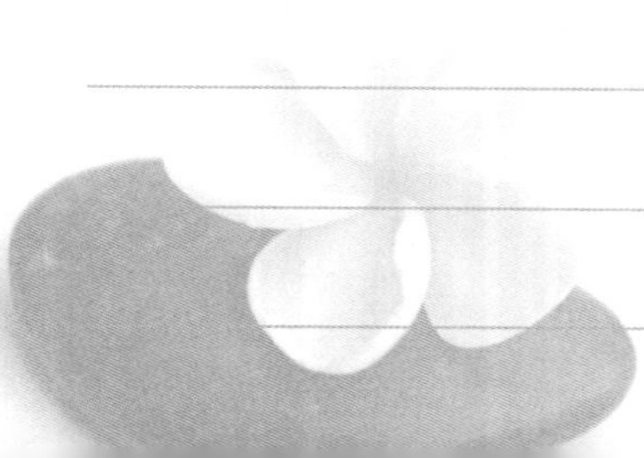

September 8

The end of life is to be like God, and the soul following God will be like Him.
Socrates

FOLLOWING

Take a day off from leading. Just follow. If you drive, don't rush to get in front of the cars ahead of you; just follow them. Feel what it's like to follow. Allow yourself the luxury of not having to know all of the answers or set the course of action.

Follow Spirit. Trust that It will guide you. Follow wherever love takes you. It is always in the right direction. Follow your best ideas; they will lead to riches. Follow joy; it will take you to a happy experience. Follow the people you most admire and respect. They will lead you to an authentic life.

September 9

Think of giving not as a duty,
but as a privilege.
John D. Rockefeller, Jr.

GIVING

You have much to give. There is no limit to the love you hold inside. Within your heart is an infinite well of joy. Passing through your mind is an endless flow of new ideas. Your spirit is boundless.

Giving to others that which you have been given by your Creator is a privilege, not an obligation. Giving your love to another isn't a duty; it's an honor. Sharing laughter and joy with others isn't a burden; it benefits your spirit as well as theirs.

That which you give is returned to you. What you send out, comes back.

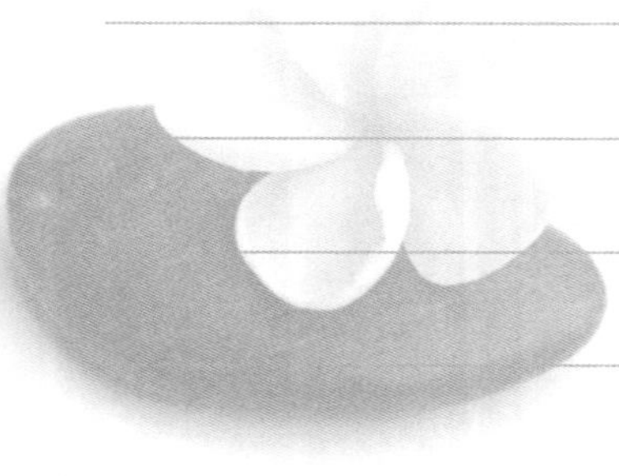

September 10

If you are still talking about what you did yesterday, you haven't done much today.
Unknown

BEING IN THE MOMENT

Be where your body is right now. Stay in the present moment. Focus on what is going on around you in this instant. Resist the temptation to relive yesterday's experience. Let go of past regrets. There is no opportunity to redo what has already been done. You can only do things differently now, in the present moment.

Seize today's opportunities. Give love to the people around you now. Grasp every opportunity for joy that presents itself. Practice being in the moment; this is where your power is; this is where God is.

SEPTEMBER 11

A babe in the house is a well-spring of pleasure, a messenger of peace and love, a resting place for innocence on earth, a link between angels and men.

Martin Fraguhar Tupper

INNOCENCE

You entered life completely pure and innocent. You did not know about prejudice. You had not yet seen hatred, cruelty, or injustice. You were unaware of any limitations. You fully expected to be loved and treated well. You had no judgment of yourself or others. You were comfortable in your body.

The challenge is to retain as much as possible of this childlike innocence as you grow older. Many people fail in this attempt and become negative and jaded. Don't be one of them.

No matter what the news reports, there is always more good in people than bad. Keep your faith in the good and you will retain your innocence.

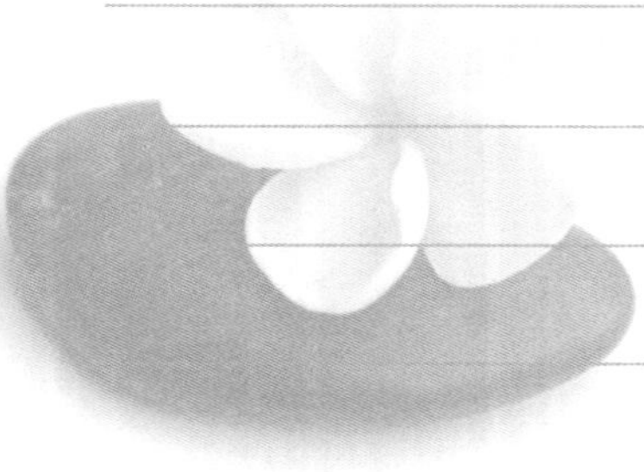

September 12

Peace comes from within.
Do not seek it without.
Buddha

ISOLATION

There is tremendous benefit to be derived from spending time alone, especially if your schedule constantly places you among people. If possible, try to arrange time today to be completely by yourself. If you are able, turn off your cell phone and stay away from your email. If you can manage this only for an hour, you will be giving yourself a tremendous gift. Later, try to arrange for a longer period of time.

It is even possible to practice isolation in the midst of people, by going somewhere unfamiliar where no one knows you. Even in a crowd, you can experience the feeling of being beautifully alone for awhile.

September 13

Peace is not something you wish for; it's something you make, something you do, something you are, and something you give away.
Robert Fulghum

JOURNALING

As you write your thoughts in this journal, take some time to occasionally review the previous entries you have made. Notice themes or recurring ideas that suggest action to which you can commit. Sometimes, we know exactly what to do to increase our sense of inner peace, yet we forget to do the obvious thing: take our own advice and do what will nurture that peace.

If you have not kept up with your journal entries as much as you would have liked to, you can still accomplish the same goal by simply asking yourself what one thing you can do today that will support a greater awareness of inner peace.

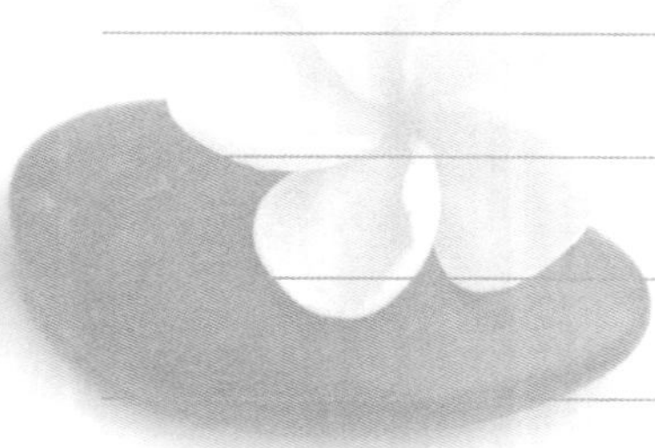

September 14

Peace begins with a smile.
Mother Teresa

OPENNESS

Practicing inner peace is something you can do wherever you are. You do not have to retire from your life or sit in a meditative state. You can nurture peace by practicing being an observer of life as it happens around you.

Adopt a friendly attitude toward life, as if you are entertaining a happy secret, and move through your day with a subtle smile. Try to be an observer as much as possible today, and notice how much peacefulness is available everywhere.

September 15

One cannot reflect in streaming water. Only those who know internal peace can give it to others.
Lao Tzu

POISE

As you become more adept at observing life while it happens around you, you also become more skilled at "going with the flow" and causing fewer unnecessary disruptions. With this new awareness of inward calmness, you become an influence for peace on those around you without ever having to preach at them or teach them a lesson. Your life becomes your message.

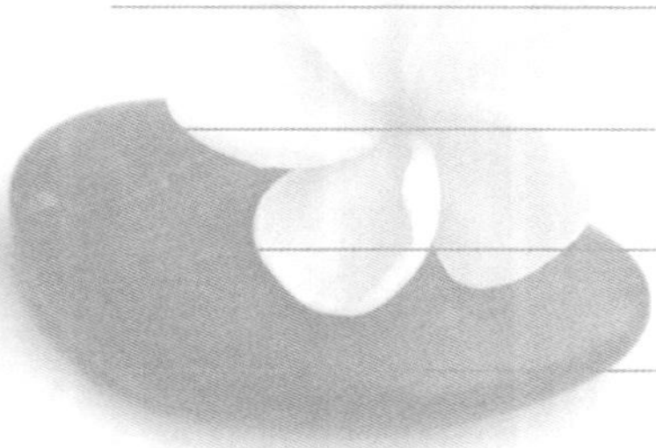

SEPTEMBER 16

He that would live in peace and at ease, must
not speak all he knows, nor judge all he sees.
Benjamin Franklin

PRIVACY

I have been learning about what cats need to be healthy and well-adjusted. It seems that cats are very complex, and so are their health requirements. Not only do they need good nutrition, exercise, and rest, they also require privacy, stimulation, and hunting time. When my cat is on his favorite cushion, I know it is time to leave him alone. When my cat is in his "private" mode, the most healthful thing I can do is pretend I don't see him and refrain from even petting him.

I've been thinking about the value of privacy in my life. I find there are several benefits of practicing privacy. I understand how a gentle step back and out of social interaction from time to time creates a sense of relief and peace. I see, also, how tempering my speech helps me feel present to others and is a form of practicing privacy.

September 17

Those who are free of resentful thoughts surely find peace.
Buddha

RELEASING

Though practicing inner peace is a wonderful idea, I notice that life doesn't always agree with my wonderful ideas. I might decide one moment to be peaceful and calm, and then I will receive an urgent or frantic phone call. Or I might be choosing joy when I suddenly stub my toe on a piece of furniture.

My recovery time is getting better than it used to be. I have learned to release moments of disappointment and distraction with more ease than I did before I started practicing. I have also learned to release personal disappointment when I don't measure up to my preconceived idea of what it means to live a spiritual life. I release the idea that a spiritual life looks any different from the one I am living now.

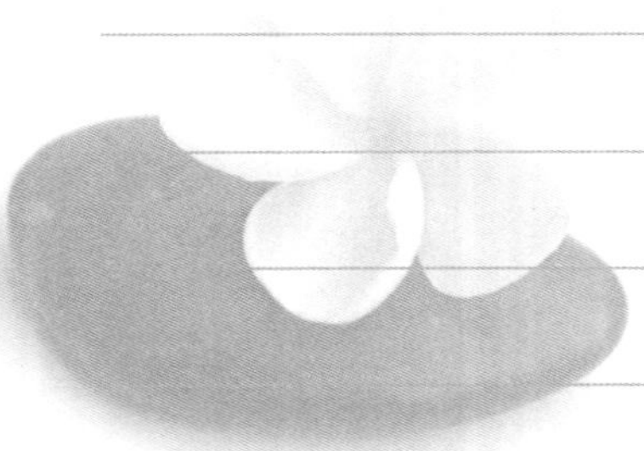

SEPTEMBER 18

When the power of love overcomes the love of power, the world will know peace.
Jimi Hendrix

RELINQUISHING

I once read a version of Buddha's "Four Noble Truths" that went something like this: Suffering exists; clinging causes suffering; clinging can cease; there is a way. I like this because it reminds me that clinging, even to something like inner peace, can result in personal distress, and that the practice of inner peace is not a war to be waged or a prize to be pursued. Rather, it is something that can be surrendered to.

From time to time, I pause to take inventory of where clinging is present in my mind. When I find it, I move to the place where I can surrender a little more.

SEPTEMBER 19

Perhaps love is like a resting place, a shelter from the storm. It exists to give you comfort. It is there to keep you warm. And in those times of trouble, when you are most alone, the memory of love will bring you home.
John Denver

RESTING

Listen to your body. When you are tired, take a few minutes to rest. If you like to take naps, make them part of your daily routine. Stop making excuses for not taking care of yourself. You can find the time to rest if you really want to.

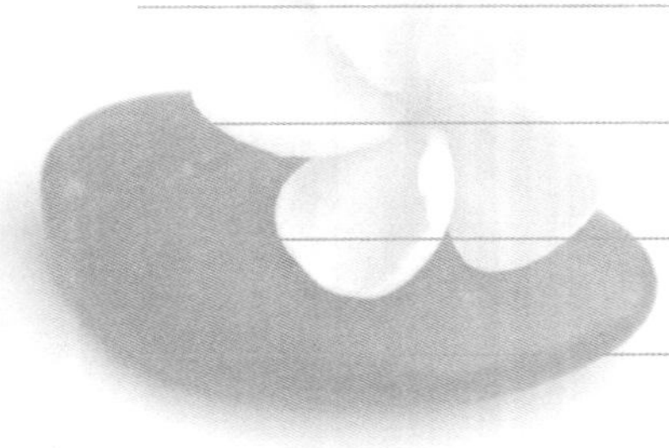

September 20

You have to leave the city of your comfort and go into the wilderness of your intuition. What you'll discover will be wonderful. What you'll discover is yourself.
Alan Alda

SENSING

As a physical being, you only have five senses: touch, taste, hearing, smell, and sight. But as a spiritual being, you have many more. Just below the surface of your conscious awareness is an infinite well of wisdom. Living inside of you is the Intelligence that creates universes. Learn to tap into that wisdom. It communicates itself through hunches, intuition, and spontaneous actions.

You are not the limited person you perceive yourself to be. You are an unlimited, spiritual being with access to everything you need to know. There is more going on around you than can be sensed with just your five human senses. Wake up!

September 21

We need to find God, and He cannot be found in noise and restlessness. God is the friend of silence. See how nature—trees, flowers, grass—grows in silence; see the stars, the moon and the sun, how they move in silence. We need silence to be able to touch souls.

Mother Teresa

SILENCE

Do you need to always have the television on at home to provide background noise? Do you turn the radio on every time you get in the car? When there is a pause in conversation, do you feel you need to say something to break the silence?

The language of God is silence. Its Presence arrives in peace and tranquility, without the harshness of abrupt noise. Join Spirit in the silence so that your soul might be touched, so that you may truly know God.

When is the last time you sat in complete silence? How long were you able to be completely still?

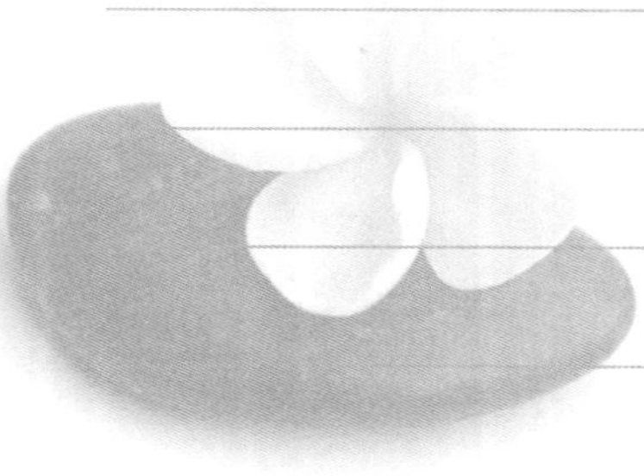

September 22

He who is most slow in making a promise
is the most faithful in performance of it.
Jean-Jacques Rousseau

SLOWING DOWN

What would happen if you just slowed down a bit? Do you think you might see things you've never seen before, or become aware of opportunities you once missed?

There is a time to move fast, but there is also a time to slow down. Practice slowing down today. You might like the new pace.

September 23

It is important from time to time to slow down,
to go away by yourself, and simply be.
Eileen Caddy

SLOWING WAY DOWN

Practice eating slowly today. You may find that you eat less and enjoy your food more. Practice talking slowly today. You may find that your thoughts move more easily and people understand you better. Practice walking slowly today. You may find that your body has its own pace and unique way of expressing itself.

Slow everything down a bit and enjoy life.

September 24

Vacations used to be considered a luxury. However, in today's fast-paced, multi-tasking world, they are now a necessity.
Chris Michaels

TAKE A BREAK

In this frantic world we live in, it is necessary to take frequent breaks in order to maintain our sanity. Take a break today and do something fun. When you return to your normal schedule, you'll find yourself more productive and in a better mood.

Schedule your next vacation. Check the flights. Book the hotel. It's time to take better care of yourself. You deserve to be treated well, but it has to start with you.

September 25

You owe it to everyone you love (including yourself)
to find pockets of tranquility in your busy world.
Unknown

TRANQUILITY

Few things are worth fighting for. Most arguments take place because of a miscommunication of intentions. Resolution will come when you back away from your position and seek to see the other person's point as clearly as you see your own.

Be careful when choosing your battles. Try not to upset the natural tranquility of the day. Let peace and serenity fill your thoughts and they will overflow into your experience.

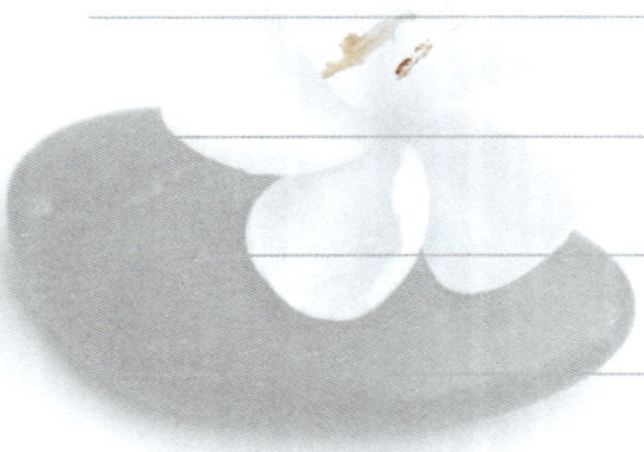

September 26

Eternal peace lasts only
until the next war.
Russian Proverb

UNDOING

I see a pattern in my life that reveals my tendency to deny the same characteristic in me that I criticize in others. Because of my spiritual practice of the Presence, though, I can also see how I don't have to do anything more than notice the tendency in me to begin the journey back to peace.

Who are the people who undo your inner peace? What is it about these people that frustrates you? Can you find examples in your behavior where you are similar to or exactly the same as they are?

September 27

Writing, to me, is simply thinking through my fingers.
Isaac Asimov

WRITING

The most valuable gift of writing is that it is slow. It takes time. It is not as fast as typing or dreaming or speaking. It is slow. My mind, though, is fast. At least, it thinks it is. Yet when I sit down to write, either a letter to a friend or in my journal, I discover that I am wrong; my mind is not fast. It is slow. It does better with slower activities.

I practice the Presence by writing words, such as *God, Spirit,* or *Kindness*, and giving myself the time to do nothing else. Then, I choose one of the words and write down every thought that passes through my mind about it. Afterwards, whether the writing made sense or not, I experience a peacefulness that is powerful.

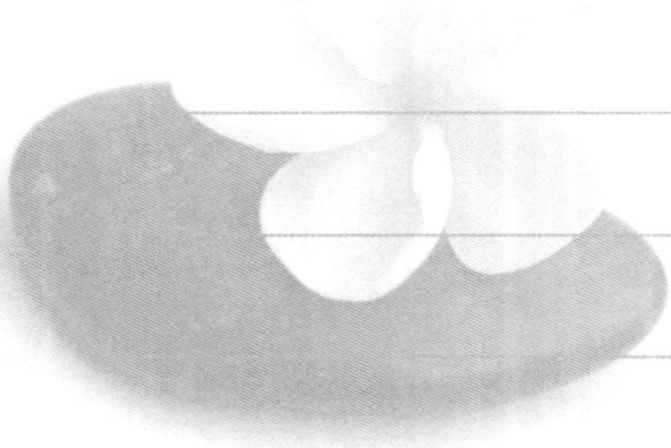

SEPTEMBER 28

Nothing can bring you peace but yourself.
Ralph Waldo Emerson

YOU

It is powerful to realize that peace is available all the time. It is not available, though, because of another person, a goal achieved, or anything like that, but because it is the natural state of your being. It is a memorable event when we successfully refrain from following a stressful line of thinking and return back to the natural state of peace within. In moments like that, it feels like being born again into a world of awe and wonder.

September 29

Each one has to find his peace from within. And peace to be real must be unaffected by outside circumstances.

Mahatma Gandhi

QUIET

The idea that "peace begins with me" is not new. The idea that peace is something initiated inside of me is not new. The idea that the quiet Presence of peace and power lives in the quiet center of my mind is not new, either. Yet each of these ideas was new to me at one time. Even though I know them now, I find that I sometimes still have to sit quietly and think about them, remember them, and relive the moments when I first discovered them, so as not to fall prey to the kind of thinking I lived in before.

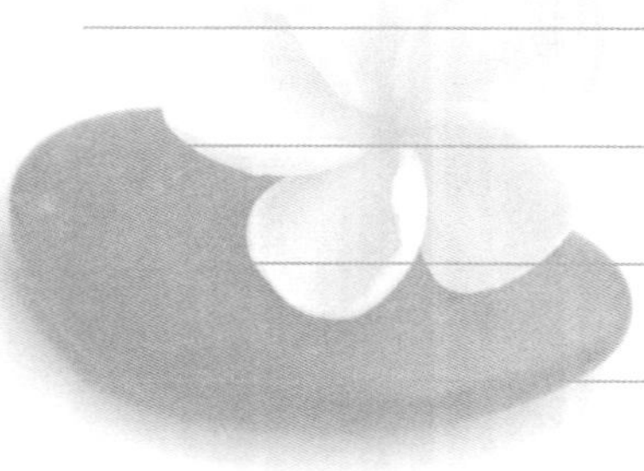

September 30

If you wish to experience peace,
provide peace for another.
Tenzin Gyatso, the fourteenth Dalai Lama

HARMONY

When I live my life in harmony with the natural peace inside of me, I become aware that this harmony influences my choices and activities. When I forget that there is a quiet Presence inside me, I begin to look to the world for my direction. Keeping my outer world in harmony with my inner world is a practice that depends on frequently revisiting this awareness of the Presence within.

OCTOBER

Practice *the* Presence *through* Generosity of Spirit

October 1

The things that will destroy America are prosperity at any price, peace at any price, safety first instead of duty first and love of soft living and the get-rich-quick theory of life.

Theodore Roosevelt

ABUNDANCE

Prosperity teachings must be balanced with emotional and spiritual maturity in order to make sense. Otherwise, ideas of prosperity or abundance result in the thinking that there is a Universal Vending Machine that doles out anything we want, no coins required. This is not how the world works.

Prosperity comes from a deep appreciation of the Presence and how it works in your life. An awareness of the Presence leads to service, love, and contribution. By implementing these practices, you will begin to notice the flow of love and every good thing in life.

Abundant living has more to do with awareness of the fullness of life as it is, rather than with amassing huge sums of money or avoiding the responsibility to contribute. As you practice charity, meditation, and sacredness, you pay the required price of knowing your true abundant self better. It is part of the natural order of things to realize that you live, move, and have your being in a Universe that works for you.

OCTOBER 2

My word is one of affirmation, rising from the knowledge that the Good, the Enduring, and the True are Eternalities in my experience.
Ernest Holmes

AFFIRMING

American philosopher Ernest Holmes's simple approach to spirituality instructs us to "Close your eyes and then very quietly, very slowly, with ample time for a deep realization of every word, say to yourself: There is One Life, that Life is God, that Life is perfect, that Life is my life now. My body is a manifestation of the living Spirit. It is created and sustained by the One Presence and the One Power. That Power is flowing in and through me now, animating every organ, every action, and every function of my physical being. There is perfect circulation, perfect assimilation, and perfect elimination. There is no congestion, no confusion, and no inaction. I am one with the infinite rhythm of Life which flows through me in love, in harmony, and in peace. There is no fear, no doubt, and no uncertainty in my mind. I am letting that life which is perfect flow through me. It is my life now. There is One Life, that Life is perfect, that Life is my life now."

Affirm this today.

October 3

Appreciation is a wonderful thing: It makes what is excellent in others belong to us as well.
Voltaire

APPRECIATION

It has been said that we only see in others that which we first see in ourselves. If we have an appreciation for our own good qualities, then we will have that appreciation for others. If we enjoy the uniqueness of our own personalities, we will find that same enjoyment in our friends and family.

Use the space provided on today's journal page to make a list of the top five things you value most about your character or personality. Now, make another list of the top five people you appreciate the most. Do the people you listed have the qualities you admire most in yourself?

October 4

Care about people's approval
and you will be their prisoner.
Lao Tzu

APPROVAL

Ironically, when you need other people's approval, you can't get it. But when you don't care about other people's approval, you will always get it.

As long as you rely on other people for acceptance and approval, you are their prisoner. They control your self-esteem because you have given your power over to them. But you have the key to the prison door and can free yourself whenever you are ready.

Begin the process of self-approval today. Bring to mind some quality about yourself that you admire and respect. Meditate on this quality until it expands in your awareness. In time, your self-esteem will rise and you will gain your own approval.

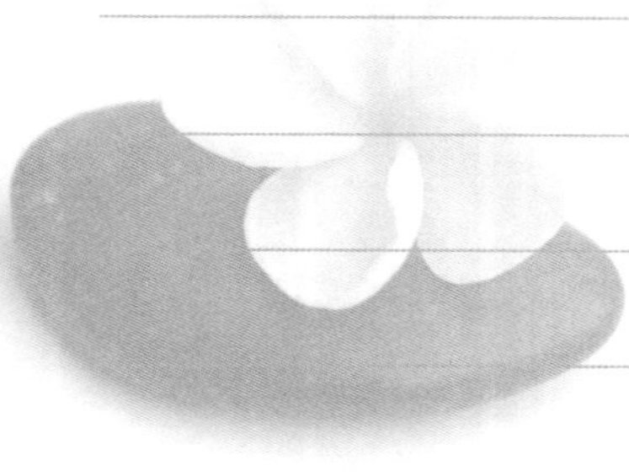

October 5

Commitment unlocks the doors of imagination, allows vision, and gives us the right stuff to turn our dreams into reality.
James Womack

COMMITMENT

It is not luck that turns our dreams into reality; nor is an abundant and happy life reserved only for a few fortunate people. It is the birthright of all who fully commit to their dreams with diligence and tenacity.

Anyone can dream, but the people who make their dreams come true are the ones who understand the power of commitment. These people never look back. They do not have a "Plan B." They have high expectations and always attract the resources to fulfill them.

To what are you fully committed?

October 6

Insist on yourself, never imitate.
Ralph Waldo Emerson

CONFIDENCE

Self-confidence comes from self-knowingness. Until you know who you really are, you won't understand your worth. Your value comes from the Presence you hold inside. Spirit lives in, as, and through you. Its beautiful Presence has been individualized as you. You are the life of God entering the world as a unique person.

Be confident in yourself. Know that God has made only one of you. Like a painting by a master artist, your value is immeasurable. Your unique character is unparalleled and cannot be imitated by others. Be yourself, and stand proud of what God made you to be.

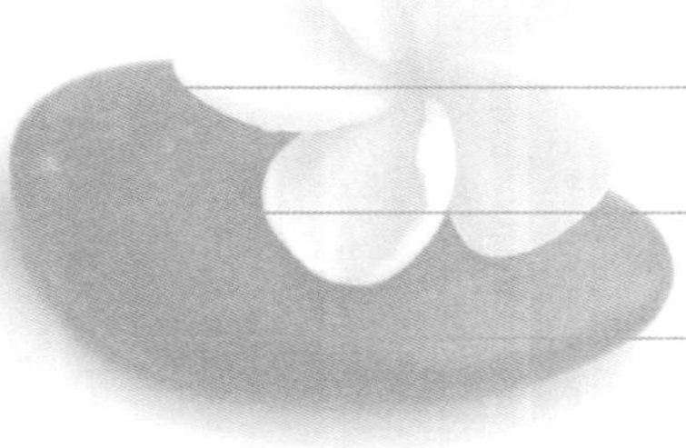

OCTOBER 7

For everything that lives is holy, life delights in life.
William Blake

DELIGHT

The universe and everything in it exists for the sheer delight of our Creator. God takes pleasure in Its own Self-expression. It rejoices in the manifestation of Its creation.

Every autumn, as the leaves begin to change colors, it's as if nature shouts at us from every viewpoint, "Look at my beauty! Rejoice with me in the magnificent array of color!"

The ground you walk on is holy. The air you breathe is Divine. The blood that flows through your body is the Presence of God's life in you. Take delight in being in God's Presence today.

October 8

No matter how qualified or deserving we are, we will never reach a better life until we can imagine it for ourselves and allow ourselves to have it.
Richard Bach

DESERVING

The Bible says, "It is the Father's pleasure to give." Spirit takes delight in giving all It has to you. It is a joy for God to share Its abundance. God's love is a gift freely given, without attachments or conditions. There is no need to earn it. You don't have to do anything to prove you are worthy. All you have to do is be willing to receive it.

Do you feel you deserve a joyful, rich life? Do you think you deserve to be loved? If so, why do you feel that you are entitled to such good fortune? Have you done something to earn your inheritance?

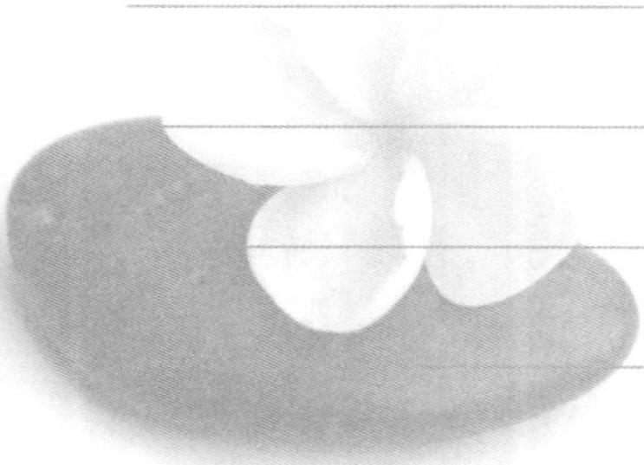

Where there is no extravagance, there is no love,
and where there is no love, there is no understanding.
Oscar Wilde

EXTRAVAGANCE

Love is God's most extravagant gift. It is an elaborate demonstration of the generosity of Spirit. It overflows into our lives from an eternal pool. It is impossible to receive it all. It must be accepted in portions. It arrives without condition. It is given without delay or hesitation.

Practice the extravagant nature of God today by letting yourself be loved. Accept everything good that is offered, and allow yourself to feel the pleasure of God's favor.

October 10

Lose yourself in generous service and every day can be a most unusual day, a triumphant day, an abundantly rewarding day!
William Arthur Ward

FRIENDSHIP

Some of the most valuable things in my life are my friendships. They become increasingly precious to me each time I realize that I neither possess nor own them. They are freely given to me, and all I can do is accept them.

My friendships give me the opportunity to practice generosity and kindness without attachment to how they are received. They repeatedly remind me that, when I begin to manipulate people around me, I become poorer and less connected.

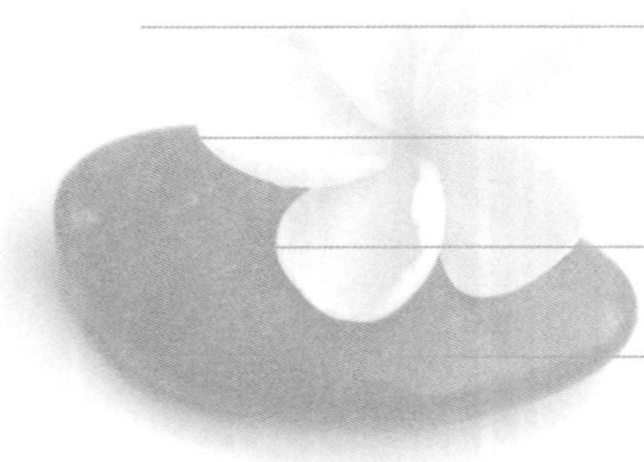

October 11

Good, the more communicated,
more abundant grows.
John Milton

GAIN

Of all the powers bestowed upon human beings, the power of love holds the most opportunity to advance our goals. But using love to achieve gain is not the same as practicing love. When love is not sincere, it ceases to be love and has the opposite effect on growth. Insincere love repels people and experiences; whereas genuine love, in the form of kindness, service, or affection, has the power to increase everything around it.

OCTOBER 12

Inventing is a combination of brains and materials.
The more brains you use, the less material you need.
Charles F. Kettering

INVENTING

Invention is another word for creation. Invention is one of the miraculous powers that comes with being human. Unfortunately, through a process of socialization, adults forget that they are naturally inventive and slowly surrender to the collective idea that some people are more creative than others.

Can you recall a time as a child when you could imagine a solution to anything? Whether your solution was practical or not, you could probably come up with some creative way to play a game, invent a toy, or solve a problem. Today, corporations spend vast amounts of money recreating that free-flowing, playful creativity, because they know people can come up with the most amazing ideas when given the opportunity.

Give yourself the opportunity to invent something today, like a new sandwich or a board game. Don't worry whether it is practical or makes sense. The point today is to let the infinite creativity you were born with have freedom to express itself.

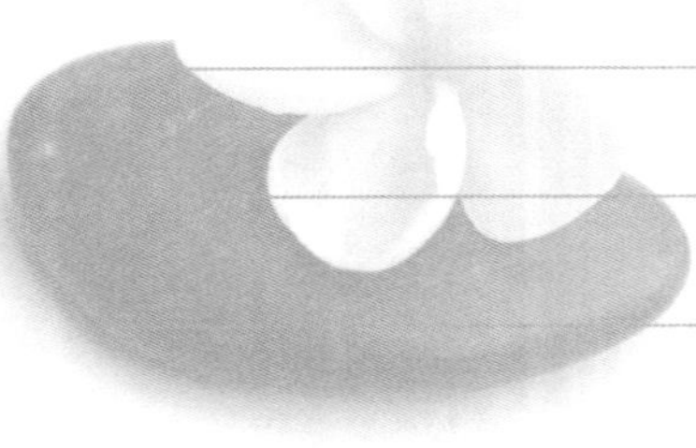

October 13

Goodness is the only
investment that never fails.
Henry David Thoreau

INVESTING

Angie M. Grainger trains people to spend according to their values. Though it may be true that we inherently spend according to our values, what Angie teaches is the difference between "surface values" and "core values." Spending according to surface values delivers the kind of quick fix that we sometimes call "retail therapy"—that which has no enduring value. But spending according to core values is quite different.

Angie writes: "Now imagine for a moment that you could step beyond the short-term and look long-term. If you've clearly identified meaningful future goals that are important to you, it becomes much easier to say 'no' to the short-term desires, for something much more important: core values. Discipline, discernment, patience, wisdom, accomplishment, self-trust, education, reliability, consistency are all stronger core values that give a deeper gratification. There is tremendous satisfaction that comes with overcoming financial challenges and getting on track with your money, and staying there!"

October 14

Expect your every need to be met. Expect the answer to every problem, expect abundance on every level.
Eileen Caddy

MANIFESTING

There is much talk in our culture about how to attract material goods through mental practice. No doubt there is something to be said about training your mind to be open in this way. Yet I have learned that there is a difference between openness and attachment. One attracts; the other repels. One is a way of living in which the Universe is a loving home, and the other imagines that personal control can be applied to the world for personal gain.

The truth is, all practices of manifestation must be based on a profound respect for the mystery of being and the elegant rightness of things just as they are.

October 15

No one wants to take from me what I give abundantly.
Sri Sathya Sai Baba

NURTURING

Giving is by far the most spiritually satisfying practice I know. An older friend who always shows great generosity to his friends, neighbors, and family is in the habit of saying to me, "You can't out-give God." Some of his friends worry that he is not being attentive to his own needs. I don't know for certain where the line is; however, I know that, among all the people I know, he is one of the most sincerely cheerful and seemingly well-adjusted.

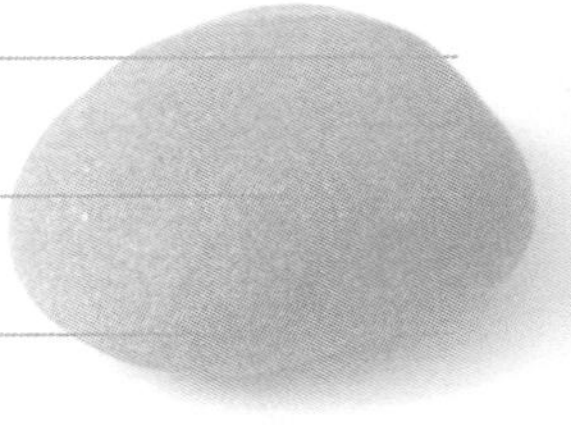

October 16

Abundance is not something we acquire.
It is something we tune into.
Wayne Dyer

PAYING ATTENTION

Practice paying attention to the concept of abundance as you move through your life. If you need a jump start on this practice, spend some time in a garden or park and notice how radical nature is when it comes to abundant expression. For some people, the idea that there is a natural flow of abundance all around them is new. Yet once they tune into it, their world view radically shifts toward possibility thinking and optimism. This practice, though, is not intended to lead you toward irresponsible excesses; it is intended to open your thoughts to the normal state of being.

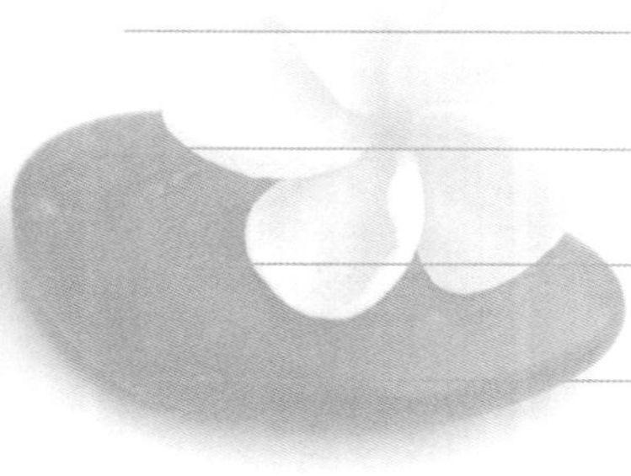

October 17

The greatest real thrill that life offers is to create, to develop something useful. Too often we fail to recognize and pay tribute to the creative spirit.

Alfred P. Sloan

PAYING TRIBUTE

You pay tribute to God through your own self-expression. Each time you engage your sense of creativity, you enact the creative nature of Spirit. Every time you give love, you bring the Presence of God into the world. Each time you forgive, you show God's compassion and honor Its nature of unconditional giving.

God does not require worship. You do not have to make sacrifices to gain God's favor. All you have to do to honor God is be yourself. Express your good nature. Give love. Enjoy life.

October 18

You can always amend a big plan, but you can never expand a little one. I don't believe in little plans. I believe in plans big enough to meet a situation which we can't possibly foresee now.

Harry S. Truman

PLANNING

Big plans come from big ideas. So make big plans! They attract big money. They draw other people to you who also like to think and dream big.

Plan to be healthy every day of your life. Plan to be rich. Plan to be loved and to attract only loving people. Plan to be vital and relevant at every age. Plan for greatness.

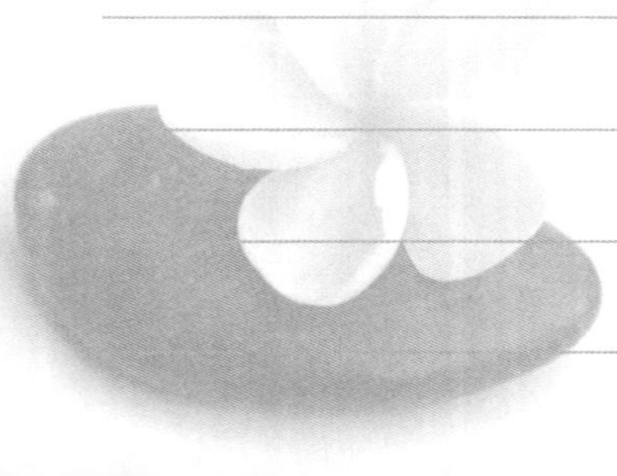

OCTOBER 19

I believe that, as long as
there is plenty, poverty is evil.
Robert Francis Kennedy

PLENTY

You live in an abundant universe. There is more than enough love to go around. No one has to be loveless in order for you to be loved. There is more than enough health. No one has to be sick, so you can be well. There is more than enough air to breathe. No one has to choke so you can breathe freely. There is no shortage of wisdom. No one has to be stupid so you can be smart. There is plenty of every good thing.

You do not have to ask God to supply your life. It has already done so. Learn to accept abundance. Let yourself prosper. Accept everything good.

October 20

As much as we need a prosperous economy,
we also need a prosperity of kindness and decency.
Caroline Kennedy

PROSPERITY

Prosperity is not limited simply to having a lot of money. Prosperity includes a healthy body; functional, loving relationships; financial well-being; a rich spiritual life; an abundance of love from family and friends; and compassion and kindness.

Poverty was never God's idea for humankind. Lack comes from an ignorance that we are all one and, therefore, not responsible for distributing the Earth's resources to each other. When we learn to act from kindness and compassion, no child will be left hungry again.

Live a prosperous life. Be generous. Give to others what you wish to receive.

October 21

Giving is better than receiving because
giving starts the receiving process.
Jim Rohn

RECEIVING

Giving and receiving are inextricably linked. You can't have one without the other. In order to receive, you must first give. It works just the way your body does; in order to inhale, you must first exhale. Proper respiration is maintained by doing both.

The spiritual Law of Circulation dictates that whatever you give out must return back to you. The cycle begins when you start giving. You set yourself up to receive something good when you give something good to another person.

Let yourself reap the benefits of giving. Allow yourself to receive the blessings you have already given to another. Feel what it's like to be blessed.

October 22

Your mind is a powerful magnet that will
attract to you the things you identify yourself with.
Alfredo Karras

ATTRACTION

The image reflected in the mirror is not who you are. Below the surface of your physical body lives your spirit. Like the tip of an iceberg, your physical, visible self is simply a small fraction of your entire being. Your spiritual self is the greater portion.

Therefore, attraction has nothing to do with external facts. It is entirely an inside job. Your mind/spirit is the powerful magnet that attracts the experiences and people that come into your life.

Do you think you are physically attractive? Do you judge your appearance by comparing it to models on magazine covers? Do others admire your appearance?

You are attractive, whether you know it or not.

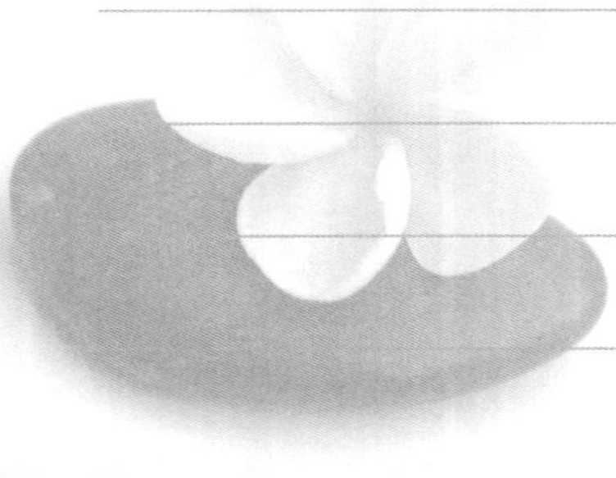

OCTOBER 23

If saving money is wrong,
I don't want to be right.
William Shatner

SAVING

Plan like you're going to live forever, but live like you're going to die tonight. Save money for your future, but don't suffer and sacrifice the quality of your life today to do it. Like everything else in life, balance is the key.

Don't save for a rainy day. If you save for a rainy day, guess what? It's probably going to rain. Save for your retirement. Save for a vintage automobile. Save for a vacation to the Greek islands. Save for your dreams, and your dreams will come into fruition.

Don't spend all of your money. Invest in your future by saving some of what you earn today.

October 24

You yourself, as much as anybody in the entire universe, deserve your love and affection.
Buddha

SELF-LOVE

Self-love is sometimes dismissed as egocentricity or the product of a narcissistic society. But neither of these things is self-love. Self-love demands compassion and commitment, and is one of the most challenging, yet rewarding, practices to sustain over time.

Many people find that their inner worlds are so filled up with crafty self-criticism that there is barely the space and time to think beautiful and affirming thoughts about themselves. Sometimes people say things in their minds about themselves that they would never dream of saying about a child. How does your internal conversation reflect the amount of self-love you have?

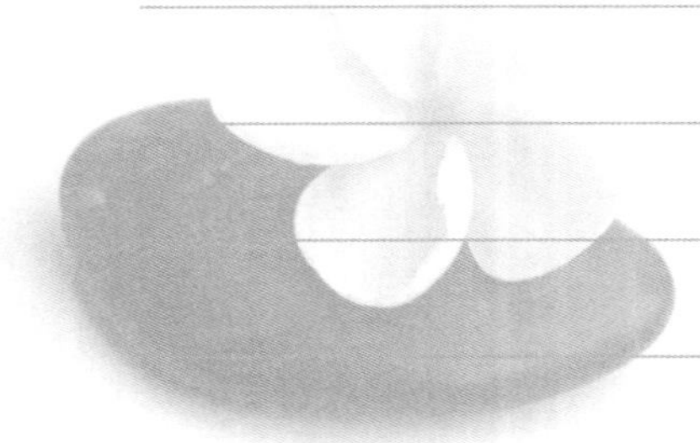

October 25

The first wealth is health.
Ralph Waldo Emerson

VALUES

Take an inventory of how you spend your time and your money. It will show you what you currently place the most value on. If you were asked a question about your highest values, would your time and spending patterns support your answer?

October 26

Wealth is not a matter of intelligence; it's a matter of inspiration.
Jim Rohn

VISUALIZING

Undoubtedly, the mental images we entertain in our minds are important on many levels. Most assuredly, they affect our moods and actions. Our moods and actions, likewise, have the uncanny ability to affect those in close proximity.

Try visualizing an activity that would make you happy to be involved in. Take some time to sit quietly and think about the activity. Then, insert yourself into this scenario. To make it as tangible as possible, imagine what you are wearing, what you are feeling, and who is present. Take time to describe the colors and sounds in the scene. This practice helps us become familiar with those states of being to which we are drawn and helps us take down the barriers built up by habitual, negative projections.

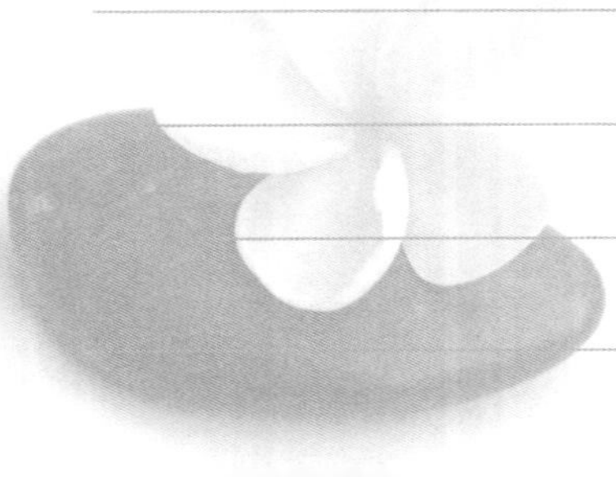

October 27

Being rich is having money; being wealthy is having time.
Margaret Bonnano

WEALTH

What is the difference between being rich and being wealthy to you? Have you taken time to describe exactly what your idea of wealth is? What would your life look like if you were wealthier than you are today? What would change for you? Would the same people be in your life, or different ones? What would you do with your time, and how would you spend your energy?

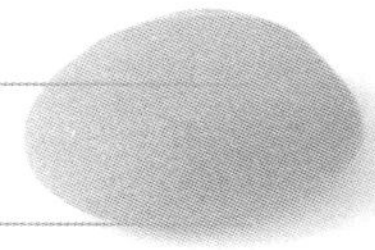

October 28

Ordinary riches can be stolen, real riches cannot. In your soul are infinitely precious things that cannot be taken from you.
Oscar Wilde

RICHES

During one of my postgraduate courses, one of my classmates lost everything in a house fire. She came home to charred remains. As she told the class the story, she spoke to the class about the incredible sense of freedom and peace that she had since the fire. She realized that she had lost nothing at all. I watched her closely, wondering if it was a kind of posttraumatic shock causing her calmness. However, she seemed genuinely content.

Oddly, this experience seemed to traumatize the other students . They suddenly had to confront what it might mean to lose everything. As an exercise, we asked each other what we might save if we had the chance for one final rescue mission into our burning home.

What would you save?

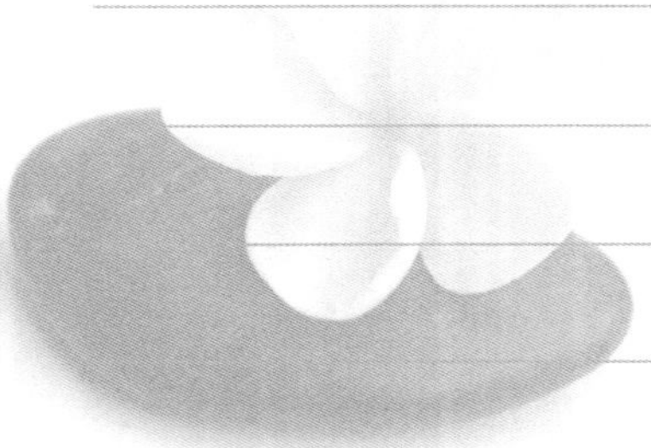

October 29

Wealth is the ability
to fully experience life.
Henry David Thoreau

AFFLUENCE

We usually define affluence as an abundance of money, property, and other material goods associated with riches and wealth. However, it can also mean having an abundant supply of such things as words, thoughts, affection, love, or kindness.

During a time of economic challenge, when I was concerned about having sufficient material things, I instead let my thoughts dwell on what I had a lot of. I had a lot of time, so I gave it away in the form of listening to friends and doing tasks and activities with them. As a result, I experienced a wealth of another kind. This small experiment reminded me how easy it is to slip into the world's definition of wealth, when everything I shall ever need is inside of me.

What do you have a lot of?

October 30

The only wealth which you will keep
forever is the wealth you have given away.
Marcus Aurelius

RESOURCES

Singer and composer Fred Small's beautiful song "Everything Possible" contains these lyrics: "And the only measure of your words and your deeds/Will be the love you leave behind when you're done." I remember the first time I heard the song—how these words rang in my thoughts like an alarm, reminding me of something very important. It reminded me that one of the infinite resources made available to me in this lifetime is the capacity to be kind, and that I had not been exploiting this resource nearly enough. I had been reserving it for certain people and withholding it from others I did not like. Things started to change when I asked myself, "What will be the measure of my life when I'm gone?"

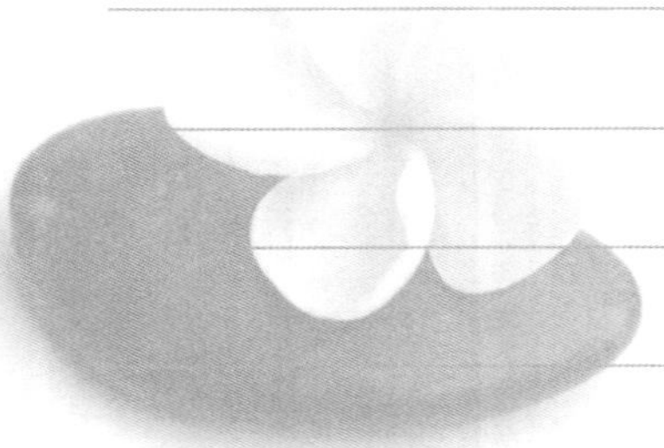

October 31

Love is the ability and willingness to allow those that you care for to be what they choose for themselves without any insistence that they satisfy you.

Wayne Dyer

SELF-INDULGENCE

Consider yourself to be someone that you care for. Then, declare today, or a portion of today, to be set aside to indulge yourself. Go to the movies, do nothing, or do something you've always meant to do. Make today, or part of it, a time for only you or "by invitation only."

NOVEMBER

Practice *the* Presence *through* Expression

NOVEMBER 1

It is the height of absurdity to sow little but weeds in the first half of one's lifetime and expect to harvest a valuable crop in the second half.
Percy Johnston

ABSURDITY

It is absurd to expect more from life than what you give to it.You can only receive that which you are first willing to give. Stop thinking about what you want to get from life, and start thinking about what you are going give.

To ensure a high-quality life experience, begin giving love. Give encouragement and praise to others. Give kindness. Give compassion. Show others your courage and strength. Let them depend on you. Give peace. Give thanks.

If you continue to practice giving, you will receive back tenfold, and your life will be blessed beyond measure.

November 2

Creativity requires the courage
to let go of certainties.
Erich Fromm

CREATIVITY

Creativity demands courage. To be creative, one must be bold enough to leave the tried and true behind and venture into the unknown. Creative people are fearless. They let go of certainties in favor of exploration into new territory. They thrive on newness.

Do you think of yourself as a creative person? How ready are you to try new things? How willing are you to step outside of the known and venture into the unknown? Are you comfortable learning new things? Are you spontaneous?

Step out of your comfort zone today. Explore something new. Create!

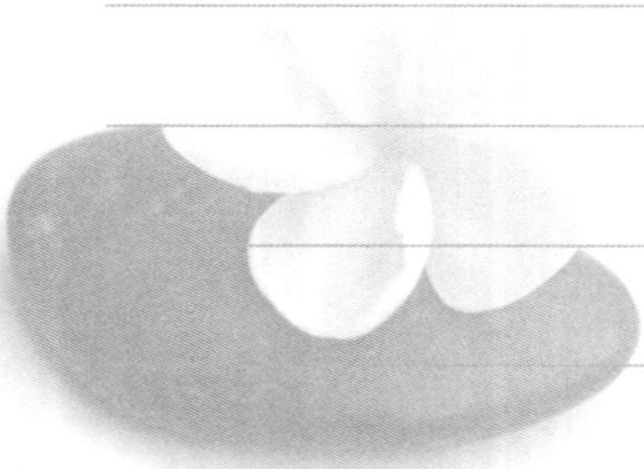

NOVEMBER 3

The minute you alter your perception of yourself and your future, both you and your future begin to change.
Marilee Zdenek

ALTERING

Things are not as they appear. There is more going on in life than that which can be seen with human eyes. The universe is mysterious and magical.

You are more than the image reflected in a mirror. Living in and through your physical body is the inner Spirit directing your experience. Some call it the soul. But it is actually your connection to God. It is your Higher Self.

Alter your perception of yourself. Stop making judgments based strictly on physical appearances. Begin to see yourself as God sees you—perfect, whole, and complete. Alter the perception of your life experiences. Stop judging them as successes or failures. Begin to see each experience as a step on a spiritual journey leading to enlightenment.

November 4

Human beings and their actions constitute the advancing front, the surging crest of an ongoing movement that never stops.
Corliss Lamont

ADVANCING

How many lives have been lived on planet Earth? How many people died before you were born? How many civilizations have advanced and then disappeared? How many fortunes have been gained and lost? How many people have found love and then lost it?

As a species, we advance slowly. We take three steps forward and two steps back. The snail's pace of our progress is not clearly visible from the viewpoint of one human lifetime. It has to be observed in thousand-year increments.

You are a link in an eternal chain of human development and enlightenment. Your life contributes to the strength or weakness of this chain. How you live affects the next generation, and the next, and so on. That is why it is so important for you to live well, be happy, and find your way to love.

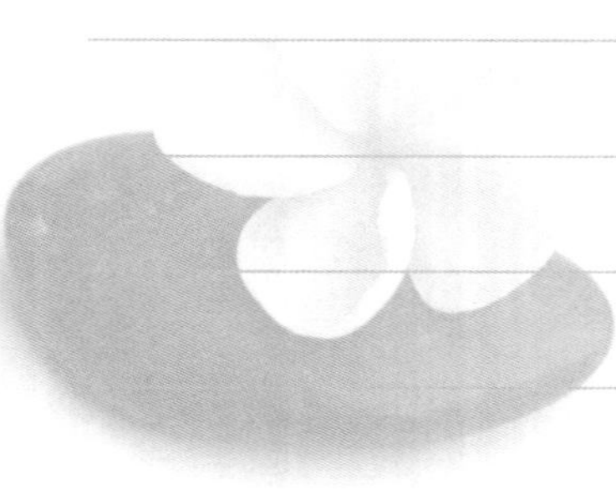

November 5

Good business leaders create a vision, articulate the vision, passionately own the vision, and relentlessly drive it to completion.
Thomas Hardy

ARTICULATING

Most people don't think much about what they want in life, because they don't know they can have it. They don't give much thought to their future. They just wake up each day and accept whatever comes along. That is why there are so many victims in the world, people who passively wait for the next bad thing to happen.

You do not have to be one of them. You can create your own future by being proactively involved with life. Make your own choices today. Choose your own dream. Create a vision for your life. Articulate your desires and plan to have your vision fulfilled.

Take one step today toward the highest and best idea you have. And then tomorrow, take another step. As you advance toward your vision, wonderful things will happen. Expect something good.

November 6

Boldness has genius, power, and magic in it. Begin it now.
Johann Wolfgang Von Goethe

BOLDNESS

Having the audacity to ask for and then go after exactly what you want from life is the reserve of a few. Not many people act boldly. Most are meek and fearful. They accept the status quo and keep their mouths shut.

What bold action could you take today that would radically improve your life? What would happen if you decided to take that action? What are your fears? What are your concerns?

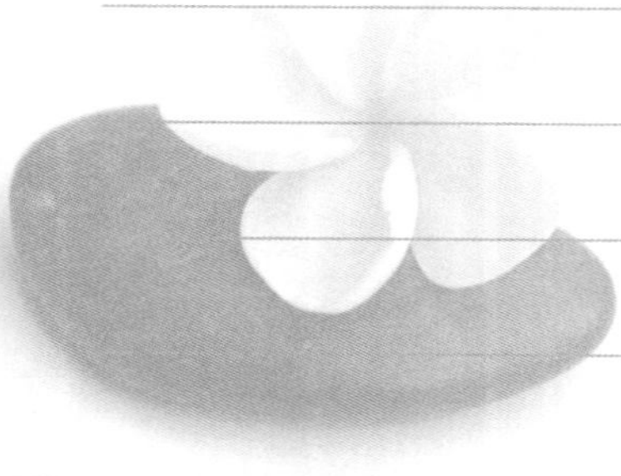

NOVEMBER 7

Creativity is piercing the mundane to find the marvelous.
Bill Moyers

BRILLIANCE

Consider holding interviews with the people in your life whom you think are brilliant. Ask them how they handle the mundane things in life. Ask them what they do when they feel stagnated. Then, listen to their responses and try their techniques on the challenging tasks in your life.

Brilliant people are not only world leaders or celebrities; they can be neighbors and friends who inspire you by their approach to life. There is a brilliant light of inspiration shining all around you. Sometimes it just takes a willingness to explore and inquire about it by asking questions.

November 8

Creativity is inventing, experimenting, growing, taking risks, breaking rules, making mistakes, and having fun.
Mary Lou Cook

ADVENTURE

Have an adventure today. Prepare something for dinner that you've never prepared before. Do something in your free time that you've never done before. Write a poem; go to a museum; enroll in a yoga class; or jumble up your schedule for the day and do routine things at irregular times. Just experiment with your world today for the sake of unleashing creativity.

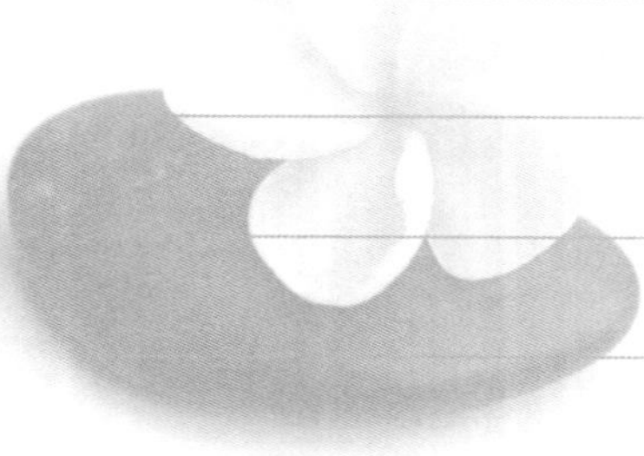

November 9

Creativity is the sudden
cessation of stupidity.
Edwin H. Land

COMMON SENSE

In Thomas Paine's *Common Sense*, he addresses a pressing issue for a nation—independence from British rule—in a way that the ordinary person could understand. He wrote with language that was direct and accessible, allowing him to reach the ordinary citizens of America.

Imagine trying to explain something complex using a similar style. Write down a description of the Presence in a way that a child could easily understand. If you have young people in your life, ask them to evaluate the clarity of your description and to point out where they don't understand what you mean.

November 10

Sometimes you gotta create
what you want to be a part of.
Geri Weitzman

BRINGING INTO BEING

We are endowed with a creative mind which, when used properly, generates possibilities, solutions, and exciting opportunities. Sometimes people sit around and wait for opportunities to present themselves; creative people simply take the first steps toward whatever they are interested in.

When we take that first step, the whole of creation conspires to get us to take the second. Think of something you want to be a part of. Ask yourself what might be the first step toward bringing it into being.

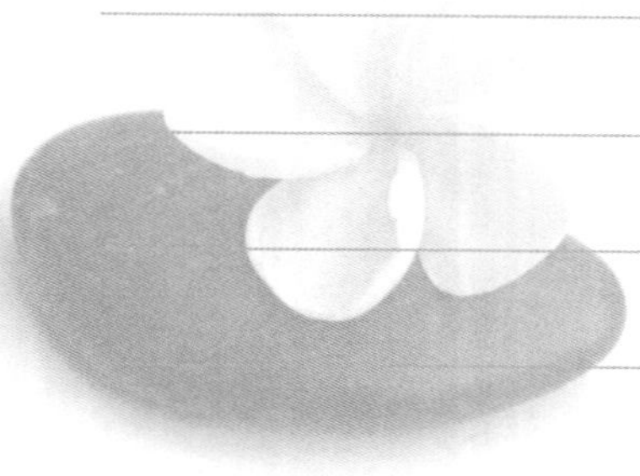

November 11

Uncertainty and mystery are energies of life. Don't let them scare you unduly, for they keep boredom at bay and spark creativity.
R. I. Fitzhenry

CONTINUING

A friend told me about a type of Chinese bamboo that has the remarkable ability to grow nine feet in ninety days. However, the surge in growth does not take place until after the plant has been alive for five years. If you want to witness the miraculous surge in growth, you must be prepared to tend to the plant for years without any visible reward.

The story reminds me of the many times I gave up just before my creativity broke ground and burst out. Is there something in your life that you are on the verge of giving up? Is there a stress-free reason you can think of to hang in there?

November 12

When in doubt, make a fool of yourself. There is a microscopically thin line between being brilliantly creative and acting like the most gigantic idiot on earth. So what the hell, leap.

Cynthia Heimel

DARING

One of the major stumbling blocks I encounter among people who want to express creativity but do not, is the fear of looking bad. Embarrassment, for some people, far outweighs the perceived benefits of creative expression. Many people I talk to have long ago given up creativity because of childhood experiences, or because along the way they have learned to compare their efforts to others.

Cynthia Heimel's recommendation to risk making a fool of yourself is something worth considering if there is an area in your life where you feel stuck.

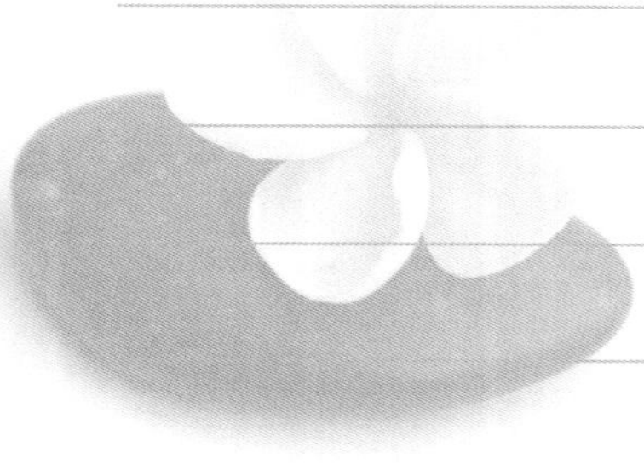

November 13

Creativity is a natural
extension of our enthusiasm.
Earl Nightingale

DETERMINATION

There is a fine line between healthy persistence and doggedly sticking to something when it is past the time to let go. Sometimes, it is advisable to step back for a moment and decide whether you should go on. After observation and investigation, determine whether you have crossed the line between beneficial engagement and unhealthy attachment. You may have to ask for a second opinion from a trusted friend, especially if you have become too close to the object of your pursuit.

November 14

Einstein was a man who could ask immensely simple questions.
And what his work showed was that when the answers are simple, too,
then you can hear God thinking.
Jacob Bronowski

DIRECTNESS

Your life does not have to be complex. It can be simple. You do not have to be filled with anxiety. You can be at peace. You do not have to rush and hurry through the day. You can slow down. Take the direct approach when it comes to life: Simplify things.

The shortest distance between two points is a straight line. The shortest distance between two people who are at odds with each other is direct communication. You do not have to fight with others. You can listen to their concerns, state your own, and ask for what you want.

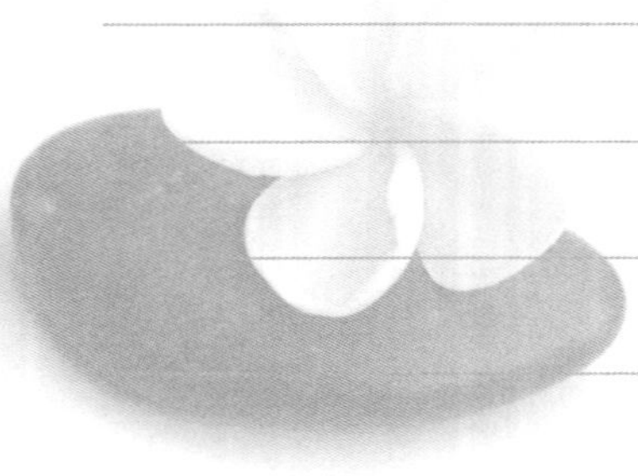

NOVEMBER 15

Common sense
is very uncommon.
Horace Greeley

UNCOMMON SENSE

Some people have too much education and not enough common sense. Advanced degrees do not always promise levelheadedness. And some people who have very little education exhibit great wisdom and practicality.

It is common sense not to spend more than you make. It is common sense to take care of the things you love so they will last. It is common sense to treat others the way you wish to be treated.

Most things that are common sense are based on spiritual principles. By practicing common sense, you are living in alignment with God's Law. You live a spiritual life, one that is very uncommon.

NOVEMBER 16

I am giddy, expectation whirls me round. The imaginary relish is so sweet that it enchants my sense.
William Shakespeare

ENCHANTMENT

Synonyms for *enchanted* include *delighted, enamored, entranced*, and *fascinated*. Do you remember the last time you had any of these feelings? When was the last time you were delighted and fascinated at the same time? When was your heart last filled with joyful anticipation?

As adults with responsibilities, we can too easily lose sight of those feelings. We forget that we are children at heart, whose only desire is for love and joy. It's easy to take on the burdens of adult life and forget our passions.

Rekindle those feelings today. Retouch your heart's desire. Remind yourself of your passions. Practice being enchanted with life once again.

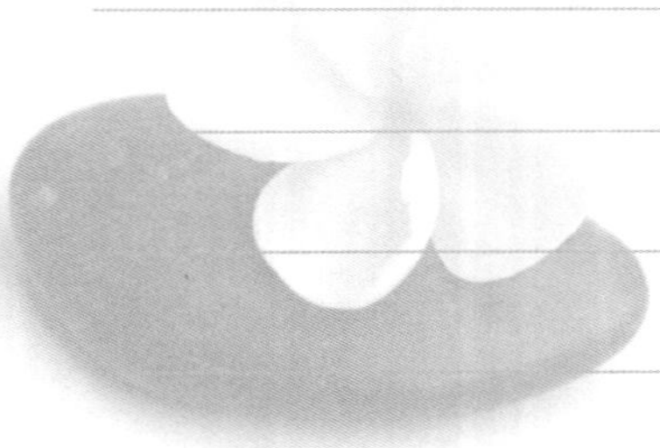

November 17

...as I reinvent myself and I'm constantly curious about everything, I can't wait to see what's around the corner...

Pam Grier

EXPLORATION

Leave the shoreline behind and set sail on a new exploration. Forget the known as you reach upward and outward into the unknown. Let the past belong to fools who always drag it into the present and relive it. Go forward. Advance boldly into the unexplored territory of a brand new day.

November 18

Making money is a hobby that will
complement any other hobbies you have, beautifully.
Scott Alexander

HOBBIES

Hobbies are good excuses to take us away from the mundane activities of everyday life. They foster creativity. They allow us to focus on something other than that which is required to survive. They create social networks as we congregate with others who share our interests.

It is important to have distractions from adulthood. We need to rekindle our enthusiasm for newness. Like children, adults also need to play.

If you don't have a hobby, consider developing one. If hobbies don't interest you, be sure to take regular playtimes.

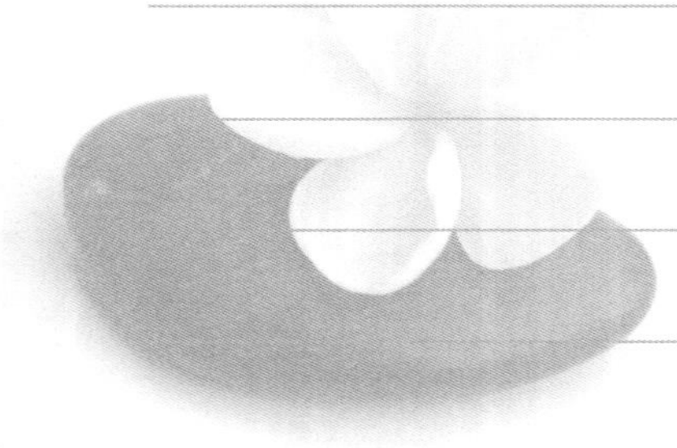

November 19

The world is but a canvas
to the imagination.
Henry David Thoreau

IMAGINATION

Take time to wonder; stare out the window. Use this time to imagine life as you want to live it. Forget about limitations for a moment, and give your mind unrestrained access to creativity.

If you can imagine it, you can achieve it. If you are passionate and tenacious enough, it will come to fruition. Don't let life carry you to places you don't want to be. Imagine something new. Take the helm and redirect your life.

Einstein said that imagination is more important than knowledge. If this is true, how much time do you spend gaining knowledge? How much time do you spend imagining? Which is more important to you? Which is more fun?

November 20

If GM had kept up with technology like the computer industry has, we would all be driving twenty-five-dollar cars that got 1,000 mpg.
Bill Gates

INDUSTRY

The industrial revolution abruptly halted agrarian culture in America and transformed it into one of manufacturing. As we entered the new age, businesses thrived. Industry giants made fortunes. The next shift came as we entered the information age. Computers, the Internet, and digital technology transformed everything in a matter of a few years.

The twenty-first century has heralded in an even newer era called the "creative age." The industry now is ideas. Today, those who are the most creative will prosper. The rise of the creative class will reconstruct our economy and society. Change is happening quickly. Are you onboard?

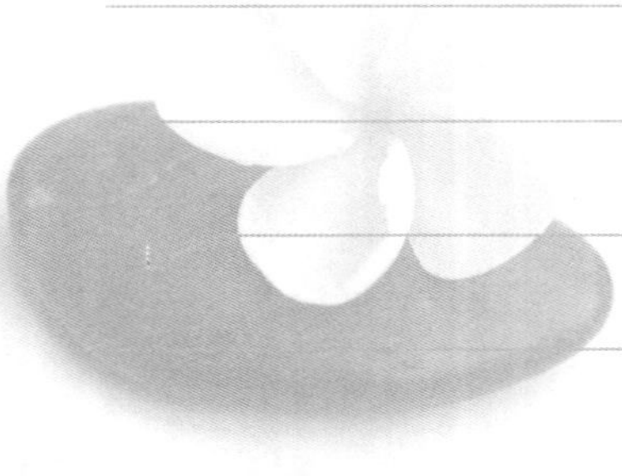

November 21

Logic will get you from A to B.
Imagination will take you everywhere.
Albert Einstein

MAKE BELIEVE

Your imagination is the creative tool you use to face difficulties and resolve them by creating solutions when none are present. To practice this art, your willingness to "make believe" will be a useful ally.

Take a situation you are facing that is a struggle or difficult to overcome. Make believe that it has been successfully resolved. Use your journal to write down the reasonable steps that led to your imagined resolution. This is a way of opening the doors of your mind to strategies that have not presented themselves so far. It works best when done with a lighthearted sense of adventure.

NOVEMBER 22

You must look within for value,
but must look beyond for perspective.
Denis Waitley

PERSPECTIVE

Roger von Oech, an author, inventor, and speaker, has enriched the creativity of millions by encouraging them to think beyond the limits of their known world. He writes: "Different words lead your thinking in different directions and bring in different assumptions. What other word or phrase can you use to describe a challenge?" You can apply a similar approach to your stressful thoughts. When you have one, write it down. Then, come up with three examples of how the opposite of the statement is also true.

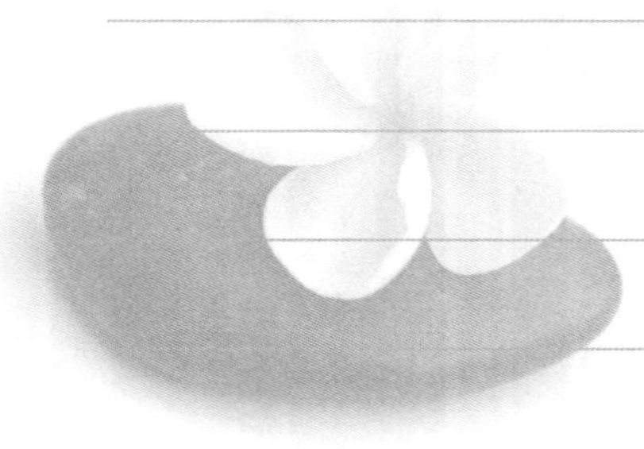

November 23

Weekends don't count unless you spend them
doing something completely pointless.
Bill Watterson

POINTLESSNESS

The phrase *down time* refers, in the world of technology, to periods when a system is unavailable as the result of a system failure due to an unexpected event, such as a crash. Planned outages are scheduled so that crashes can be avoided. During a planned outage, the system will be cleaned up, maintained, repaired, and updated.

Human beings require down time on a regular basis, too—preferably on a schedule. During these down times, some of the best maintenance practices include doing nothing and letting the system rest. When last did you do nothing?

NOVEMBER 24

The sharp thorn often
produces delicate roses.
Ovid

PRODUCING

Attachment to the outcome of a project or idea is written about extensively in many of the world's faith traditions. Frequently, we are warned not to be overly fixated on the results, but to be clear on the goal. The reason for this paradox is that nothing seems to be produced in our lives without creative steps toward a goal.

Yet it is frequently the case that, as we step toward our intention, the landscape of our lives changes due a shift in priorities and interests. As a result, we often end up producing something different from what we intended. Sometimes, it is a delightful surprise; other times, it is a mystery.

November 25

The secret of getting ahead is getting started. The secret of getting started is breaking your complex, overwhelming tasks into small, manageable tasks, and then starting on the first one.
Mark Twain

STARTING

To generate energy, one of my favorite and most successful strategies is to start by tidying up some small area in my office or home. I can easily become overwhelmed if I see too much in front of me. When I tidy up one bookshelf, meticulously paying attention to order, shape, and cleanliness, I seem to achieve peace and hope in the midst of whatever else is going on. Consider tidying up one part of your world today as the first step toward releasing your creative energy.

November 26

OBSERVATORY, n. A place where astronomers conjecture away the guesses of their predecessors.
Ambrose Bierce

SPECULATING

In the business world, speculation suggests transactions with considerable risk, in the hope that large benefits will be reaped at the end. It suggests the idea of taking a risk by thinking outside of the norm. In spiritual practice, speculation means to indulge in conjecture or, more simply put, exercising the imagination.

You can practice this by writing down how you would like your life to be five years from now. In this exercise, don't worry about being outrageous. Simply get involved in being creative. You aren't trying to create a new you; you're just exercising your imagination.

November 27

There is no greater agony than
bearing an untold story inside you.
Maya Angelou

STORYTELLING

I remember the day I realized that my grandmother was not going to be available to me for much longer, and that I had grown used to talking to her whenever I wanted. I realized that she had been so attentive to her grandchildren that we expected her to listen to every word we said. And she did. Even as an adult, I would pour out my day's experiences to her, unedited. One day, I stopped and asked her to tell me about her life. I asked her to start at the beginning, omitting nothing, and share every detail. What followed was a beautiful story that I almost missed because I had been too busy telling my own story.

Try asking someone in your world about his or her life's story, and expect a fantastic moment of connection and wonder.

November 28

Whatever you are by nature, keep to it; never desert your line of talent. Be what nature intended for you, and you will succeed.

Sydney Smith

TALENT

The key to your success and prosperity is to find your talent and use it. There is something you can do like no one else. God has given you specific gifts. Explore their depths. Practice using them. Follow where they lead. Don't be distracted by other people's dreams or expectations for your life. Stay on course.

Many people will try to discourage you. They are fools. Don't listen to them. They will show anger as you step away from the mediocre path of the majority. They will tantalize and ridicule you. Let their fearful chatter be the background noise you have trained your mind to ignore.

Stay true to your natural talent and God will reward you with a rich life.

NOVEMBER 29

There are victories of the soul and spirit.
Sometimes even if you lose, you win.
Elie Wiesel

VICTORY

You will be victorious in life. You will get exactly what you want. You will succeed at love. You will prosper. You will know what it's like to feel powerful and relevant. You will achieve self-respect and honor. All of this is within your reach. Nothing in the universe can stop you, because there is no greater power than God, whose only desire is for your happiness and well-being.

Never give up! Never stop pursuing your dreams. Don't let others discourage you. Don't allow setbacks or delays to dampen your spirit. Keep moving in the direction of your best ideas, and you will arrive at your destination triumphantly.

NOVEMBER 30

Instead of begging OPEC to drop its oil prices, let's use American leadership and ingenuity to solve our own energy problems.
Pete Domenici

INGENUITY

What is challenging your life right now? What issues need to be resolved? Assuming that you have tried everything you know, now try a different approach. Apply some ingenuity and inventiveness to the situation. Observe things from a different angle. Try to think outside the box of conventional wisdom.

Many people continue to do the same things yet wonder why they don't get different results. After you've tried everything you know to do, start to look in another direction. Knock on a different door, and apply a new strategy.

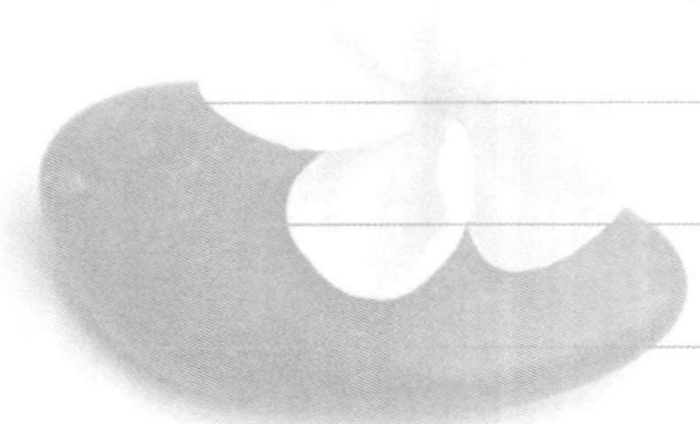

DECEMBER

Practice *the* Presence *through* Gladness

December 1

Courage and cheerfulness will not only carry you over the rough places in life, but will enable you to bring comfort and help to the weak-hearted and will console you in the sad hours.

William Osler

CHEERFULNESS

Like a boat in the water, your actions leave behind ripples to be absorbed by others. To ensure that you are affecting people in a positive way, be cheerful. You have an opportunity to heal the world every day, simply by expressing your enthusiasm and joy for life.

Give gladness. Be happy. Show the world that you live close to your heart, and enjoy God's Presence in your life. There's no reason to be sad any longer.

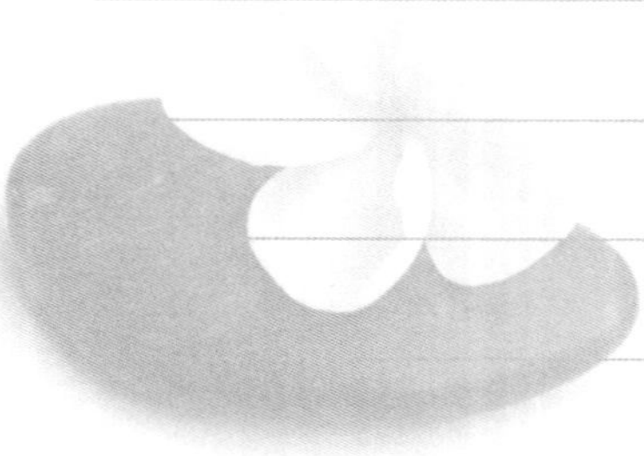

December 2

There is no value in life except what you choose to place upon it, and no happiness in any place except what you bring to it yourself.
Henry David Thoreau

CHOOSING HAPPINESS

Choosing happiness is a choice you must make every day. It is not merely the effect of a positive experience. Many people who have struggled with hardship and fought to stay alive still remain happy, regardless of the negative circumstances which affect them.

The challenges before you do not have to steal your joy. There are many things that can be taken from you in human life, but no one can steal your happiness unless you choose to let them. Choose happiness today.

December 3

Enthusiasm releases the drive to carry you
over obstacles and adds significance to all you do.
Norman Vincent Peale

ENTHUSIASM

Everyone feels enthusiastic on occasion. But the person who can remain buoyant through anything is the one closest to God.

One of the benefits of creating and maintaining a close, personal relationship with Spirit is a complete sense of well-being. With it comes a knowing that, no matter what happens to you, everything will be just fine. In God's Presence, nothing can go wrong.

It is easy to be enthusiastic when you trust in God. You no longer require hope, because hope is replaced with the complete trust that, no matter what goes on around you, God has guaranteed a perfect and loving result.

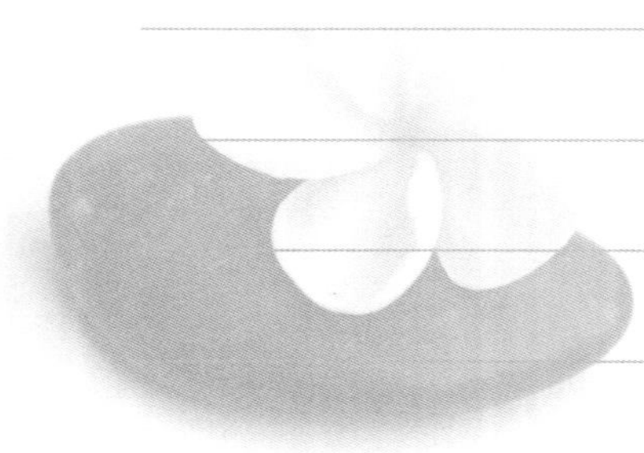

December 4

Without leaps of imagination, or dreaming, we lose the excitement of possibilities. Dreaming, after all, is a form of planning.
Gloria Steinem

EXCITEMENT

Are you excited about your day? Do you understand the potential that resides within a twenty-four-hour period? Wonderful things can happen at any time. New opportunities to love will present themselves today. New potentials will rise up from within. You will make a new discovery. You will have a chance to laugh.

Yesterday ended last night. It's over. It's finished. Nothing can bring it back or make it different. All of the opportunities for change and healing are in the present moment. Today is the one day you have to live. Get excited!

December 5

I don't like spinach, and I'm glad I don't,
because if I liked it I'd eat it, and I just hate it.
Clarence Darrow

FREEING

I had a relative who was opposed to happiness. She would ask, "Can you imagine what it would be like if everyone just did exactly as they wanted?" I don't know why her question would always reduce me to crumbles of laughter. Maybe I couldn't understand that she had a deep-seated belief that people were basically prone to trouble. Perhaps, in my innocence, I thought differently about people. It seemed to be a marvelous idea that every person should do exactly as they wanted.

Today, as an adult, being well aware of my connection to all life and to other people, I find more and more that what I want is for those around me to do exactly as they want.

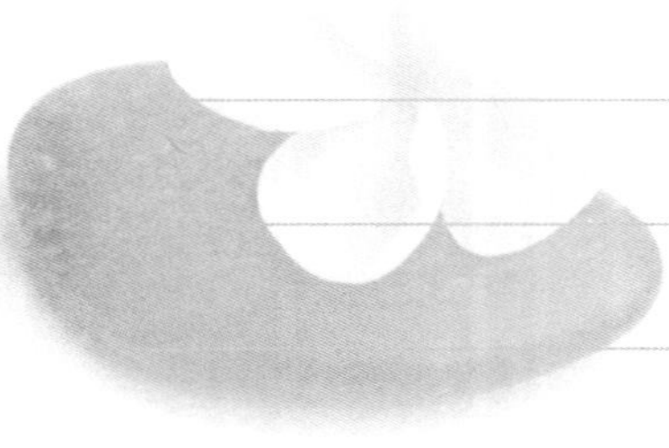

December 6

Our brightest blazes of gladness are commonly kindled by unexpected sparks.
Samuel Johnson

GLADNESS

When Samuel Johnson was born in 1709, there was some doubt that he would survive infancy, due to severe health challenges. He was scarred from tuberculosis, deaf in one ear, and blind in one eye, the results of being nursed by an infected nursemaid. Nevertheless, he was fiercely independent and driven to get along in life with as little assistance as possible. In his writings, he reveals a passion for life that is inspiring.

Sometimes it is possible to let setbacks rob us of our gladness. Take a moment to consider where you may have allowed yourself to lose your natural enjoyment of life due to challenges.

December 7

A kind heart is a fountain of gladness, making everything in its vicinity freshen into smiles.
Washington Irving

GLEE

The word *glee* has its roots in Old English, where it had something to do with the enjoyment and merriment that went along with entertainment. An entertainer was a *gleuman,* someone who brought about jubilant delight or joy. The word itself sounds like an infectious smile, and I can't imagine glee without imagining smiling faces.

What makes you break out in a gleeful smile? What or who has the ability to make you feel pure delight?

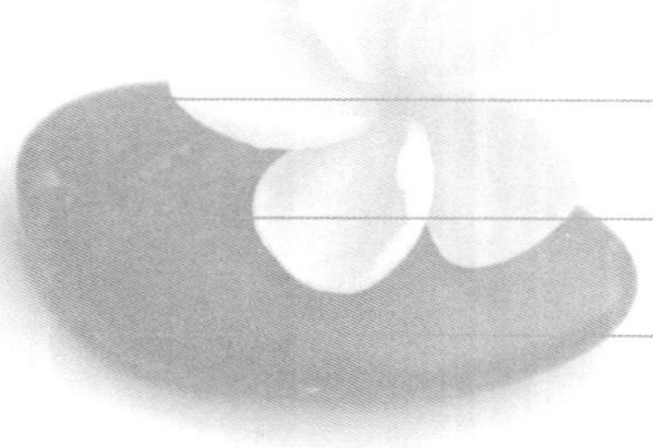

December 8

I know that two and two make four—and should be glad to prove it too if I could—though I must say if by any sort of process I could convert two and two into five, it would give me much greater pleasure.

Lord Byron

HUMOR

What causes one person to experience humor may have no such effect on another person. Humor, apparently, is as personal as our taste in food, lovers, or anything else that is influenced by culture, age, education, intelligence, or context. I particularly enjoy watching children when they experience something as funny, not so much because I see it as funny, too, but because their laughter and gladness is infectious and helps me feel like I am in the Presence of Holiness.

What do you consider to be funny and entertaining? When last did you enjoy funny entertainment, and how did you feel afterwards?

December 9

In the sweetness of friendship, let there be laughter and sharing of pleasures. For in the dew of little things, the heart finds its morning and is refreshed.

Kahlil Gibran

LAUGHING

When laughter is shared, people are connected. Laughter has the ability to spread in a disarming way. A belly laugh is difficult to ignore and can easily bring a smile to other people, even if they have no idea what the laughter is about. Vigorous laughter gives the body a release from tension and is reported to boost the immune system and stimulate the chemicals our bodies use to feel good.

What makes you break out in laughter? Who has the ability to make you laugh, and when last did you spend time with them? How can you get more laughter in your life? What was the last funny joke you heard? Learn a new joke and tell it to a friend.

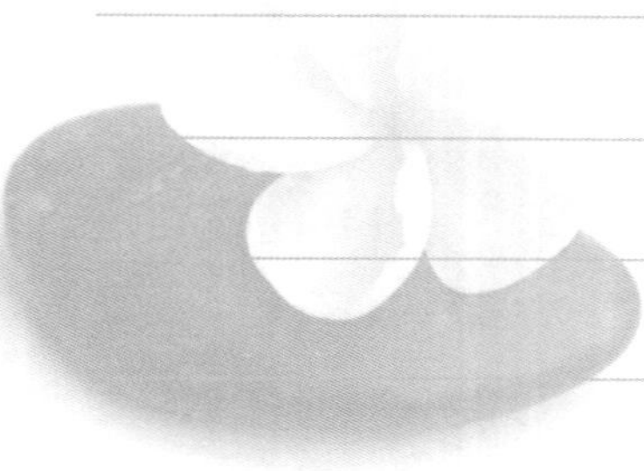

Everything you can imagine is real.
Pablo Picasso

PLAYFULNESS

A playful approach to life is an easy way to spread gladness. And it is a wonderful way to exercise childlike creativity and nurture your capacity to dream up fantastic stories with impossible futures and wonderful endings.

Spend some time making up a fantastic story in which you are the main character. Be outrageous and include elements of humor and whimsy. After all, nature does it all the time.

December 11

Pleasure for one hour, a bottle of wine.
Pleasure for one year a marriage;
but pleasure for a lifetime, a garden.
Chinese Proverbs

PLEASURE

The philosopher Epicurus defined *pleasure* as the absence of suffering. Imagine that. American philosopher Ernest Holmes believed that the ultimate goal of life is the complete emancipation from discord of every nature. Imagine that!

I ruminate on these ideas from time to time to remind myself to nurture the suffer-free moments in my life. It is easy to take a walk around the neighborhood or indulge in an ice cream sundae or spend uninterrupted time with a good book. And the benefits are immense. I have noticed that I don't take as much pleasure as I could in the things, people, and places that I take for granted. For example, I see the sunrise over the trees from my bedroom window so frequently that I forget to marvel at it. It's a pity, because seeing a sunrise makes it so easy to feel the Presence.

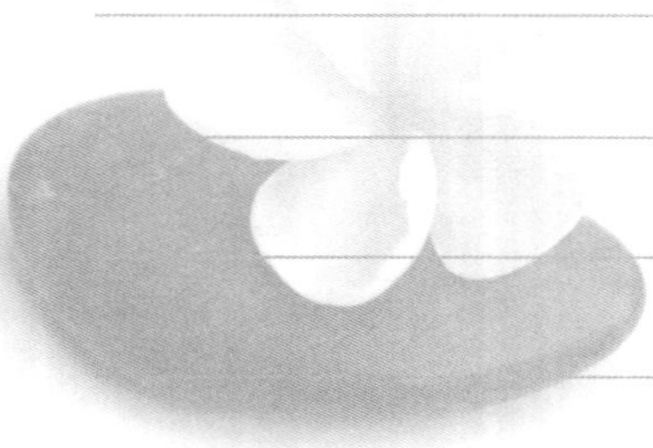

December 12

You and I want our lives to matter. We want our lives to make a real difference—to be of genuine consequence in the world. We know that there is no satisfaction in merely going through the motions, even if those motions make us successful.

Unknown

SATISFACTION

Are you happy with what you do for a living? Do you end most days feeling you've made a contribution to the betterment of humankind? Are you satisfied with the amount of love you give and receive? Are your relationships healthy and functional? Are you happy with your appearance?

Your goal should be to live in such a way that if you die tonight, you will be completely satisfied with the choices you made and the life you lived. If today happens to be your last day on earth, will you feel proud of what you accomplished? If not, today is the day to begin making changes.

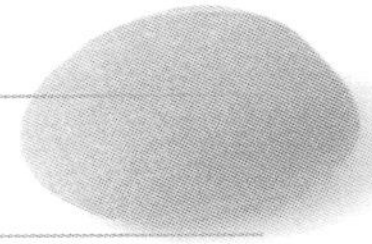

DECEMBER 13

Remember that there is always a limit to self-indulgence, but not to self-restraint.
Mahatma Gandhi

SELF-INDULGENCE

You do not have to endure hardship to prove that you are worthy to God. There is no virtue in self-denial or martyrdom. God is not well-served by your lack and limitation.

If you want to truly honor your Creator, live well, be happy, and find love. Dive into the deep end of the pool of life and get soaking wet. Explore the depth of your innate potential. Indulge in the luxuries of joy and love. Live an abundant life filled with all good things.

When you live from the wisdom of your Higher Self, self-indulgence becomes a good thing.

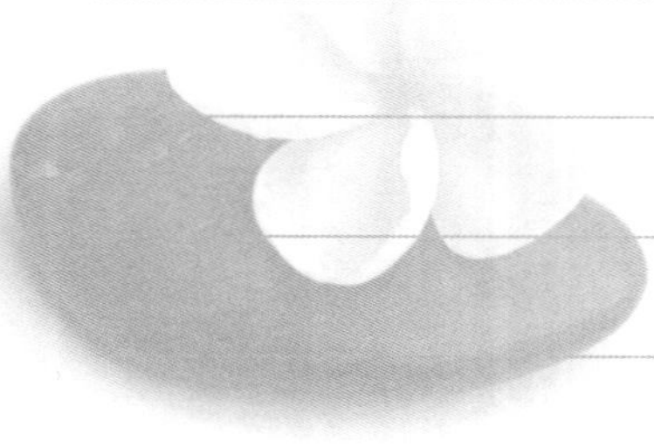

December 14

Simplicity and repose are the qualities that measure the true value of any work of art.
Frank Lloyd Wright

SIMPLICITY

The greatest pleasures in life are the simple ones. If you can make the person you love the most smile today, it will bring more joy to your heart than anything else. If you can go to sleep tonight knowing you are loved and feeling satisfied that you have given love in return, you will have accomplished all that your Creator requires.

We don't really need much to be happy. We just need to know that our lives have meaning and purpose. We need to be appreciated and feel accomplished. Don't waste your money on extravagant gifts for others. Give the simple gift of love, and trust that it will mean more to them than anything you could buy at a store.

December 15

Sometimes your joy is the source of your smile,
but sometimes your smile can be the source of your joy.
Thich Nhat Hanh

SMILING

How do you think people would respond if you started smiling more often? What would your spouse or partner do if they caught you smiling at them from across the dinner table? What would your boss say if you looked up from the meeting table and just smiled? Would they think you've gone mad? Try it and see what happens. I think you'll find the results quite amazing.

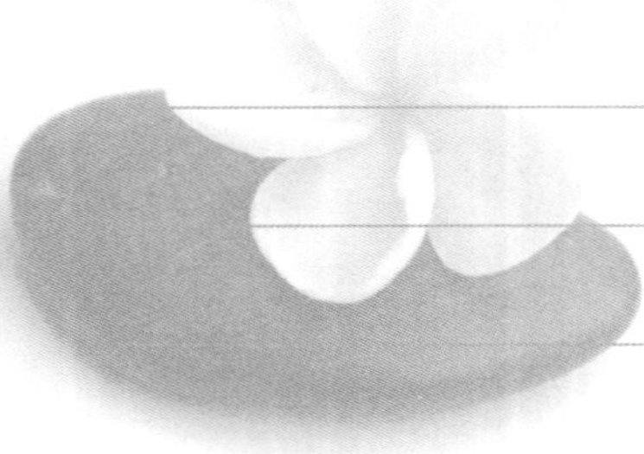

December 16

Life is a crowded superhighway with bewildering cloverleaf exits on which a man is liable to find himself speeding back in the direction he came.

Peter De Vries

SPEEDING UP

You probably have a lot to do today. With the holidays coming up, you more than likely have a long list of errands.

Try not to move so quickly that you miss out on the simple pleasure of the upcoming season. Remember, it's not how much you accomplish that's important; it's how you treat the people around you.

Take some time for yourself today. Steal it if you must. If you have to get up early or go to bed a few minutes later, take that time to center yourself. Remind yourself of the joy of the season.

December 17

If the only prayer you said in your whole life was, thank you, that would suffice.
Meister Eckhart

THANKFULNESS

God is not a giant Pez dispenser, popping out one candy after another. Don't ask God for anything today. Don't beg or beseech. Don't try to make a deal with God, offering one thing for another. Just say, "Thank you."

In prayer, say, "Thank you God for my health. Thank you for all of the love that's in my life today. Thank you for the blessings I have received and for the ones on their way to me. Thank you for the peace in my heart and the calm knowing that all is well. Thank you, God, for the wisdom you give me and the freedom to never be a victim again. Thank you for loving me and for forgiving my mistakes."

Use this prayer frequently.

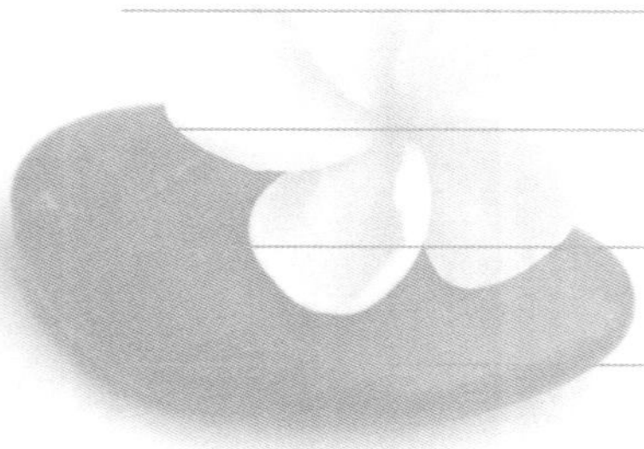

December 18

Always seek out the seed of triumph in every adversity.
Og Mandino

TRIUMPH

In the biblical story of David and Goliath, David faces what seems to be an insurmountable task. He literally has a giant of a problem. And yet the story is so popular because David emerges triumphantly from the battle.

You represent the character of David. Some of the challenges you face seem gigantic. Yet what you may be unaware of is the power you have inside you to meet those challenges. This innate power is the Presence of God, and it can overcome any obstacle set before it.

Your challenge—the giant Goliath—is there to call forth the Presence of God in your life. Its only purpose is to bring you closer to God, so that you can see just how powerful this partnership really is. Face your challenges head-on. Know that you will come through them unscathed. You will emerge triumphantly. With God, all things are possible.

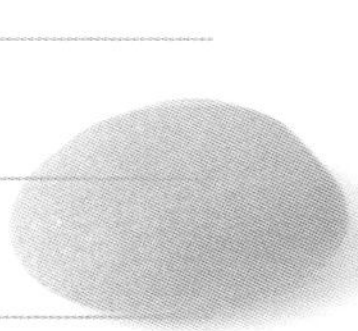

December 19

Pleasure may come from illusion, but happiness can come only of reality.
Chamfort

WATCHING

My best friend brought his niece and nephew to my home while he was babysitting them. We got out the inflatable pool, filled it up with water, and sat on the deck to watch the elaborate interactions of the kids as they devised the most comfortable way to ease themselves into the water. I was fascinated to see how completely present they were for the task at hand. Without any editorializing of how they presented themselves, not caring whether their swimsuits were of the latest fashion or how their bodies looked, they carried out their task, bursting out with shrieks each time they touched the cold water. Panting with excitement and apprehension, they culminated the experience with a wild plunge and more shrieks of shock. I could have watched for hours. And I did.

DECEMBER 20

Most men pursue pleasure with such breathless haste that they hurry past it.
Søren Kierkegaard

GRATITUDE

Gratitude is often thought of as a feeling or experience caused by getting something. For example, I might feel grateful and happy when I receive a gift or compliment. Or I might feel thanksgiving rise up within me when a prayer seems to have been answered. I might be filled with gratitude for the time my grandchildren spent with me, or the note my colleague left to acknowledge something I did.

But there is another side to gratitude that has everything to do with a prosperity mindset. Thanksgiving or gratitude is not only the result of something; it is also the attitude which prepares us to receive. Try to imagine that gratitude is a cause, not only a result.

December 21

The power of accurate observation is commonly called cynicism by those who haven't got it.
George Bernard Shaw

WIT

Wit is the ability to see the world in an interesting way, and cleverly make connections between ideas, things, and situations in a humorous manner. The phrase "living by your wits" means that you use this ability to make your way through the world with an interesting and resourceful approach.

You can practice your sense of wit by considering how to do ordinary things in new ways, or by observing friends and family and identifying characteristics they have in common. An archaic use of the word *wit* means, simply, to know. What can you discover and know through observation today?

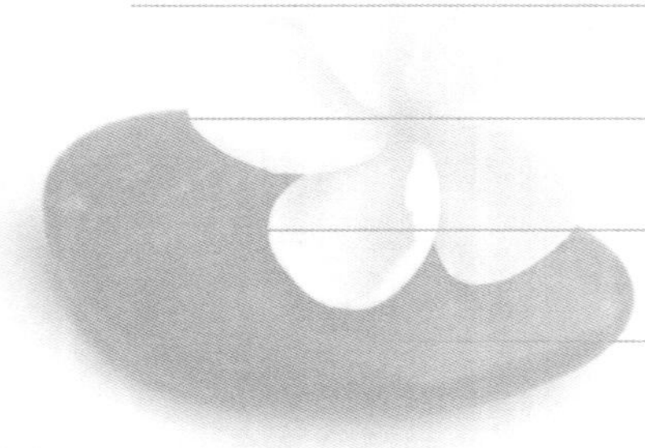

DECEMBER 22

He who can no longer pause to wonder and stand rapt in awe, is as good as dead; his eyes are closed.

Albert Einstein

WONDER

When we encounter something new or are surprised by something, we frequently experience the feelings of wonder and astonishment. It is as if we experience a moment of pause to take in the event or object with rapt attention.

We can practice being aware of the Presence by consciously feeling wonder at ordinary objects and events. Another way of practicing this is to appreciate everything and everyone you encounter in the next hour. Try to notice how the items and people you observe support your existence, and silently say a few words of gratitude for their Presence.

December 23

Miracles are a retelling in small letters of the very same story which is written across the whole world in letters too large for some of us to see.
C.S. Lewis

MIRACLES

A *miracle* is commonly defined as a noticeable interruption of the laws of nature, which can sometimes be explained by Divine intervention. But there is another way to look at a miracle. Think of it as seeing the ordinary with careful attention. Think of it as noticing the details, mystery, and wonder of everything around you.

For a meditative practice today, choose something to examine closely. It could be a flame on a candle, a plant in a pot, or a sleeping pet. Look at it for a long time, and let yourself imagine how it came into being.

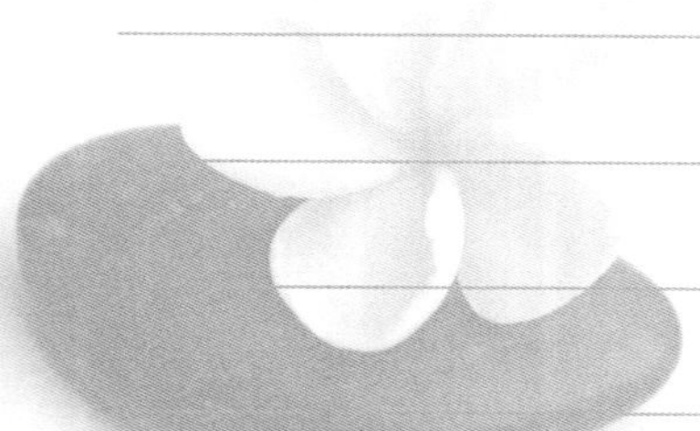

December 24

Life is the first gift, love is the second,
and understanding the third.
Marge Piercy

GIFTS

Make a conscious decision today to give your love in the form of understanding, and you will discover the most powerful way to enhance your life and the life of everyone around you. Without insisting that your love be received or even appreciated, consider this an experiment on how much you can listen to those around you. You can express this kind of love in a few words and with few actions. At the end of the day, you will be able to look back and assess the effects of giving your love.

December 25

Thousands of candles can be lit from a single candle, and the life of the candle will not be shortened. Happiness never decreases by being shared.
Buddha

HAPPINESS

Author Dennis Prager realized that most people tend to regard the pursuit of happiness as selfish, as opposed to a moral demand. He writes, "When we think of character traits, we rightly think of honesty, integrity, moral courage, and acts of altruism. Few people include happiness in any list of character traits or moral achievements."

Happiness is an important way of contributing to the world and making it a better place. Sharing your happiness could be one of the greatest gifts you'll ever give.

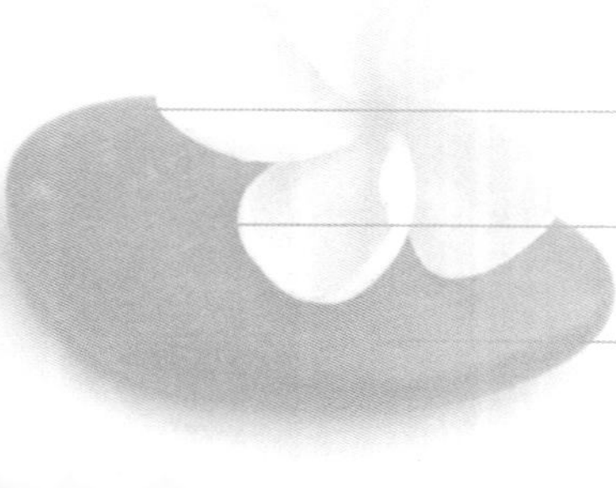

DECEMBER 26

When you can think of yesterday without regret
and tomorrow without fear, you are near contentment.
Unknown

CONTENTMENT

You are growing in wisdom. You are learning about love. You are facing your fears. You are coming into your own authority. You are becoming authentic.

Each experience in your life brings you closer to God. Every challenge you face and overcome teaches you how powerful you really are. With each passing year, you mature spiritually.

Spiritual maturity has a side effect called *contentment*. It arrives gracefully, as a peaceful knowing that all is well. You begin to live a serene life, unmoved and unaffected by the chaos of human life. When others are crazed and worried, you remain calm and peaceful. Enjoy this contentment. Make your home in it.

December 27

To insure good health: eat lightly, breathe deeply, live moderately, cultivate cheerfulness, and maintain an interest in life.
William Londen

CHEERFULNESS

Wherever children play and laugh, you may be sure that God is present. Our Creator takes pleasure and joy in Its creation. Life is not meant to be a burden. It was created for joy and ease. Children know this. That's why their primary activity is play.

Try to get back in touch with your childlike nature today. Go play. Spend time with someone who makes you laugh. Go see a comedy or watch a comedian on television.

Regardless of what challenges you have faced, try to end this year in joy. Bring to mind all of the joyful moments you have had this year. Make a list of the top three.

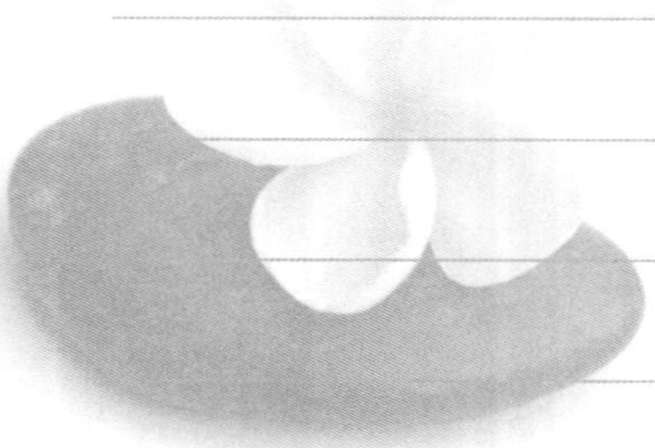

December 28

Love consists in desiring to give what is our own
to another and feeling his delight as our own.
Emanuel Swedenborg

DELIGHT

There is never going to be a time in your life when absolutely everything is perfect. There will always be some issue to face, challenge to overcome, or problem to solve. That is the nature of human experience.

This is why it is so important to take delight in those moments in life of sheer pleasure and ecstasy. Wallow around in the joy of friends and family as they come together. Let yourself be absorbed in those joyful moments. Lose yourself in gladness.

Set down your burdens for a while, and take refuge in those moments in life when nothing can disturb your happiness. You can always pick up your troubles later. They will be waiting for you. However, you will notice they have somehow become lighter.

DECEMBER 29

There is delight in singing, though none hear beside the singer.
Walter Savage

CELEBRATION

There is cause to celebrate. You have made it through another year. You have faced your challenges, solved your problems, and somehow come through it all without too much damage.

Use this journal to make a list of your top three successes this past year. It is important for you to see your progress and notice how much you have grown. Once you have made your list, decide how you want to celebrate your successes. It's time to party!

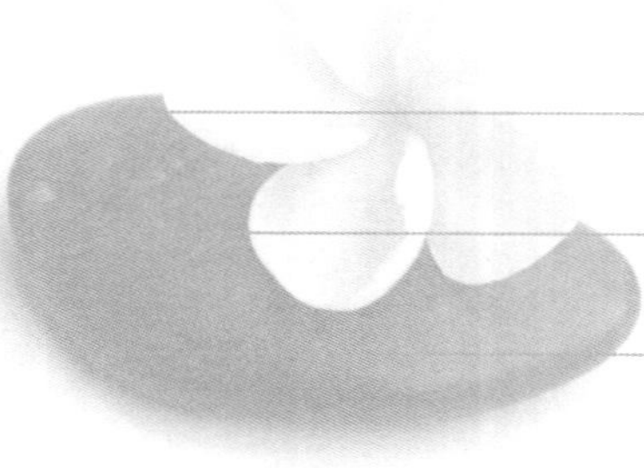

December 30

A good beginning makes a good ending.
Proverb

ENDINGS

Life is full of stops and starts, beginnings and endings. Everything has a lifespan, a designated birth and assigned death. Things have to end so that we may have new beginnings. Death has to occur so resurrection can follow. It is natural and normal to mourn the loss and feel the sadness of an ending.

Some endings are joyful. We are always glad to end a spoiled relationship or unfulfilling job. There is a feeling of accomplishment at having ended a struggle or overcome a difficult challenge.

You can try to delay the inevitable, but things that need to end will always do so. There is a natural process that will occur if you don't stand in the way. Don't try to keep things alive that need to expire. Let go of your fear.

December 31

Life without a purpose is a languid, drifting thing; every day we ought to review our purpose, saying to ourselves, "This day let me make a sound beginning, for what we have hitherto done is naught."

Thomas Kempis

REVIEW

A whole year has passed since you started journaling. Congratulations on keeping up with your writings. Now, take time to review what value this spiritual practice has brought to your life.

Do you feel closer to God? What has changed? What is new in your life? What has passed away? What challenges have you overcome? What new wisdom do you possess? How have you grown spiritually?

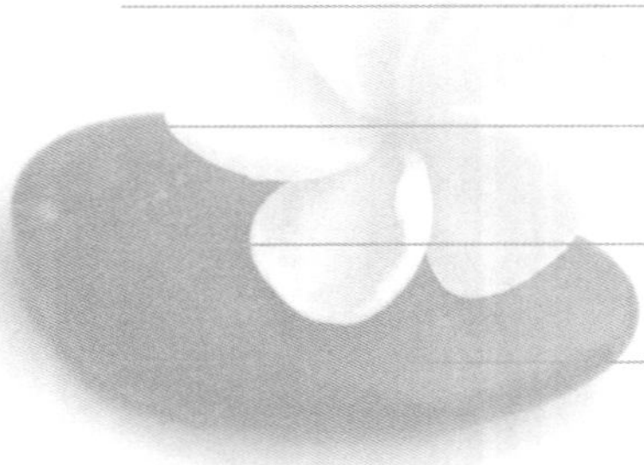

My Notes

My Notes

My Notes

My Notes

My Notes

Notes

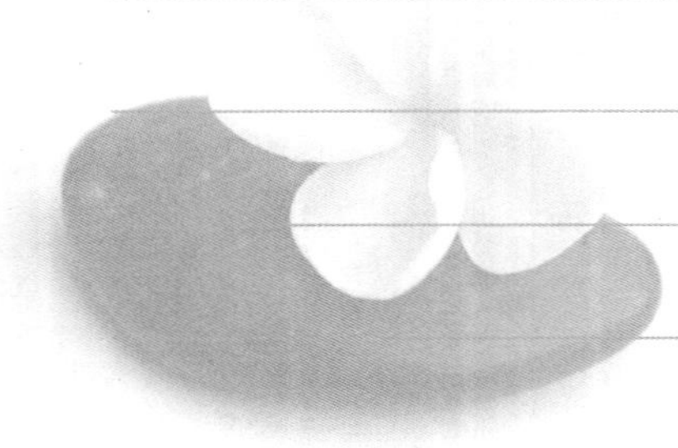